ETHNOGRAPHIC EXPLORATIONS

In *Ethnographic Explorations: Surrender and Resistance*, Whitaker and Atkinson, two experienced ethnographers, explore the complexities of fieldwork, analysis and writing from new perspectives. It takes the opportunity to reflect on Ethnography not just as a methodological perspective, but at a fundamental level.

In general terms, Ethnography is seen not just in terms of a set of data-collection methods, but as a more profoundly transformational perspective. The book explores a series of tensions and differences in the conceptualisation and conduct of ethnography, among them: Surrender and Catch; Strangeness and Familiarity; Intimacy and Distance; and Romanticism and Modernism. It emphasises disruptions and interruptions rather than an idealised model of smoothly untroubled research. The book covers a variety of theoretical and methodological perspectives, illustrated with research in many social settings.

The book is intended for researchers at postgraduate and postdoctoral levels and at experienced researchers who want to read a different, sometimes challenging, take on ethnographic research and its outcomes.

Emilie Morwenna Whitaker is a Lecturer in Social Policy at the University of Salford, UK, and an Honorary Lecturer at the School of Social Sciences, Cardiff University, UK. Her recent publications include *Reflexivity in Social Research* (Palgrave 2021) also with Paul Atkinson.

Paul Atkinson is Distinguished Research Professor (Emeritus) of Sociology at Cardiff University, UK. His recent publications include the last two books in his Ethnography quartet *Writing Ethnographically* (2020) and *Crafting Ethnography* (2022), both for SAGE Publications; the fourth edition of Hammersley and Atkinson, *Ethnography: Principles in Practice*, was published by Routledge in 2021.

ETHNOGRAPHIC EXPLORATIONS

Surrender and Resistance

Emilie Morwenna Whitaker
and Paul Atkinson

Routledge
Taylor & Francis Group
LONDON AND NEW YORK

Designed cover image: Alison Chan, reproduced with permission

First published 2023
by Routledge
4 Park Square, Milton Park, Abingdon, Oxon OX14 4RN

and by Routledge
605 Third Avenue, New York, NY 10158

Routledge is an imprint of the Taylor & Francis Group, an informa business

British Library Cataloguing-in-Publication Data
A catalogue record for this book is available from the British Library

ISBN: 978-0-367-17440-8 (hbk)
ISBN: 978-0-367-17441-5 (pbk)
ISBN: 978-0-429-05680-2 (ebk)

DOI: 10.4324/9780429056802

Typeset in Bembo
by KnowledgeWorks Global Ltd.

CONTENTS

PREFACE AND ACKNOWLEDGEMENTS

This book is not another addition to the growing literature on research methods that seek to instruct novices on 'how to do ethnography'. Equally, this is not a series of autobiographical reflections, or what is often called autoethnography, although from time to time we allow ourselves to include some personal materials and reflections. This is also not a book about 'qualitative research'. On the whole, we are in favour of qualitative work, but we are not enamoured of a lot of it as currently practised. We do not, for instance, think that being qualitative is an inherently superior commitment. We also try to avoid, as far as possible, that sort of methodological dissension that pits qual against quant, positivism against interpretivism or postmodernism. Nor do we endorse approaches that seem to equate qualitative research with under-analysed unstructured interviews. We do insist on ethnography as a distinctive form of social research, based on participant observation in particular social settings. We subscribe, therefore, to a classic, perhaps even old-fashioned view of the centrality of fieldwork, a perspective that PA has promoted throughout all his published work. We are not particularly impressed by the rapid succession of 'innovations' and varieties of 'post' that have populated recent methodological discourse. We are not, therefore chasing novelty for the sake of it. Rather, we want to encourage our readers to *think* about research in ways that are faithful to ethnography in terms of personal and intellectual commitments. In doing so, we want to challenge some cherished images of ethnographic work. There is no single orthodoxy or set of methodological precepts that can inform ethnography unequivocally. It is too easy to imagine ethnographic fieldwork as conceptually and practically straightforward, and time in the field as a relatively untroubled period of productive and sociable relationships. Rather, ethnographic research is always poised, metaphorically speaking, in a field of conceptual opposites, ideas that are in tension, and with unresolvable dilemmas. We prefer to view it from the perspective of interruptions and disruptions.

Our approach is informed throughout the book by the phenomenological perspective of Kurt Wolff, who coined the idea of Surrender-and-Catch, in trying to capture the two sides of ethnographic research, in the field and in the study, in person and in texts. We use that perspective as a springboard to discuss some of the many tensions and polarities that characterise the ethnographic enterprise. They include Strangeness and Familiarity; Intimacy and Distance; and Romanticism and Modernism. Our general approach is informed by literary theory as well as the traditions of anthropological and sociological ethnography.

Our collaborations stem from the time when we were colleagues at Cardiff University. Although circumstances have kept us physically apart since Emilie moved to Salford University, we have continued to work together. This book is the outcome of several years of publishing together. The book itself was sketched out during a rather dull session at a conference we were both attending. It seemed to capture some of our shared ideas, and our frustrations with superficial accounts of qualitative research and ethnography, and we find striking the extent to which our ideas, born of different biographies and environments, converge.

We are very grateful to Hannah Shakespeare, our editor at Routledge, for her support and patience, and to Sara Delamont, who read and commented on all the chapters in draft. Between us, we wish to acknowledge the colleagueship and friendship of members of the Cardiff Ethnography Group. We should like to thank especially Kate Moles, Robin Smith, William Housley, Tia DeNora and Steve Fuller for their generosity of spirit and encouragement. Emilie would also like to thank the many women writers who invite us to see, think and feel as we go, without way-markers and maps.

1

COMMITMENTS AND THE FIELD

An uncertain undertaking: ethnography as commitment

Ethnography has been written about on multiple occasions. Published work ranges from introductory methods texts to more advanced discussions. Many books are devoted to practical advice as to the conduct of ethnographic work, while others discuss specialised aspects (such as digital or visual ethnography). We make no attempt to compete directly with such methods texts. Rather, this book consists of a series of closely linked essays, each of which addresses some fundamentals of ethnographic research – intellectual, personal, emotional, methodological and textual. Clearly, as authors, we have our own orientations and preferences, and they inform all of our remarks, but we are not advocating a single orthodoxy. Contemporary ethnographic research is too diverse and complex for that. It encompasses a wide range of approaches, and it is to be found in an ever-wider array of social science disciplines. Ethnography never was the preserve of any one of those disciplines, whatever anthropologists might claim. But now ethnographic fieldwork is practised by criminologists, cultural geographers, media and communication scholars, and by researchers in education, health and nursing studies. It is to be found in business and organisation studies. It is not conducted with equal felicity by all its practitioners and advocates, perhaps, but its persistence and pervasiveness are indisputable. In the course of these chapters, we illustrate our arguments with reference to classic studies and more contemporary ones. We make no apology for including references to some older texts. They remain reference points for subsequent studies, and there is no intrinsic merit in novelty. We have also, from time to time, included our first-person accounts. They are indicated as being either by EMW or PA. As our arguments include reference to some of the personal aspects of ethnographic work, it seems appropriate to permit the incursion of our own voices.

DOI: 10.4324/9780429056802-1

'Ethnography' has a variety of meanings and connotations, and it is not our intention to reduce them to one perfunctory definition. Nevertheless, there are some commitments that we think characterise ethnographic research, and those will inform our subsequent discussions. We shall, therefore, begin by outlining those – and our – core commitments. These issues are methodological, intellectual, emotional and existential. Together, they call for a distinctive level of personal investment: of time, effort, concentration and imagination on the part of the ethnographer. We should also make it clear that we are *not* here dealing with that broader array of research strategies conventionally referred to as 'qualitative research' or 'qualitative inquiry'. Those latter terms and synonyms include methods that ethnographers certainly may use (such as interviewing) but do not involve ethnographic fieldwork as we understand it. So, ethnography and qualitative research are not equivalent. Indeed, we believe that fieldwork needs to be rescued from some current versions of 'qualitative research' (cf. Atkinson 2015).

We take it as axiomatic that ethnography depends, in part at least, on the conduct of fieldwork, understood as a period of time engaged in participant observation in one or more social settings. While such settings may be offline or virtual, we shall deal exclusively with face-to-face encounters in the field. It is conventional to describe such engagements as involving extended periods of time – up to a year or more – of 'immersion', although we also believe that it is possible to learn significant things in shorter bursts of fieldwork within a restricted social or cultural domain (see Atkinson 2022). 'Participant observation' itself covers a multitude of personal and intellectual engagements. It alludes to the fact that ethnographic fieldwork necessarily implies direct, interpersonal engagement with others and that it calls for a heightened sense of observation. Here observation does not refer to visual perception alone but to all the senses. It means the cultivated capacity to attend to and note the dense variety of actions (including spoken actions), spaces, things, sounds, smells and so on that constitute the fabric of everyday social settings. This then involves going beyond seeing, for observing means paying explicit attention, watching and recording. Here recording does not refer just to the use of digital recording devices such as cameras, video recorders or voice recorders. It also means writing concretely detailed notes and analytic texts, exploring the possibilities of textual and other forms of representation and reconstruction. As Stewart (2007, p. 27) puts it, 'it's the paying attention that matters – a kind of attention immersed in the forms of the ordinary but noticing things too'.

Ethnographic fieldwork is not undertaken in mindless ignorance, and the ethnographer is not a *tabula rasa*. Fieldwork is undertaken in order to explore fundamental questions about everyday life. The ethnographer asks herself deceptively simple questions, such as 'What is it like to live as a …?', 'How do they do that?', 'What resources and skills do actors bring to bear in doing…?', 'What rules inform everyday conduct here?' and 'What coping strategies help people to get by in…?'. Simple questions such as those – and one can readily compose others in the same vein – invite complex answers. It is in the very nature of everyday life that the bases of orderly conduct and interpersonal comportment are multiple and subtle. The knowledge and skills that social actors use – often tacitly – are dense and demand a great deal of detailed observation and analysis. The sensory and material worlds of everyday activity call for careful, sustained attention and detailed recording.

Ethnographic research is iterative, processual and unpredictable. As one may imagine, attempting to understand and document the culture and organisation of a given social world is no easy task. It requires patience. With a few exceptions, we do not undertake compressed periods of observation, except perhaps for the purposes of a methodological experiment (Atkinson 2022). It takes time to observe the cycles and routines of an organised activity and for recurrent patterns of activity to be apparent. Moreover, the research process itself is iterative, not linear. It is certainly not a matter of hanging about in the field and simply waiting for things to happen or for sociologically and anthropologically gripping things to become apparent. It requires active reflection, analytic work and conceptual clarification throughout the project, extending beyond the fieldwork into the construction of ethnographic texts. It also extends back before any fieldwork is embarked on.

Sometimes, the trajectory of ethnographic inquiry is likened to something akin to a funnel. It begins with a very broad scope, and by means of 'progressive focusing' the analytic frames are narrowed, becoming more precisely framed and more fully documented. It is a metaphor that works up to a point, but it is too pat. It suggests a smoothly progressive movement, from the general to the particular, from a wide to a narrow field of vision and towards greater clarity. The progress of ethnographic fieldwork, if it can be described in such terms at all, is much more variable, both in reality and as an ideal. It is, at its best, an iterative process whereby fieldwork should lead to the formulation of preliminary ideas that in turn inform further fieldwork attentiveness. New ideas can arise at the same time that previous insights are being explored further. It is a process that has been glossed as 'analytic induction' and as 'abductive' reasoning (Tavory and Timmermans 2014; Atkinson 2017; Timmermans and Tavory 2022). Later, in the book, we shall be advocating abductive reasoning, but even that kind of designation is an idealised version of the processes of exploration, speculation, confusion and uncertainty.

It is, in many ways, a leap of faith to embark on fieldwork in a new setting. That is true whether the field is distant – as in classic anthropological fieldwork overseas – or near at hand. There is no firm guarantee that we shall cope with the fieldwork, intellectually, personally or interpersonally. There is no certainty that, however diligently we conduct our research, it will yield the sort of outcomes that make for a satisfying monograph or thesis. Of course, all scholarship is like that to some extent. No outcomes are guaranteed. If they were there, there would be no need to conduct the research in the first place. Many experiments fail and many surveys generate no findings of any consequence. Many quantitative studies fail to identify any substantial effects or correlations that are sufficiently strong to justify firm conclusions. Yet ethnographic fieldwork seems to involve a special degree of uncertainty. Our presence in the field is always provisional, always conditional: things can go wrong and relationships can turn sour through no fault of our own. We may find ourselves struggling to make coherent sense of what we observe and participate in. Likewise, it requires some sort of faith that our fieldwork *will* yield comprehension that will in turn result in publishable 'findings'. On a more cheerful note, fieldwork can always yield *something* to think and write about.

The autobiographical accounts of many an ethnographer provide ample evidence of the uncertainties of fieldwork, including projects that – for a variety of reasons – had to be abandoned, or had to be conducted in unforeseen ways (see, for instance, the essays edited by Smith and Delamont 2019). Compromises abound, as do changes in direction. Such unpredictability is not always for the worse, however, and there are also accounts of research epiphanies and breakthroughs, when the hard graft of fieldwork is made to yield fruitful, if unforeseen, outcomes. If there are few cases of smooth fieldwork following clear research plans and designs, there are many accounts of the uncertainties and contingencies of field research. Ethnographic research is both intellectually and personally demanding. One has to manage and cope with those uncertainties and to respond to unforeseen events. Moreover, there is clearly no consensus as to the methodological claims of ethnography itself (Hillyard 2010). It is conventional to point out that ethnographic work can yield barely manageable overloads of sensations and potential 'data'. For instance, Jerolmack and Khan (2018, p. xii) point out that:

> ... even when gaining access is easy (and routinely, it is not), the ethnographer becomes quickly overwhelmed by the field – there is simply too much data, too many potential directions the research can take. Every moment is a potential observation, and it is quickly succeeded by new moments. Despite the neatly packaged holistic accounts of 'primitive' groups that make up the canon of anthropology, the truth is that even the most punctilious ethnographer studying the most bounded field site cannot record and analyze everything.

We realise that some of these preliminary statements may seem redolent of nostalgia for a 'golden age' of 'proper ethnography'. As Weston (2008) writes, there is detectable within anthropology – and it could be true of sociology too – a recurrent nostalgia that is based on 'a certain historical consciousness, a particular understanding of the way anthropology was done in the imaginary era when Big Men were Big Men and ethnographers were ethnographers, when expeditions were well funded, when Self and Other stayed separate and stayed apart' (pp. 127–128). Even a 'golden age' of anthropological fieldwork had its martyrs, such as the murdered American ethnographer Henrietta Schmerler, who was raped and murdered in 1931 (Schmerler 2017). One might suspect a similar nostalgia, *mutatis mutandis*, among sociologists looking back at the apparent certainties of the first and second Chicago schools of urban ethnography, when the conduct of fieldwork seems – in retrospect at least – to have been less troubled by doubt or the vagaries of postmodern theorising. As Weston goes on to suggest,

> In addition to nostalgias ventured and nostalgias abjured, there are latent nostalgias that are no less powerful because they elude naming as such. Methodological discussions are loaded with assumptions about what constitutes ethnography, even at its most innovative. Embedded in many usages of the term *ethnography* is a certain reverence for the way things used to be, when face-to-face meant a few strides away rather than Web-cams at two ends of an Internet hookup, when fieldwork meant immersion in a fixed place rather than a series of mobile encounters strategically designed to create a research space.
>
> (*p. 135*).

We recognise those sentiments, but in alluding to ethnographic commitments that we think are important and significant, we are not trying to put the clock back in order to celebrate or advocate a golden age of fieldwork, although we do think that much is to be gained by paying our dues to earlier generations. We do not yearn for an imaginary time when everything was cut-and-dried, and the ethnographer (whether at home or elsewhere) could proceed with all possible self-assurance. On the contrary, as we pursue our ideas in this book, we shall try to demonstrate the many ambiguities, tensions and troubles that impinge one way or another as a consequence of our intellectual and personal commitment to fieldwork and to an ethnographic imagination. Recent years have seen an erosion of self-confidence, as anthropologists in particular have become uneasy at the association of fieldwork and colonialism. Fieldwork itself can be represented as inherently exploitative, while the explication of other cultures can be seen in terms of cultural appropriation. Jackson (2017) takes a somewhat recondite approach to express this. He discusses composers' use of folk song and melody in the early twentieth century in the context of his own work on Janáček:

> …I mentioned other composers, including Dvořák, Kodály, Bartók, and Vaughan Williams, who used folk music as the basis for their own compositions, often without specific acknowledgment of their sources. Undoubtedly, my misgivings reflected my own anxieties as an ethnographer, recording oral traditions, interrogating informants, and collecting the stories of strangers. Even when given carte blanche by those who allowed me to live among them and know their secrets, I was often unable to rid my mind of the thought that I was profiting from things that did not, strictly speaking, belong to me. There lurked a suspicion that I was part of an underhanded and ongoing Western tradition of pilfering and piracy, and that this was somehow connected with what I construed as the impertinent jargon of anthropology itself.
>
> (*p. 49*)

In some ways, such sentiments are understandable, and ethnographic research certainly lends itself to feelings of guilt over appropriation and exploitation. But there is a diametrically opposite sentiment that can be equally appropriate. Far from being dubious, ethnographic fieldwork is highly ethical (cf. Atkinson 2015). No other approach to scholarship implies such a personal commitment as giving up months and years of one's life to comprehend the everyday lives of others and to spend months and years subsequently in crafting a text. This is far removed from the sort of exploitation and plunder of an imperial power. It depends upon a certain intellectual humility that is at odds with imperial arrogance. At the same time, one must also recognise the force of individual and collective feelings of 'betrayal', when those texts and the understandings they enshrine are inevitably incomplete and fall short of their author's aspirations (Brettell 1993). Undoubtedly, we ethnographers 'take' from the field, and then our many commitments inevitably lead us away from the field. We interrupt others' lives, and we impose on them (see Chapter 4). But this is a long way removed from the imperial extraction of surplus value, or the display of 'exotic' others as demonstrations of primitive development or superstitious mentality. In fact, one can argue in all seriousness that anthropologists have for over a century resisted such 'Western' mis-readings of others' lives. For many sociologists, the study of 'Western' social worlds does not have the same taint of overseas or internal colonialism, perhaps. But there can still be accusations of exploitation, especially when one is 'studying down'.

In conducting ethnographic fieldwork, we have to be attentive to the phenomena that confront us. That may be obvious, but it is by no means straightforward. While participant observation seems simple, it is rarely so. The close observation of what is actually going on can readily escape a field researcher who is personally engaged but phenomenologically blinkered. Observation is active: it implies a reaching out to identify and record the multiple and complex phenomena of everyday social and cultural life. Without such active observation, the rest is idle. When we come to write about 'surrender' to the field, this should not be understood to mean a passive reception of sensory impressions. Rather, we approach the physical and intellectual labour in the spirit enunciated by David Thoreau (2000) in *Walden*:

> But while we are confined to books, though the most select and classic, and read only particular written languages, which are themselves but dialects and provincial, we are in danger of forgetting the language which all things and events speak without metaphor, which alone is copious and standard. … No method nor discipline can supersede the necessity of being forever on the alert. What is a course of history or philosophy, or poetry, no matter how well selected, or the best society or the mot admirable routine of life, compared with the discipline of looking always at what is to be seen? Will you be a reader, a student merely, or a seer?
>
> *(p. 96)*

One does not need to endorse Thoreau's individualism in order to acknowledge the force of his observations on observation: the power of an ethnographic gaze derives in no small measure from one's membership of a community of practitioners and the cultivation of a shared sensibility. But if anthropologists and sociologists cannot bracket out bookish attitudes and cannot focus on what is in front of them when they are together with their fellow women and men, then any speculation and theorising will be ill-informed at best and vacuous at worst. Surrender implies a kind of radical empiricism, born of phenomenology and nurtured in cultural anthropology and interactionist sociology.

Irrespective of whether one is recapitulating classic fieldwork, or attempting some contemporary version, the commitments of ethnographic fieldwork require a personal investment as well as an intellectual one. More than any other social research strategy, ethnography rests on the researcher her/himself as the 'research instrument'. Fieldwork depends on a capacity to sustain social relationships, to pay close attention to the phenomena, to transmute those 'observations' into documentary materials and to synthesise 'findings' into analytic ideas. Paying close attention and maintaining social relations in the field are not just intellectually demanding. The relationships of field research are tiring and can be emotionally draining too. Hours spent in the field are tiring in themselves, calling for sustained concentration on people, places, events and sensory experiences. One has to try to cultivate a form of multi-sensory awareness. On the one hand, there is the requirement to maintain 'normal' presence, acknowledging other participants and interacting with them. One is not the proverbial (but misleading) 'fly on the wall', except insofar as the ethnographer and the fly might both hope not to be sprayed, swatted or expelled. The fly on the wall, the passive observer, is not required to keep up ordinary social interactions and to cultivate productive relationships over time. The ethnographer in the field has to do those things, while remaining alert and 'noticing' things that are going on, in order to record them, think about and analyse them. Observations that are not recorded in some way soon become useless.

Ethnographers have traditionally been trained to construct fieldnotes as they go along. This is rarely, if ever, a matter of writing in a notebook or clipboard while observing (as if one were some sort of inspector). Rather, fieldnotes need to be worked up and worked on as soon as possible after the event. Proverbially, one should not let the sun go down on unrecorded fieldwork. Memory for concrete detail and for the ordering of events can fade quickly. We all know that fieldnotes are selective. Nobody could possibly reconstruct all that is said and done over a short period of time, let alone for several hours, a day or a work shift. But we do try to create detailed texts that preserve as much as possible of the phenomena. In itself, this task will require the investment of several hours in the day. As a purely practical piece of advice, it is better to have shorter periods of participant observation that are well documented than long, exhausting ones with no time left to write them up.

PA has in his possession an archive of fieldnotes created in the 1950s by the American sociologist Julius Roth. Having suffered from TB himself, Roth decided, after his recovery, during which he kept a detailed diary, to undertake fieldwork in a TB hospital. There he worked as a porter and kept a field journal. So, each working day (there were 100 in all) he wrote several thousand words of detailed fieldnotes and analytic memos. That was in and of itself a major undertaking. The key issue is not the temporal extent of his ethnographic work, but the fact that he attended to the details and practicalities of everyday work in that context and recorded them. The result is a remarkable ethnographic and historical document on the practical management of an infectious disease in a hospital of that time. It has powerful resonances for studies of infections today, not least the airborne COVID-19 virus. Roth's account of ritualistic practices of infection control remains pertinent. In many ways, his identification of the hospital's boundaries, its timetables and its ceremonials paralleled Goffman's account of the total institution (Goffman 1961a; Roth 1963). It exemplifies the sort of investment of time and concentration that is required.

The spirit of ethnography resides in paying close attention to what is ordinary as much as – usually more than – what is extraordinary. It means noticing and observing what is there in front of us. There is no need to expect only the remarkable. The conduct of everyday life is informed by the complex conventions and rituals of the interaction order (Goffman 1961b, 1967). It is suffused by everyday practices and affects. As Stewart (2007, p. 2) suggests,

> The ordinary is a shifting assemblage of practices and practical knowledges, a scene of both liveness and exhaustion, a dream of escape or of the simple life. Ordinary affects are the varied, surging capacities to affect and be affected that give everyday life the quality of a continual motion of relations, scenes, contingencies, and emergencies. They're things that happen. They happen in impulses, sensations, expectations, daydreams, encounters, and habits of relating, in strategies and their failures, in forms of persuasion, contagion, and compulsion, in modes of attention, attachment, and agency, and in publics and social worlds of all kinds that catch people up in something that feels like *some*thing. (emphasis in original)

There is a moral order through which are expressed mutual obligations or their infraction. Composure or its failure can result in stigma and embarrassment, pride and self-esteem. Small worlds present the potential ethnographer with microcosms that teem with possibilities, social worlds that *matter* intensely to their members. Attention must be paid through our openness and surrender to those phenomena.

Paying attention to the phenomena as we have just written is not perfectly straightforward. Even in relatively unfamiliar settings, it is easy to overlook or to gloss over actions and events. And in social settings that are familiar to the ethnographer (such as domains within her 'own' culture), it is undoubtedly easy to take things for granted or to assume that one 'knows' what is going on or what it 'means'. Consequently, part of the intellectual work of the ethnographer is to try to treat things as 'strange'. It is the work of strangeness to create the process of transforming the stream of doings and events into phenomena. There is an often-repeated maxim that the ethnographer (amongst others) tries 'to make the familiar strange and the strange familiar'. In many ways, that *is* telling advice, and it alerts one to the general issues of strangeness. But perhaps it is too glib, too pat. It is more pertinent to suggest that the ethnographic observer should always be working with and through strangeness.

In this context, strangeness means something quite specific, and it is not equivalent to something being 'unfamiliar'. Familiarity certainly needs to be worked against (Delamont and Atkinson 1995, 2021) but so too does unfamiliarity in a certain sense. The familiar and the unfamiliar both need to be transformed into researchable, accountable and describable phenomena. Estrangement is a key intellectual commitment. It involves the suspension of ordinary, everyday attitudes towards things, events and persons. While this is an attitude of mind associated especially with the phenomenologists, it is also to be found among the English Romantics. For instance, Berlina (2017), in a discussion of the idea of strangeness, quotes Coleridge describing poetry as: 'Awakening the mind's attention from the lethargy of custom, and directing it to the loveliness and the wonders of the world before us; an inexhaustible treasure, but for which in consequence of the film of familiarity and selfish solicitude we have eyes, yet see not, ears that hear not, and hearts that neither feel nor understand' (Coleridge 1840, p. 308). This is in the context of Berlina's introduction to the work of Victor Shklovsky. Shklovsky's key concept was *ostranerie*, applied to literary and artistic work, conventionally translated as estrangement (or otherwise as 'enstrangement'), which he himself summarised as 'The representation of the usual as strange, as seen anew, as if at a remove – this was something I regarded as a phenomenon shared by romantic, realist, and so-called modernist art' (Berlina, ed. 2017, p. 272). Estrangement comes in many guises, but it is a recurrent strategy in fiction, visual art, philosophy and the social sciences.

For a social scientist, strangeness and estrangement are most associated with the social phenomenology of Alfred Schütz. Summed up in his essay on 'the Stranger', Schütz (1971) begins from the person who is literally a stranger: someone who finds her/himself in a novel social situation. The new arrival may soon find that their own everyday assumptions concerning social reality do not hold true in this novel social world. Everyday routines and recipes for action may not 'work'. It follows, therefore, that the stranger needs to suspend ordinary – if tacit – assumptions based on prior experience, and to assimilate new ones. The latter may involve explicit learning or may be a more insidious process of acquiring a new version of common sense. This process of un-learning and re-learning is, therefore, a concrete exemplification of the more general principle of social phenomenology: in order to make sense of everyday life and of actors' constructions of reality, it is necessary to suspend one's own common sense and to pay sustained attention to that of others. This is the process of 'bracketing' that holds up understandings and assumptions – however obvious or habituated they may be – to analytic scrutiny. There is a crucial difference between the philosopher or social investigator and the acculturated newcomer. The stranger in everyday life needs to assimilate new cultural forms in order to become a member of the new social group. The ethnographer, by contrast, is not content simply with acting 'as if' she or he were a fully competent member. Rather, the ethnographer needs to maintain an explicit, theoretical attitude towards the processes of learning and what has been acquired. The ethnographer, in the guise of a cultural learner, adopts an analytic stance, rather than swapping one 'natural attitude' for another. (The natural attitude describes the taken-for-granted assumptions and actions of ordinary, everyday life in the absence of any disruptions.)

Lost and found

The upshot of this perspective is that the ethnographer must commit herself to being some sort of 'stranger'. This in turn means that one can become – if temporarily – lost in an unfamiliar social world or attempting to make the familiar strange. In either event (and we recognise once again that the dichotomy is an exaggerated one), this implies a certain kind of ethnographic disorientation. In the interests of ethnographic exploration, one must be prepared to lose one's way and indeed to lose oneself. To extend that metaphor further, one can suggest that ethnography is always a matter of the lost and found. It is a repeated, oscillating process of losing and finding. Everyday phenomena rush towards us in all their pressing immediacy. They recede if we lose focus once again, searching for their possible significance. The loss, partial perhaps and temporary, means that the ethnographic enterprise can always arouse regret. For many anthropologists and sociologists, ethnographic fieldwork is an activity of one's youth. To remember and to re-visit one's first major fieldwork is not merely to glimpse the now shadowy figures of one's research participants. One catches sight of a lost, youthful self. Both that earlier self and the past hosts may be faded through the passage of time, and the focus of the here-and-now softened. Revisiting one's first field experience, such as re-reading one's earlier fieldnotes – can therefore be an act of ambivalent remembrance. It is but one aspect of ethnographic chagrin.

Chagrin also arises from the fact that even in the immediate ethnographic present, we know, or at least suspect, that there is much that is 'lost'. It really does not matter whether we are writing fieldnotes, collecting recordings or harvesting other kinds of materials and traces, we are so often conscious that there is always 'more than' we can ever gather, more than we can encompass on our stuttering analyses. We fill in the hazy outlines as best we can, but there is always a regret that the vividly coloured 'now' fades to the penny-plain outlines of our partial understandings. The local colour can – like certain pigments – prove to be fugitive, fading over time. So repeated senses of loss and getting lost are recurrent existential and emotional accompaniments of ethnographic research. These are not roots of failure, however. Losing and finding are productive moments in everyday life and in social research alike. As Walter Benjamin noted:

> Not to find one's way in a city may well be uninteresting and banal. It requires ignorance – nothing more. But to lose oneself in a city – as one loses oneself in a forest – that calls for quite a different schooling. Then sign-boards and street names, passers-by, roofs, kiosks, or bars must speak to the wanderer like a cracking twig under his feet in the forest.
>
> *(Benjamin 1986, pp. 8–9)*

The wanderer listens, collects clues, tunes into the hums and the silences, pays attention to the details of the place – its pockmarks and ruins, its shifting scents. They do so without mastery, yet with knowledge. Guiding them is not a grand theory or blueprint, more a tactile, embodied on-the-hoof learning. Benjamin's joy lies in 'seeking out' the deliberately unexpected, the lesser known, the emergent rather than planned. The adventure lies in not having a pre-determined, well worked out, regimented plan. The art and sensibility lie in learning with openness, of subjecting oneself to whatever lies ahead with a preparedness of spirit, of 'going along' to experience what unfolds. Benjamin would refer to this as the 'art of straying.' It is the inventive, experiential, evocative path of discovery. The planetary ethnographer is not, however, a *flâneur* or *flâneuse* (Tester 1994; Elkin 2016). The flâneur wanders with conscious aimlessness in search of experiences; the ethnographer wanders, metaphorically, alertly, even purposefully.

The ethnographer does feel this in their bones, even if it is a challenge to articulate. In the field, every time we have taken a turn – perhaps to a new street, perhaps in receiving unexpected news, perhaps in having a brief conversation which changed our perspective – the world is remade and shifts under our feet. We are less certain of our direction. It is as though you only get closer to the phenomenon by putting to one side the original map you drew of it. The familiar ethnographic maxim holds true: when we are too familiar with a place, we stop seeing it; when we shift direction or perspective, we are able once more to become entangled with it. Benjamin is encouraging us to try to balance that unsettling against the freshness of ideas which emerge from being turned around once more.

Kurt Wolff shares this phenomenological commitment. We shall be visiting his ideas throughout the book. His key idea, running through much of his published work, is the binary of 'surrender and catch'. On surrender, Wolff writes:

> to surrender means to take as fully, to meet as immediately as possible whatever the occasion may be. It means not to select, not to believe that one can know quickly what one's experience means, hence what is understood and acted on.
>
> *(Wolff 1976, p. 20)*

For Wolff, therefore, the phenomenologist and the ethnographer (he was both) must commit to the here-and-now of fieldwork and other experiences of a world within reach. To surrender is to immerse oneself in the contingencies and interpersonal relations of a social world. For Wolff, and indeed for us and the great majority of ethnographers, such surrender is not enough. We need what Wolff called the 'catch'. That is, the analytic, theoretical payoff. The catch is what transforms experience and observation into sociological or anthropological interpretation. Surrender and catch are but two sides of the same thing: the ethnographic capacity to engage with the field and its actors while simultaneously being able to estrange oneself from the phenomena and to make the phenomena strange to oneself.

Both Benjamin and Wolff imply a losing of oneself in the moment, in the matter in hand, in the encounter. To find oneself transformed, perhaps puzzled, potentially confused, reconfigured. To move on with new knowledge and new questions. Whilst Benjamin writes of the city, or – more acutely – the possibilities of experiencing the city, Wolff seeks to craft a methodology from a similar sentiment. The art is to approach the phenomenon not as a fully formed externalised entity to coax or breach or besiege but to 'become entangled in the ribbon' (Benjamin 1986, p. 28).

Etymologically the words 'lost' and 'surrender' hold a family resemblance. In the Old Norse, 'los' refers to the disbanding of an army. The result of a truce, victory or defeat sends soldiers falling out of formation, scattering and dispersal – finding new ways home. The verb 'surrender', similarly militaristic in tone, is about a giving over to, but this is not necessarily submission or domination. In the Old French form 'surrender' is to 'give back' or 'return'. It is less the hoisting of a white flag and the great shame of defeat, but rather a yielding. For some psychoanalysts, surrender can connote a 'quality of liberation and expansion of the self' (Ghent, 1990) through the wilful collapsing of defensive barriers. Here, surrender is less 'giving up' and more 'letting go'. Surrender, in the common-sense understanding is also deeply relational in nature, marking the shift from one state of being to another, the transition commonly marked by ritual, witness or certification. 'Rendre', 'to render', focuses attention on representation and translation – forms of knowledge, tools and ideas that are transferred from one place to another, transmuted and transfigured to 'render' the transformation from one of state to another.

Ethnography is not aimless. But it has no single predetermined goal or end point. It is always, in principle, an open-ended as well as an open-minded undertaking. Insofar as we enter into social worlds without the teleological comfort of a defined outcome, the ethnographic journey can feel like losing one's self and losing one's way in a confusing hubbub of voices, actions, conventions and narratives. Existentially, such loss – however temporary and conditional – can feel like a loss of identity. It can also be experienced as a loss of status and authority, especially for the more experienced ethnographer. In order to acquire the sapiential authority of ethnographic understanding, one must surrender secular authority as an intellectual, expert, and academic. Consequently ethnography is always in a state of unstable equilibrium, poised between finding a way and losing one's way, losing oneself and finding oneself again.

As Wolff (1976) himself acknowledges, surrender can seem to imply what used to be called 'going native'. That is, the loss of analytic distance and the consequent loss of anthropological or sociological perspective. But it is clear that such a form of surrender is not intended, and it is not in that sense that we employ the term here. Wolff helpfully draws a distinction between overwhelming and unexpected surrender and the work of a sensibility, which he deems 'surrender-to'. This is the frame within which we operate here. Surrendering-to depends on becoming lost, giving oneself over to phenomena, to finding different and myriad ways of making sense. It is about crafting and working at a certain sensibility or disposition. Of this, Wolff (1976) writes, 'I can try to surrender to something or somebody. To surrender-to is to concentrate, to dedicate or devote oneself, to pay utmost attention' (p. 26). Like the Old French, it is a yielding to the phenomenon at hand. Going native – which has a long history of existential and epistemological repugnance – derives from over-familiarity. Closing the social and imaginative space between the ethnographer and the host participants implies the loss of intellectual distance and a consequent loss of disciplinary, intellectual perspective. Familiarity implies thinking as usual, and therefore threatens the capacity to undertake anything resembling phenomenological suspension of tacit assumptions: it blunts the analytic edge of ethnographic discomfort. (cf. Gherardi 2015 on Kurt Wolff).

'Going native' has many connotations that we would reject: in the colonialist period, going native could imply a moral contamination, and the anxieties it provoked were based in part on the imperative to preserve social distance and cultural superiority. But it retains idiomatic force in relation to ethnographic work. Those 'natives' today are as likely to be elite lawyers or biomedical scientists as 'exotic' inhabitants of a distant country. The ethnographer who goes native in the contemporary climate may be found guilty of a different kind of transgression. The ethnographer who loses her sense of distance and confuses the categories of ethnographer and other, of researcher and researched, may still appear to be an abomination. The fear of going native can also speak to an existential anxiety – of losing oneself and losing one's identity through immersion in the field. Yet, this hesitation, this resistance, comes at a price. It can inhibit the thorough, experiential and sensory engagement that encompasses everyday knowledge, technique and skilled activity. The fear of going native can also speak to an existential anxiety about losing oneself and losing one's identity, and the fear of being absorbed by the other'. There is, therefore, a recurrent desire to remain hesitant, reluctant, restrained. The 'marginal native' is not necessarily navigating and traversing those margins but can remain 'stuck' at the margin – a wallflower.

Getting lost

We pick up the thread of getting lost and being lost once more. Loss and getting lost can be experienced as threats. But they can also be positive. Forms of being lost, getting lost, are productive phenomena. We begin our projects by an active engagement with getting lost. Whether that may be in the laboratory, in the hospital or in the city's back alleys, we start by deliberately entering into spaces, places and lives that to some extent or another are unknown to us. That is, we actively give in to the idea of getting lost. A phenomenological commitment to estrangement implies losing one's sense of certainty, while Wolff's 'surrender' implies losing oneself in the moment, in the matters at hand; and then finding the phenomena, and hence finding oneself once more, equipped with new perspectives and understandings.

But *getting lost* is not the same as *being lost*. When we enter into those unknown spaces, we have engaged in preparations which we all too quickly forget have been undertaken. Firsthand accounts of fieldwork contain many examples of fieldwork projects where original research designs and research problems were overtaken by local circumstances. It is a recurrent trope among the classic urban ethnographies: Whyte's *Street Corner Society* (1943) and Liebow's *Tally's Corner* (1967). The ethnographer found him or herself in a given spot, in company with a group of others, and simply stayed and followed local realities. Such 'losing' is, of course, supplanted by 'finding' one's spot, and then finding ways to explore that locale. Such a spot might be the local *kafeneion* for the ethnographer of Greece (e.g. Herzfeld 2003) that functions as the right place for a male ethnographer to talk to male customers, or somewhere like 'Slim's table' at the Valois cafeteria in Chicago (Duneier 1992); it might well be a hairdressers (Shortt 2015). While those street corners and cafés may be concrete places, they may also be thought of more metaphorically, through acts of finding oneself and others. The act of getting ethnographically lost is not an activity without knowledge, lineage or tools. These are the preparations. They form the backdrop to our craft.

If and when the ethnographer finds her 'spot', then intellectual and personal surrender means that it can become endowed with significance through close attention and a willingness to explore the social relations and cultural meanings of the phenomena they encounter. The ethnographic spot can thus become a microcosm for matters of moment, the particular becoming generic in scope. That place of signification for Stewart (1996, p. 8) was an Appalachian settlement:

> I spent the first year in Egeria – a place named after a biblical story of an idyllic oasis – in a remote mountain cabin with views on all sides of dispersed settlements where people still kept chicken and cows and pigs and had fields of hay and huge gardens. It was imagined, locally, as well as in my own 'American' imaginary, as an *old timey* place indexing a nostalgia for a time and place apart from the cities and the postindustrial present of life in the cities. Yet people here, like those living in the fragments of the old coal camps in the hollers below, worked in the mines when they could or in the new supermarkets in town or were enabled to 'return' to this place to 'retire' only through devastating disabilities incurred in long decades of backbreaking work in the mines and in the northern cities.

Through the ethnographic analysis, and in particular in the treatment of the ethnopoetics of narrative, that place becomes translated into an iconic kind of space – the 'space on the side of the road' of Stewart's title. In her words, 'In West Virginia, and in other like "occupied", "exploited", and minoritized spaces, it stands as a kind of back talk to "America's" mythic claims to realism, progress, and order' (p. 3). So, finding one's place means transforming that place, intellectually, experientially and textually, so that it can stand for wider and more profound processes.

It should be apparent that our sense of 'lost' should not be interpreted too literally. Ethnographers *do* get lost. Belmonte (1979) describes vividly how he arrived in Naples to do fieldwork, speaking no Italian (let alone *dialetto*) and having no knowledge of the city. His initial experience of that city might charitably be described as 'wandering. Behar (2007) also gives an account of feeling and being lost in Cuba, having no sense of direction as well as a sense of panic induced in busy public spaces, coupled with a sense of insecurity as an American citizen there. More generally, a sense of dislocation is a common experience for ethnographers in the field. Even when they may seem socially embedded and acceptable, they frequently lack an unequivocal social space, being in some sense an anomaly. Graham (1981) conducted fieldwork in a company mining town (Townsite). Despite the fact that – like most women of the town – she was married to a company employee, she was an anomalous woman. Indeed, she was also something of an anomaly among anthropologists:

> In Townsite a complete woman did not have a career; at that time in the academic world a complete professional woman did not have a family. To Townsite residents I was a marginal female because I was also an anthropologist; to many of my professors, women as well as men, I was a marginal anthropologist because I was also a wife and mother.
>
> *(p. 109)*

These are the way-markers, the noticings and happenings of others who we have read, spoken to and challenged; insights and imaginaries interwoven into the ways in which we approach our own sites of getting lost. They prepare us, challenge us, frustrate us, provide us with 'sensitising tools' (cf. Blumer 1954 on sensitising concepts) in order to begin to reorient and move through the experience of getting lost. We are never 'outside' what we have read or heard or have been taught, any more than the walker can totally 'forget' the hillsides of their childhood – the ancient burial cairn with the sole rowan hints that it's three miles south to the village and the *Rose and Crown*.

As Rebecca Solnit (2006) has it, to get lost is to have ceased paying attention to your surroundings – to the landscape you have moved through – to arrive at where you have ended up. To get lost is to fail to notice the way-markers, the changes in flora and fauna, speech and sound, to neglect to look over your shoulder to familiarise yourself with the return. Or perhaps more tellingly, *to not to know how to pay attention to it in the first place.* Getting lost through negligence leads to panic, haste and hurry. Conversely, like Benjamin and Wolff,

Solnit argues that becoming lost can be enlightening, but to experience that one has to inhabit the place in which you move, rather than moving against it, or feeling that it is moving against you. This is a sense of possibility that is captured by Winn (2018) in her description of setting off to walk a coastal path from Somerset, through Cornwall, to Dorset, with her ailing husband. It is a purposeful, directed (if ill-prepared) journey but is quite literally a series of steps into the unknown, an act of faith that is constantly challenged by an environment to which one must adapt.

From a phenomenological perspective, and hence from an ethnographic stance, getting or being 'lost' is not a matter of confusion. Equally, 'surrender' does not imply an abandonment of intellectual engagement. Both – metaphorically – seek to capture the open and exploratory spirit that informs the ethnographic intellect (Delamont 2019). Finding our way and finding a way are inherent in the processes of ethnographic fieldwork and indeed of the creative work of reflecting on and writing about those engagements. The capacity to 'surrender' to the chosen field and to be open to the phenomena observable there implies an open-mindedness and a willingness to work in uncertainty. It is something of an ethnographic cliché, but it bears repetition that an open mind does not equate to an empty mind. The ethnographer – whatever their career stage – does not go into the field without a repertoire of generic ideas. We do not embark on fieldwork as ignoramuses. This is a caricature sometimes derived from a misunderstanding of the ethnographer's strategy. We bracket our everyday understandings and assumptions, in order to approach things as 'strange'. But that does not mean that we wipe clean our social science ideas. Those ideas are not a uniform set of ready-made concepts. Obviously they depend on one's disciplinary origins, one's primary research field, and one's prior training. But we bring to bear an array of concepts that inform our general thinking. We have guiding ideas about the nature of social organisation and sociality, about cultural forms and processes, and about institutions and their regimes. We have, in other words, broad, but well-informed, notions about our subject matter. We also have precedents: there are key works – probably generationally defined – that can inspire and inform our work. For a review of some such guiding ideas and relevant studies, see Atkinson (2017). No anthropologist going into the field could possibly be ignorant of classic texts written by leading anthropologists of their day; no sociologist would be unaware of similar key ethnographies. At the same time, it remains to be seen *how* those generic issues will be manifested in the unique setting of the fieldwork site.

Consequently, ethnographic fieldwork is always characterised by well-informed faith tempered by uncertainty. Embarking on fieldwork is an act of faith – faith that we can make sense of a novel social world, that we can understand the local phenomena that make it unique and can render that understanding into sociological or anthropological knowledge. At the same time, our uncertainty reflects the fact that each project is experienced by the researcher as a novel one. It is rare for ethnographic research to follow the sort of logic of a laboratory science research group: 'We have identified X, and have purified it, so now we need to go on to do Y...'. Rather, each ethnographic project feels like starting from square one. So, we come to it forearmed with social-scientific competence, yet uncertain of what to expect and how it will work out. One has to live with and within that uncertainty. We echo Rilke and his advice to a young poet:

> ... be patient towards all that is unresolved in your heart and try to love *the questions themselves* like locked rooms, like books written in a foreign tongue. Do not now strive to uncover answers: they cannot be given you because you have not been able to live them. And what matters is to live everything. *Live* the questions for now.
>
> *(Rilke 2016, p. 17)*

To live the questions, to avoid premature and simplistic answers, is to adopt the ethnographer's patiently watchful stance. This does not mean that uncovering answers must be delayed indefinitely, but it does remind us that tentative uncertainty is productive in and of itself. Janeja and Bandak (2019), writing on the anthropology of waiting, suggest that:

> The temporalities of waiting are critical to the translation of data into information, and further into knowledge; the deliberate and patient production of ethnography; the processes of imagination, flight, maturation... and retrospection as fundamental to analysis; the transformation of ethnographic boredom into productive engagement – have been increasingly put under pressure in a neoliberal era where people are not allowed to wait.
>
> *(p. 23)*

'Maturation' suggests pertinent culinary metaphors: ideas can certainly 'ferment', and the process of analysis can often be more like dough 'proving' or 'rising' It is not only neoliberalism in the academy that makes ethnographic waiting difficult. To hasten forward purposefully is recurrent in many areas of research and is not just a contemporary phenomenon. Attempts to make procedural or mechanistic protocols of ethnographic analysis can be appealing because they can seem to short circuit the long duration of a process of maturation. But they serve us poorly.

Consequently, as ethnographers we have to work with and from within a kind of uncertainty. In his letters Keats wrote of a quality found in those who create great works of literature that he called 'negative capability'. He described it as an ability to 'be in uncertainties, mysteries, doubts, without any irritable reaching after fact and reason' (see Rollins 1958). This accomplishment of embracing the unknown, looking it in the face, and sitting with it for a while is a difficult one. It is the willingness to remain in doubt and ambiguity. To possess negative capability is to launch a raft into a sea of uncertainty and not head for the first piece of land that emerges on the horizon. So ethnographic work is shot through with negative capability (cf. Jackson 2017, p. 56). This kind of uncertainty is not something to be got over as an initial hindrance. Ethnographers need to bide their time and not to rush towards premature conclusions. A certain tentativeness or hesitancy is an ethnographic virtue. A reluctance to jump to early conclusions and instead choose to explore different tangents within ethnographic work tends to lead to different insights and nuance which are likely to have been overlooked. We need always to maintain a sense of balance between unpredictable and purposeful fieldwork.

Sometimes, the realities of ethnographic research are described as being 'messy'. Well, any research *can* in principle get messy; any human enterprise can. But it is potentially misleading to describe fieldwork in terms of mess. As Matthews (2021) points out, ethnographic research remains purposeful and methodical, even when there are unpredictable and uncertain contingencies: 'Messy denotes clutter, confusion and incoherence, whereas the intertwined process of thinking about academic ideas and collecting data most commonly has a justifiable and coherent, if dynamic structure…' (p. 117). Keats is extolling the importance of allowing oneself time to sit with so far unrevealed suppositions in the faith it will lead to a much greater and subtle understanding. Negative capability can be utilised as a sort of analytical method which seeks to prevent established frames of reference from becoming rooted and dogmatic, enabling other interpretations of events or courses of action to arise. This disposition acts as a check that the backpack of readings, concepts and ideas we carry is not weighing us down to the point of exhaustion. Negative capability encourages us to work with what is present, observable, local. Yet it extols the virtue of being unafraid to try out ideas, regardless of where they were birthed, because it is an ethos of deviancy and intellectual curiosity. It encourages us to look for and give voice to the outliers, the misfits and the disconfirming because negative capability is at peace with contradiction and simultaneity. In this sense, Keats would very much have stood against the cleaning up and sanitisation of ethnographic accounts.

Negative capability should not be read as fickleness or lacking the confidence of one's convictions, nor should it be read as a reluctance to spend time with and work on some ideas more heavily than others. After all, at some stage, pen does have to meet paper, decisions about weight and direction do need to be taken both in and out of the field. Here, negative capability as an ethical proposition is about maintaining qualities of fairness and compassion towards the phenomenon. As we move from regular interactions with participants into a more cerebral phase, differences between our ideas and those of participants and may well arise. These are likely to be less over matters of fact, but more over issues of analysis and interpretation. Here, it is the responsibility of the researcher to account for decisions taken and conclusions drawn – that openness of spirit which Keats extols matters here too. What negative capability provides is a reminder of the power of consistent mundane reasoning over the drive for security and conclusion; we are forced to confront ourselves once more with doubt as an important ethical check.

Ethnographic work needs time to mature. Surrender to the phenomena should never be passive or subject only to fleeting sensations. Surrender is purposeful. So too is reflection. We need always to reflect on what we have understood and what is yet to be uncovered. Consequently, the fruitfulness of fieldwork does not always depend on the absolute amount of time that elapses in the field. It rests as much on the quality of ethnographic attention and equally on the quality of analytic reflection (the necessary condition for Wolff's catch). As Atkinson (2022) suggests, what is needed is an 'aliquot' of fieldwork – the right amount for one's purposes at hand. That may prove to be relatively short or may turn out to demand the sort of long-term immersion in a chosen field. Either way, one must allow for ideas to be worked on. They do not emerge from one's experience in the field, nor do they spring out of obsessive churning of data. They derive from our active engagement with the phenomena in the first place, and our equally active engagement with a world of ideas and possibilities (Atkinson 2017). The outcomes always remain open to further revision, however, and the complexity of phenomena – their multivalent significance – cannot be wished away or ossified into apparent certainty.

We accept that it is hard to maintain negative capability as a disposition when confronted by the temporal boundaries of contemporary ethnographic work. It may well be tested when well-meaning peers seek conclusive arguments that feel premature. It is likely to be tested by the hopeless misunderstanding of policy-makers and 'impact' agenda-pushers, who prefer clean lines to the contingencies and complexities of practice. As supervisors of graduate students or as mentors of early-career researchers, it is difficult to encourage intellectual wandering when submission deadlines are enforced and metricised. Keats of course did not have to contend with the enforced departure points of university life which forcefully signal a need to become definitive and final. Negative capability will inevitably be tested when attempting to piece together a huge jigsaw puzzle of ideas, descriptions, notes and transcripts. Yet in many ways this is when it matters most. Social life and its enquiry can only ever be reinvented and reinvigorated by living the questions, as opposed to grasping for definitive answers. If nothing else, Keats's brief lines on negative capability should help to settle nerves, not that we have solved a problem, but that hopefully we have inspired five more.

Ethnographic surrender, in the service of anthropological or sociological understanding, opens up the researcher – and hence the research enterprise – to rendering social worlds accessible to one another. To render, in that sense, is to make a social world intelligible. It is not exactly a matter of translation since that could imply the search for equivalences across two or more linguistic and cultural domains. It is, rather, the attempt to reconstruct a social world *and* the processes that led to that reconstruction. It is always an approximation. Moreover, ethnographic work involves the migration of culture and action between media of expression. Everyday practical activity – as observed and participated in – is transposed into conventional forms of representation. They are normally couched in textual forms: first in the form of fieldnotes and transcripts, and secondly in the form of published ethnographies. It is a commonplace to observe that the term 'ethnography' refers simultaneously to the conduct of the research in the field, and to the monograph that is the habitual product. The two are inextricably linked historically and epistemologically. It is as much like musical transposition as it is like linguistic translation, with the added complication that a different harmonic system is called for, not just a different key, and different instruments as well. Hence, there can never be complete closure, the work being always open to scrutiny and revision (by the original author as much as by others).

Hinting at the catch

Neither Wolff, nor Solnit, nor Rilke nor any others who extol the virtues of becoming lost or surrendering to a phenomenon come with clean hands. Every encounter we, or they, have with tentative understanding reminds us of our status as being *in mediis rebus* – we are always already having intimate encounters with existing 'webs of signification' (Geertz, 1973a). These webs precede us, are embellished and remade constantly, can capture and rename and slip away that which we thought we were dealing with. But knowledge of these webs – symbols, traditions, concepts, myths and works – should not compel us one way or another, because these are the webs from which we weave new configurations for ourselves. The task is not to take those for granted, let alone treat them as gospel, but to put them into play and, as Geertz (1973, p. 30) puts it, 'to plunge into the midst of them'. They provide a degree of praxis, 'knowledge of use', or 'knowledge for use' which is core to the practising of any craft. They may provide starting points for questions we can ask of what we experience, witness, avoid, divulge, hide, overhear, put together and pull apart. They may act as bulwarks against fruitful understanding or feed it. They are the contents of the wanderer's rucksack, ripe for new additions to be dropped in, others perhaps discarded or put back in the cupboard. They are there to be carried for a time, but they should not burden us so heavily that we are no longer able to move. Crucially the collations of ideas, texts, concepts, myths, signs and tales we collect do not comprise the wandering itself. Their utility as is that of a way-marker when placed in creative tension with the ideas we generate in the field, where outliers and interactions push against the journals and stocks of ideas we carry, helping to foster new questions, questions that likely loosen the grip 'tradition' has on us and enable us to see the phenomenon at hand in new ways. But we have to allow ourselves to become lost in the first place.

The practice of attention is central to a phenomenologically informed ethnographic endeavour. Attention is active, and it is generated by our engagement(s) with a social world in all its complexity and ambiguity. Attention is the antithesis of disengaged watching or seeing. It seeks to *grasp* the actions of others through concrete engagements with them. To pay attention is actively to be conscious of the effort involved and to recognise the intention to observe, memorise and reconstruct. In that sense, and in Wolff's sense, phenomenological engagement is the opposite of introspection or intuition. It calls for reflection, certainly, but it is not an excuse for narcissistic self-absorption. For it is always directed outwards, towards Others, their doings and the life-worlds they collectively create.

The practice of ethnography is neither science nor art, or it is both. It is a form of craft activity, informed by the investigator's stance of cautious exploration. It is grounded in a practical engagement with the world, material and cultural, in the production of robust knowledge about a particular social world and through that to generic social science understanding. The ancient Greeks called this capacity *Metis*: a practical wisdom bound up with the imagery of the competent sailor and hunter. As Stavros Stavrides (2010) describes *metis*, it has:

> more general characteristics of a peculiar and distinctive wisdom. This kind of wisdom, multifarious and inventive as the wisdom of an experienced navigator should be, was not the wisdom of the philosophers, but an everyday intelligence, appropriating every means available in order to cope with changeful situations. *Metis*, as it was called, was a kind of inventive competence acquired in practice, immersed in the universe of social practices, molded through practice.

As Vernant and Detienne (1978) also describe it:

> ...there is no doubt that mêtis is a type of intelligence and thought ... it implies a complex but very coherent body of mental attitudes and intellectual behavior which combine flair, wisdom, forethought, subtlety of mind, deception, resourcefulness, vigilance, opportunism, various skills, and experience acquired over the years. It is applied to situations which are transient, shifting, disconcerting and ambiguous, situations which do not lend themselves to precise measurement, exact calculation, or rigorous logic".
>
> *(Vernant and Detienne 1978, p. 3)*

For the ancient Greeks, the image of an unknown sea with no recognisable points of reference and no seashore in view was one of absolute alterity. That is why it was considered appropriate to describe metaphorically the Nether World. To cross the sea, the sailor must actually invent a passage, a *poros*. Navigation thus acquires the form of an activity paradigmatically confronting alterity and therefore providing meaningful images of an intelligence coping with the everyday emergence of otherness. As we have already implied, navigation is a most appropriate way of thinking about the processes of ethnographic exploration, provided one thinks of it in terms of navigation without charts, picking one's way across new terrain, moving from point to point rather than following a predetermined route. It seems to us that inhabiting being lost and developing the practical and inventive competency – *metis* – to be able to deal with 'changeful situations' experienced in the flow of fieldwork chimes very much with Wolff's notions of surrender: the better to encounter, to know, without having things settled or prescribed. That is particularly so if we think about wandering and becoming lost as a threshold experience and practice – as an act of opening out to risk, as being and becoming incomplete, in embracing encounter and the unfamiliar and unknown, and, in doing, so to potentially becoming Other too.

2

ETHNOGRAPHY IN TENSION

This book is in large measure about where we observe, and where we wander. Cavafy's poetry, written in Alexandria, was grounded in the everyday scenes and doings of the city's inhabitants in the early decades of the twentieth century. He reported on them with clarity and candour. In so doing, he endowed them with special significance, evoking erotic and mythologised resonances:

> *Surroundings of home, of meeting-places and of the neighbourhood,*
> *Where I observe, and where I wander, year after year.*
> *I brought you into being, with pleasure and with pain,*
> *With so many events and with so many doings.*
> *(C.P. Cavafy, 'In the same place', 1929, from a free translation by PA)*

If erotic knowing seems an odd point of reference here, it is something that we elaborate on later. In many ways, that is the aim of ethnography as we conceive of it, and it is certainly the aim of this book. To some extent, the book is the antithesis of a normal textbook on research methods. At least, it is intended to be so. The textbook mentality tends towards a comprehensive treatment of the research process, which is itself simplified and codified. The textbook teaches us 'how to do it', although textbook accounts can often seem far removed from how researchers actually conduct their research in practice. We are not trying to simplify or codify. If anything, we are making things more complicated, more unpredictable, more difficult: difficult in the sense that we remain faithful to the phenomena of research rather than reproducing easy formulae and precepts. We acknowledge those personal and intellectual difficulties that make up the heady mix that is fieldwork, together with its transformative possibilities. We recognise the tentativeness of ethnographic speculation and analysis in addition to its intellectual rewards.

DOI: 10.4324/9780429056802-2

We also reflect on the undoubted pleasures – personal and intellectual – that accompany fieldwork. To a considerable extent, the pains and the pleasures, the triumphs and the tribulations, reflect the same recurrent issues. Some of those are the subject matter of this chapter.

In exploring some of these issues, we are not tied to any one 'school', any single theoretical tradition or any one epistemological perspective. Ethnographic research is not tied to one overarching theory, and neither are we. The successful conduct of ethnographic research is flexibly responsive, and we believe that ethnographers should be eclectic in their use of ideas. That does not mean that we pay no heed to theory, or to the ideas that have informed ethnography in sociology, anthropology and other disciplines. On the contrary, we draw on various disciplinary traditions, in the social sciences and the cultural disciplines.

Conceptually speaking, ethnography is always conducted between contrasting but complementary poles. It is in tension between: Surrender and catch; Finitude and transcendence; Familiarity and strangeness; Intimacy and distance. These are ways of summarising some of the recurrent tensions that recurrently characterise anthropological and sociological ethnography. They do not define specific theoretical or conceptual traditions or the equivalent of research paradigms. They are common to ethnographies of whatever theoretical or disciplinary stripe. They are intrinsic to ethnographic research: they help to define its characteristic personal and intellectual character. They are what constrain our work, and what make it productive; they convey simultaneously the biographical and intellectual implications of ethnographic encounters.

These polarities and tensions are, of course, all metaphorical. And metaphor is perfectly right for the ethnographic enterprise: *metaphorein*, Greek for 'to carry over'. The ethnographer carries over from one or more social world(s) into the discourse of her or his academic domain. S/he transfers from private, local worlds into the public world of published, filmed or photographed intellectual work. Ethnography carries over from embodied, practical activity into textual and theorised reconstructions. The metaphorical contrasts are not mutually exclusive. Rather, they stand in dialectical relationships. We do not proceed by choosing one or the other extreme but recognise that the polarities are always in a state of tension. Indeed, tensions of various sorts are recurrent features of the personal and intellectual conduct of ethnographic fieldwork. Ethnography is enacted within the intellectual and personal force fields that lie between the opposites and that hold them together. Intellectually as well as physically, the ethnographer shuttles back and forth within and between different social worlds. An ethnographic mentality calls for a certain kind of flexibility – the ability to immerse oneself thoroughly in one or more social settings, and the ability to transcend any one of them

The ethnographer is intellectually mobile as s/he explores (with varying degrees of the facility) those tensions. We shall therefore be tracing the fractures and ambiguities of ethnographic exploration: the existential and intellectual satisfactions and frustrations. Such an exercise could easily appear to be an essentially *negative* one, stressing intellectually problematic issues, rather than a self-help manual for young researchers. But the book should not be read in that spirit. In exploring some of the tensions, antinomies and troubles of ethnography, we also develop an understanding of its intellectual and personal gains. While ethnographic knowledge may be hard-won, it is all the more precious for that. But the conduct of ethnography is not a matter of recipes and formulae. Textbook knowledge is all very well, but it can promote a breezily optimistic view of what can be an intellectually and personally complex enterprise. There is nothing wrong in understanding ethnographic research as inherently complex, involving ambiguities and tensions. We study everyday life by engaging directly with it, in multiple settings, with social actors of every kind. Ordinary social activity is itself thoroughly complicated, as are our fellow women and men. And so we might well expect to find field research with them to confront us with complexities of their own.

Surrender and catch

We deploy the idea of surrender-and-catch, developed and expanded upon by Kurt Wolff. Wolff's notion of surrender and catch is pertinent and attractive. He derives the idea in part from his own fieldwork experience of a community study of 'Loma' (New Mexico), although he acknowledges that the explication of his approach post-dates his work at Loma and the publications that flowed immediately from it. In Wolff's hands, surrender-and-catch is spun into an idea that extends much further than the narrow confines of ethnographic fieldwork. The imagery of surrender implies an unconditional commitment to the field or object of our inquiry. It calls for personal exposure; it leads to a risky and precarious identity. Surrender means that a chosen field of experience enfolds us, as we embrace it. That is not merely a prerequisite or a preliminary to real research and analysis. It *is* the creative research process, or at least it is a moment of it. In terms of traditional fieldwork, our participant observation means that we participate wholeheartedly. It is at once a personal, even existential, commitment and an intellectual one. Surrender means that we launch ourselves into unanticipated events and towards as-yet-unknown others. In the act of surrender, we necessarily suspend our taken-for-granted, common-sense ideas, in order to recapture a renewed understanding of a social world about us. Surrender is akin to erotic love. And like erotic knowing, it demands the embodied commitment of the ethnographer. In surrendering to the here and now, the ethnographer participates fully, in the sense of using all of her or his senses and faculties to make sense of and come to grips with a given social world. As we shall explore much more fully in Chapter 5, ethnography is an incarnate discipline and participant observation implies a thoroughly physical commitment.

Wolff (1976, pp. 22–23) makes cognitive love central to his conception of surrender:

> Total involvement in surrender as in love itself .... In surrender as in love, differentiation between subject, act, and object disappears.
>
> Suspension of received notions: matters that I feel have anything whatever to do with what I want to learn or know, with my exploration, are suspended, that is not affirmed, not denied, but put it question.
>
> Pertinence of everything: 'everything' is everything within the surrenderer's awareness – as for the lover it is everything about the beloved and the love. In the extreme concentration on the moment of surrender, 'everything' is important, but 'everything else' vanishes.
>
> Identification: in surrender the individual identifies with it, its occasion, moment, object, self....
>
> Risk of being hurt: this meaning characterizes not only surrender but also acting on the catch and, obviously, many other activities and situations.

One does not need to adopt all of Wolff's florid formulation, perhaps, in order to appreciate the degree of engagement and commitment that the ethnography commands. It is a way of knowing that calls for the researcher's unqualified attention. As Gherardi (2015, p. 120) summarises it:

> Cognitive love should be understood as openness to knowledge and a mode of knowing that is similar to love, a love for knowledge, since surrender results in existential knowing – the catch that transcends the already constituted meanings.

Clearly, Wolff's formulation owes much to the phenomenologists. But it also adds something. Social phenomenologists like Alfred Schütz also emphasised the need to approach a given social domain as a stranger. The process of estrangement implied the suspension or bracketing of everyday assumptions, of our 'thinking as usual'. This *epoché* means that while our own common sense is bracketed out, we can treat common-sense, practical knowledge as a topic of inquiry. But there is a profound difference between the two formulations. The implied social researcher in Schütz's version remains at a cognitive level. He or she may find the process discomfiting, but that always seems to be a loss of intellectual poise. The phenomenologist who brackets her or his own cultural categories is at a loss until the new field of experience is grasped through intersubjective engagement with the host community. Wolff's estranged researcher is a more existential explorer. It is not merely the loss of common sense that marks or initiates the process of surrender. It is closer to being a loss of self. It certainly can imply a loss of control. It is effective as much as cognitive exploration. Insofar as they must abandon their social status and their stock of cultural competence, ethnographers cede control to their hosts in the field.

If surrender means an impulsive and creative imagination, then catch implies the rational and reflective or analytic capture of experience, of knowledge gained, of theorised understanding. In terms of George Herbert Mead's social psychology, surrender is a commitment of the impulsive I, while the catch is the prerogative of the socialised Me (Mead 1934). For Mead, understanding, including self-awareness, derives from the internal dialogue between the I and the Me. They are not separate entities. They are aspects or moments of the generic process of engagement with the world and our fellow social actors, through which the self is constituted. In the same way, surrender and catch are not separate phases of inquiry or methodologically distinct moves. They are dual aspects of a process of engagement and reflection. The social explorer surrenders to a social world, to fellow women and men, while the catch is an emergent process of reflection (often itself tacit) that is a necessary moment in any such encounter or activity.

As Wolff himself acknowledges, 'surrender' can seem to imply what used to be called 'going native'. That is the loss of analytic distance and the loss of anthropological or sociological perspective. But it is clear that such a form of surrender is not intended, and it is not in that sense that we employ the term here. On the other hand, it can imply something different from and more than simply the intellectual suspension of the ethnographer's own preconceptions and taken-for-granted categories of knowledge. We think it means something more akin to an appreciation – in the fullest possible way – that for the participants, the here and now of their everyday activity is the paramount reality. It means, therefore, an engagement – however temporally bounded – in the work of making that reality happen. It means experiencing that when we observe a social scene, *nothing else can matter so much at that time*. It means an openness to one's fellow women and men that encompasses, to the full, the spirit of *empathy*.

A collective unease or anxiety at going native, of being seduced by the host culture, is clearly embedded in the profoundly ambivalent orientation to the 'others' of exotic and 'primitive' societies that characterised the early decades of the twentieth century. As Torgovnick (1990) describes it, literature (Lawrence and Conrad), fine art theory (Fry) and anthropology (Mead, Malinowski and Leiris) had distinctive attitudes towards the 'primitive' (usually Africa). They struggled to find the right intellectual apparatus and vocabulary within a framework of colonialist discourse. They simultaneously resisted and re-cast moral and aesthetic appreciations of negritude and exotic cultures. Authors/artists like Roger Fry tried to find a workable way of expressing the plastic and graphic vitality of African art and artefacts, while still inhabiting the imperialist language and cultural categories of Edwardian England. The aesthete and the anthropologist could understand and appreciate the cultural manifestations of Others and could develop an appreciative critical vocabulary. But it must always stop short of assimilation. At worst, any degree of surrender would be conditional and temporary. Going native would imply a loss of intellectual distance and an equal loss of that reticence that was the mark of the European intellectual. To go native would be to lose credibility: it would damage respect and self-respect and would be a loss of autonomy. In the contemporary intellectual and political climate, we no longer endorse any residual repulsion in the face of the primitive and the alien. We do not have to find new frames of reference that are not overtly racist. Degrees of affiliation, association and assimilation are more common, even commonplace.

Empathy, feeling with, derives from what Schütz (1967) described as the process of 'growing old together'. The passage of time and presence in the company of others is what – however temporarily – distinguishes ethnographic fieldwork from any other approach to social research. As we shall see in Chapter 4, it does not automatically yield intimacy. We shall argue that in fact growing old together often adds up to mutually interrupted lives. It is not a synonym for the kind of Romantic imagery conjured up by the over-worked term *rapport*.

Finitude and transcendence

We complement Wolff's ideas with some that also derive from the phenomenological movement. They are summarised by Adams (2018) as *finitude* and *transcendence*. Both those terms, taken separately and together as a contrasting pair, have a host of connotations, and they, or closely related ones, are to be found in an array of contexts; here we do not seek to explore them in all their metaphysical connotations. Rather, we want to develop them in relation to our overall project, in capturing some of the recurrent features of ethnographic research. In combination with the ideas of surrender and catch, they will help us to develop some of the tensions and possibilities inherent in the conduct of ethnography.

Finitude refers to the circumscribed practicalities of concrete, practical existence and action. It recognises that we are, as actors, constrained by the here and now. Such constraints are physical and cognitive. Both reflect directly on how we might think about ethnographic practice. As Adams summarises it, finitude means that our everyday life is constrained by time, by place and by one's body. One is hedged about by one's physical being, and by that constellation of experiences, feelings, thoughts and sensations that are ingredients of identity and a sense of self. Such attributes and orientations are by no means private, being themselves constructed from culturally shared resources, including the resources of language. Finitude is, therefore, cognate to the existentialists' notion of *facticity*. Everyday activity is circumscribed within a given, concrete *situation*. We are tied to particular places, events and engagements with others. Our understandings and competences are derived from such situations: the definition of the situation is not an arbitrary imposition but derives from our practical engagement with persons and things that comprise the situation. This carries with it 'all the limitations associated with the physicality of my body: its fragility, its deformities, and its vulnerability to fatigue, to disease, to aging, to hunger, to thirst, and to desire' (Adams 2018, p. 6). So finitude is given by the temporal and spatial limits of situated activity. It is limited by our physical embodiment and our sense of self, permeated as it is by cultural codes and our habitual patterns of thought. Those habits of thought are productive, in the sense that they make everyday activity and understanding possible. They are the bases of thinking as usual and acting as usual. But they are also constraining, in that they put limits and boundaries on what is thinkable and what is achievable.

Transcendence, by contrast, refers to the capacity to escape the limits that constrain concrete activity. We have the capacity to step outside ourselves, as well as make ourselves into topics of reflection and understanding. In ordinary ways, we can imaginatively transcend finitude when we make plans and plan a future. We can undergo transformations through encounters with new and strange situations. We can learn new patterns of thought and action, voluntarily or as a consequence of changed circumstances. We can seek out new experiences that are different from and challenge our habitual patterns. We can undergo conversions and experience epiphanies. We can transcend the here and now by acts of imagination that confer alternative realities and possibilities. Conceptual thinking (in the broadest sense) allows actors to think beyond the immediate practical and concrete situation. It is possible to think in terms of 'What if?' for instance. One can consider other possible situations – from memory, from conversation, vicariously from the experiences of others. Consequently, the transcendence of the here and now, however absorbing and urgent its reality may be, is always possible. Such possibility is not given only by imaginative flights. Physical transport to other places, with other people, into culturally strange situations, may generate the possibilities of transcendence. Altered states of sociability, from loneliness to the intimate presence of strangers, can induce disruptions to one's normal state of knowledge and belief.

So, in terms used by Adams, finitude induces us to think and act within limits; transcendence leads to think beyond our limits. This is a recurrent tension in everyday life. Accepted ideas are challenged, and responses may remain within the limits of thinking-as-usual or may end up beyond those boundaries. Cherished ideas may remain cherished or may be questioned. This is the recurrent tension of ethnographic exploration. If we combine these insights with Wolff's ideas, then we can see that we surrender to the here and now of finite situations. For the duration of our engagement, the given situation becomes our paramount reality, shared with others. There is no more urgent task than to come to terms with that finite situation on its own terms. But equally, Wolff's catch demands a distancing from that here and now and that implies transcendence.

Transcendence is not a mystical process. It does not depend upon an altered state of consciousness. (Although it can certainly rest on a consciousness of altered possibilities.) Indeed, it depends in the first instance on normal human qualities. For instance, it is predicated on the elementary human capacities outlined by Mead (1934). The social actor in Mead's social psychology is capable of reflecting on her or his own actions and being therefore simultaneously the initiator and the topic of scrutiny – subject and object simultaneously. The actor has the capacity to 'take the role of the other'. Her or his perspectives are not necessarily restricted to those for which s/he is the point of origin. Hence the social actor has the uniquely human capacity to imagine action divorced from her or his immediate circumstances. S/he can anticipate the future effects or proposed actions. S/he can shift perspective, from one interactant to others, from the self to a generalised other. Action and reflection are only possible by virtue of the human transcendence of purely reflex behaviour. Such a general perspective on reflection and action is at the heart of symbolic interactionism (Atkinson and Housley 2003).

The reciprocity of perspectives also evokes Scheler's treatment of *sympathy* (Scheler 1954). Sympathy here does not mean the rather wishy-washy sentiment of feeling sorry for another. It means something much more profound within the phenomenological movement. It is a theme taken up by Stein (1989) in her phenomenology of empathy. Here, the discussion centres on the capacity of the social actor to comprehend others as human subjects, not merely as the objects of scrutiny. This is not a matter of mind-reading but is the foundation of sociality. Moreover, it relates to our ability to comprehend *acts*. So, the reciprocity of perspectives derives from action in a shared social world. The ethnographer, therefore, does not claim to be able to second-guess actors' true motives or private feelings, but her or his comprehension derives from participation in a shared world of collaborative acts, including speech acts. That understanding is not given; however, it means that participation, just as much as observation, is intensive *work*.

Empathy-sympathy, taking the role of the other, or the reciprocity of perspectives all imply that the ordinary social actor has the capacity to go beyond – however partially and imperfectly – the limitations of selfhood. This is not unlimited: we cannot traverse the whole gamut of others' experiences. But it is clearly possible to engage with the world around us in ways that are not solipsistic. We recognise the existence of other actors, and to varying degrees recognise the existence of their differences from us and their similarities to us. Only the dyed-in-the-wool bigot refuses to acknowledge difference, and only the most purblind cannot recognise the nature of the difference between Self and Others. Consequently, ordinary competence implies some degree of transcendence. Obviously this is not socially or existentially homogeneous. There are known and unknown domains that can be differentially comprehended. There are contours of acquaintance that facilitate or hinder transcendence. Horizons of understanding and empathy can be narrowed or widened. Professional social scientists themselves ought to be able to transcend the ordinary finitudes of everyday life and the everyday transcendence of human action. Professional competence does not depend simply on the mundane notions of others and rests on informed knowledge of the variety of social types, activities and strategies of everyday life. Such knowledge is not perfect, and it does not furnish simple recipes for taking the role of the other or comprehending others' actions. But we should expect social scientists to use their trained competence to seek some level of transcendence from the limitations of ordinary thinking-as-usual.

This, after all, was the message of social phenomenology, as articulated by authors like Alfred Schütz. Thinking as usual is the 'natural attitude', meaning the frame of mind wherein the practical actor relies on tried and trusted patterns of thought and action. It is relatively unreflective. In this frame of mind, the actor is unconcerned as to *how* things happen or get done, but retains the purely pragmatic orientation, focused on *that* they happen in a predictable fashion. By contrast, phenomenologically informed social scientist approaches social realities from a theoretical, reflective perspective. The phenomenological *epoché* implies a suspension of everyday thinking. The kinds of typifications and recipes that inform common sense must be bracketed, treated as *topics* of sociological investigation, rather than as unexamined *resources*.

These are the intellectual resources that encourage the kind of transcendence envisaged in Karl Mannheim's sociology of knowledge. Mannheim (1936, 1993) described the intellectual as having the capacity to be 'free-floating'. The translation and the image it conjures up can be misleading. Free-floating (or some similar phrase) can readily suggest an image of a completely disengaged and omniscient observer, who floats in a totally unrestricted manner, surveying social worlds from a great height, with a completely disengaged gaze. Such an intellectual would be a bloodless creature, totally unfettered by any ordinary finitude of identity, body or circumstance. Moreover, simplistic versions suggest that this is a privilege granted to the intellectual *because* s/he occupies the role of an intellectual. It thus has the appearance of being a privilege, effortlessly achieved by virtue of position. The déclassé, white male intellectual is readily evoked by such imagery. But the capacity to move, in imagination and sustained analysis, from one's immediate circumstances to new, other temporal, spatial and moral worlds is not a privilege: it is a hard-won intellectual achievement. It is the outcome of sustained work. And it is not the preserve of white male privilege, even though white males have been the predominant category among the intelligentsia. Indeed, as a number of feminists have argued (such as Stanley and Wise 1983, 2002), the conditions of being a woman can give rise to a variety of phenomenological bracketing that is in itself a form of estrangement – both from everyday life and from the taken-for-granted categories of social analysis.

Our view here is the complete opposite of privileged understanding. Relative freedom, or transcendence, is not *given* to the intellectual (the social scientist in our case), rather it is the outcome of hard work. Rather than being given or granted, it is a professional competence and is the outcome of successful disciplinary work. In the case of the ethnographer, it derives from a willing suspension of her or his everyday life, in order to participate in the everyday life of others. It involves a certain degree of existential and intellectual risk, as the outcomes of ethnographic fieldwork are never guaranteed beforehand. It certainly involves hard intellectual labour. It needs a disciplined approach to comparative analysis. It is not unique to the ethnographer, or even to the social scientist. The historian, the biographer, the expert in comparative religion – they must all work at transcending their own cultural milieu in order to make sense of other times, other cultures, other actors.

The ethnographic tension and movement from finitude to transcendence implies the equivalent motion from the immediate circumstances of the field to the generic possibilities offered by comparative perspectives. And that in turn depends on the intellectual ability to treat the everyday world as strange. Strangeness also means treating oneself as strange. One's scrutiny is turned back on oneself. The ethnographer glimpses herself in the mirror of those 'others' who are being studied. She treats her own assumptions as strange, just as she treats those of others. This is the ethnographic realisation of Cooley's famous formulation of the 'looking glass self (Cooley 1902). Ordinary social actors find themselves reflected back in the perceptions and judgements of others, and in that reflection feels pride or mortification. The ethnographer constantly and repeatedly places herself before that interpersonal mirror, and in doing so places her identity and cultural competence under scrutiny (real or imagined). Moreover, far from enjoying intellectual self-assurance the contemporary ethnographer recognises that she is poised in a state of unstable equilibrium, uncertain not only of her hosts' knowledge, but uncertain of her own too. Mannheim's intellectual, therefore, is not, nor ever was, a self-confident thinker who moves effortlessly from one cultural setting to another, between historical epochs or between intellectual fields. By virtue of her intellectual commitments, she recognises that understanding – however hard-won – is partial and tentative. Equally, her own identity is destabilised. The contemporary ethnographer is not an omniscient observer but is conscious of the imperfect nature of transcending both the immediate circumstances of the field, and the trappings of her own biography.

Staying and moving

Ethnography is based on lingering, on being in place. The notion of the field implies a temporary coming to rest. Indeed, long-term fieldwork implies a sense of remaining. But ethnography is not a static undertaking. We are now familiar with the ideas and practices of mobile methods in ethnography (Büscher and Urry 2009). They include such strategies as the go-along, a form of walking-with and talking-with social actors (Kusenbach 2003). Here, however, we wish to emphasise a different order of mobility: that is, the intellectual or imaginative mobility that reflects a distinctive kind of surrender (and catch). The outcome of the catch is not a final position. One does not come to rest at a single point of intellectual mastery. The catch implies further mobility: the capacity to move, in thought and imagination, between social worlds and between ideas. That is, the intellectual mobility to wander, drift and even to lose oneself in the course of fieldwork.

Ferrell (2018) suggests that *drift* is simultaneously a condition of later modernity and a way of thinking about such phenomena. He bases his own study on fieldwork among 'drifters' – hobos, tramps and gutter-punks. Rootlessness, homelessness and nomadism, he suggests, are symptomatic of global social conditions: 'Lives adrift, folks waiting for nothing or on the way to nowhere known – these circumstances circle the world today' (p. 6). He also suggests that such actors are 'ghosts', insofar as their condition is one of absence. But drift, in Ferrell's terms, is not just a way of life for some marginalised, liminal individuals. It also implies a way of knowing:

> For ethnography and ethnographers ... the problem comes when the subjects of study are drifters and ghosts, coming and going haphazardly, moving through settings more than occupying them .... The problem is redoubled when ethnographers, trained to record what is present, and on its own terms, are faced mostly with what is absent. Absence may be present, but knowing how to notice it, record it, and account for it is another matter.
>
> *(p. 190)*

We can perhaps extend the drifting metaphor. Constructively engaged drift enjoins the ethnographer to a form of intellectual surrender. Like the hobo, the ethnographer is a kind of intellectual nomad, or a ghostlike semi-absence, who occupies a social and physical space on a transient basis, who works and explores without dwelling. So purposeful drift – the counterpart to late-modern rootlessness – becomes a productive metaphor for the ethnographer's imaginative and personal commitments. Just as Mannheim's intellectual becomes detached and déraciné, so the ethnographer traverses social scenes, settings and actors – crossing and re-crossing physical and symbolic borders. S/he is present and absent in surrendering to the situation while grasping the catch of analytic reflection (fully realised in her absence from the field).

Such disruptions and transitions are analogous to border crossings. These can be physical transitions or metaphorical ones. Often they are both. Here, we interpolate a biographical account by PA, who travelled from London to Athens, aged eighteen, in 1966 to spend a period of three months with a Greek family and to help out at the English-language evening school they owned. In it PA reflects on the phenomenology of some borderland transitions.

PA's border crossing:

> I travelled by train from London to Athens, aged eighteen, alone. I did not really know what to expect, only that I had a seat reserved all the way, and it had cost us virtually nothing, as my father worked for British Rail. I was going to stay with an Athenian family and do some English teaching at the evening school that they owned.
>
> The journey, the train, took me through Holland, Germany, Austria (briefly), Yugoslavia and finally Greece. Each country needed a separate packet of currency so that I could buy food and drink in the successive restaurant-cars that joined and left the train. Yugoslavia needed a separate wallet all to itself, as the dinar was so inflated that one needed a large-denomination note just to buy a cup of coffee.

As we moved through each country, the train's character changed. Through Germany it was the 'crack' Lorelei Express, following the course of the Rhine, with efficient staff, dressed in remarkably imposing uniforms. When we crossed into Yugoslavia, it changed. It took on the character of the country itself: slow and dour. Its feeling – what in Italian opera we would call its *tinta* – was grey. As we entered Yugoslavia itself, the border crossing took on a new seriousness.

I had been joined in southern Germany by a youngish Yugoslav *Gastarbeiter*, returning from work in a German car factory. We conversed in broken German, Learning that I was English he sought my advice on the best way to knot a tie. My attempt at the half-Windsor for him was inept. After we had passed through the Yugoslav border he lifted the seat I had been sitting on to reveal a row of contraband watches. The bastard had left a schoolboy sitting on smuggled goods, which he had secreted there while I was out of the compartment.

Entering Yugoslavia, a communist state in those days, was more of an event, and more memorable, than any of the other border crossings my journey had involved. It was very early in the morning. It was, as everything seemed to be, a grey pre-dawn. The guards boarded the train and woke us up, demanding our passports. They took mine for checking. Giving it up was frightening, and for the first time I felt vulnerable. We were apparently in for a longish wait at whatever station we were at, so we got out onto the platform. It was chilly and misty. But it was suddenly alien, a little alarming, a little exciting, and very intriguing. The sharp tang of Balkan cigarettes mixed with the pervasive smell of trains and dank dawn. It was romantic. It was, after all, the Cold War and I was crossing the Iron Curtain. Tito's regime was not the most authoritarian. But it was still a communist state. The border guards were real enough and they were certainly armed. It felt like being in a Len Deighton novel, a gritty story of espionage in Eastern Europe. It was the prelude to what seemed like an interminable trundle through the country: it lasted twenty-four hours or so. There was little to relieve the boredom, and the train compartment filled up with local travellers.

The following day – the third full day of my journey – brought a complete change. Entering Greece was a much more relaxed affair, although I had little confidence I would ever see my passport again. But the day was flooded with new light. An opalescent light seems always to belong to Greece. The light shone with the cool brightness of mother-of-pearl. Borders are real. They have real consequences and real effects. In those days there were no European passports, No Euro currency, no free movement between countries. Borders, however, were not just matters of border-controls, checkpoints and passports. There were and there remain real differences in *tinta*.

We passed by Mount Olympus. The light fell on it from the East. It was not my first time in Greece, which already felt like a spiritual home. My classical Greek was excellent; my Modern Greek rudimentary. Musicians

> boarded the train, going from compartment to compartment. They were put out to discover that I had no change to give them having only large notes (old drachmas). But the music was unlike any 'Greek' music I had heard previously (such as the popular theme from the film *Zorba the Greek* by Theodorakis. It was the 'oriental' sound of northern Greece, with a high-pitched wailing clarinet. My border crossing was complete.

Ethnography always implies border crossings. Not just those 'big' borders of national states and other cultures. But the everyday borders of institutions, families and biographies; the borders that demarcate what is private, intimate or sacred; the borders between the known and the unknown, the familiar and the strange. We cross and re-cross them in the course of our fieldwork. Border crossings are always pregnant with the possibility of separation and loss; of renewal and reunion; ofdeparture and return; of reconciliation or separation; and of discovery and disappointment.

The intellectual borderlands are places of dislocation and rediscovery. They are spaces in which one can be lost and yet find oneself again. They hold the promise of what is not yet discovered while reminding us of what has not been fully left behind.

Wandering and wondering

Paul Klee once described drawing as taking a line for a walk. Ethnographic work can entail taking ideas for a walk. Intellectual mobility and ethnographic exploration imply forms of imaginative wandering. It is proverbial that in the course of their fieldwork, ethnographers can experience losing their way, as well as a temporary loss of self. The latter reflects the suspension of social position (as academic, as expert) or status in the interests of surrender to the field. It leads to what we have referred to as the 'imp of fieldwork' (Whitaker and Atkinson 2019). That is, the nagging voice of self-questioning. The imp pops into one's head, asking 'What are you doing here…'. (… in the middle of nowhere; … in this uncomfortable place…; … on your own…; with all these strange people…). It is, indeed, a third voice between surrender and catch. It represents a residue of resistance and the germ of self-doubt. While it can be suppressed for the purposes of fieldwork itself, it also provides the germs of ideas that one must confront in seeking analytic purchase.

Wandering, losing one's way, imaginative bimbling. These are all productive, irrespective of momentary doubts. The essential unpredictability of ethnographic fieldwork means that being unsure of the direction taken is common. Rather than seeing that as a source of trouble, one might follow Solnit (2006), who in turn follows Benjamin, in celebrating creative and fruitful loss:

> "Not to find one's way in a city may well be uninteresting and banal. It requires ignorance – nothing more", says the twentieth-century philosopher-essayist Walter Benjamin. "But to lose oneself in a city – as one loses oneself in

> a forest – that calls for quite a different schooling." To lose yourself: a voluptuous surrender, lost in your arms, lost to the world, utterly immersed in what is present so that its surroundings fade away. In Benjamin's terms, to be lost is to be fully present, and to be fully present is to be capable of being in uncertainty and mystery. And one does not get lost but loses oneself, with the implication that it is a conscious choice, a chosen surrender, a psychic state achievable through geography.
>
> *(Solnit 2006, p. 6)*

Again, the phenomenological and existential commitment implies losing oneself in the moment, in the matter-in-hand, and in the encounter. One is 'lost' only in the sense of not knowing what comes next and remaining open to whatever that may be. But then, we find ourselves again, just as we 'come across' episodes and encounters that nourish our thoughts and reflections. We are potentially confused, certainly. But we come to ourselves with new and changing questions as well as partial answers and connections. Finding oneself in the 'catch' of discovery is always, therefore, an act of self-discovery too. Such discovery is itself unfinished: the self assumes the shape of a question mark. Our stance remains interrogative, not declarative; the indicative (what this is) mingles with the subjunctive (what this might perhaps be):

> The question then is how to get lost. Never to get lost is not to live, not to know how to get lost brings you to destruction, and somewhere in the terra incognita in between lies a life of discovery.
>
> *(Solnit, p. 14)*

Our terra incognita is sometimes our *nullius terra*, which is not quite 'no man's land', nor the neutral ground where duellists met in New Orleans. But it is the neglected terrain that nobody else much wants to claim, either because it seems too banal, or is too marginal, or too esoteric. We inhabit, explore and get lost in what is seen but unnoticed, what is overlooked, and even what is arcane. So terra incognita is re-discovered in the process of surrender and exploration. We find ourselves, and we find social fields that were strangely recalcitrant rendered into new forms of understanding. Our wanderings are sometimes akin to the geographical and psychological explorations of authors like Iain Sinclair (2002, 2021), not least in the ever-present need for sensory and conceptual alertness. Social worlds, like landscapes, are animated by the acuity of the observer's vision and imagination.

Strangeness and familiarity

These interpersonal and intellectual tensions are understood in terms of the phenomenological movement. Wolff's surrender-and-catch, transcending-and-finitude, the intellectual – these all owe their inspiration to phenomenological ideas. One does not have to 'be' a phenomenologist in order to derive insight as to the relevance of certain phenomenological insights to the conduct of social research. Here, strangeness and familiarity have distinctive meanings. Estrangement is fundamental to phenomenology. It is first and foremost an attitude of mind that leads us to suspend our taken-for-granted assumptions and experiences of the world about us. That is an intellectual exercise referred to in the philosophical literature as the *epoché* or 'bracketing'. It means a willing, and willed, suspension of belief in one's cherished, common-sense world. Likewise, 'familiarity' has an analytic meaning here. It refers to our socialised cultural competence, which means we can find it hard to identify things that are so habituated that they are seen but unnoticed. Coping with cultural familiarity can be a recurrent problem for ethnographers conducting fieldwork 'at home' or 'nearby'. 'Fighting familiarity' is an imaginative and intellectual challenge (Delamont and Atkinson 2021).

Consequently, there is a direct parallel between the destabilising effects of phenomenological bracketing and the estrangement effects of ethnographic fieldwork. Both encourage a self-conscious kind of scepticism and promote a close inspection of phenomena, in order to generate renewed understanding of those phenomena – cultural or natural. There is, therefore, every reason to 'surrender' to the phenomena, in order to make them strange. In other words, we commit ourselves to ordinary, everyday activities and encounters (surrender) while holding them and ourselves at arm's length in order to interrogate them rather than simply losing ourselves in them (catch). (As we shall see, losing one's way is also a productive way of thinking about the process.) This is explicitly argued by Geană (2018), who traces parallels between the phases of anthropological research and the moments of a phenomenological programme, in the spirit of Schütz and other phenomenologists.

It is sometimes stated, or implied, that ethnographic conduct with others in an unfamiliar setting is sufficient to generate anthropological strangeness. (Here 'anthropological' does not mean that the phenomenon would be confined to anthropologists.) Proverbially 'first days in the field' are taken by sociologists to be prime occasions when the ethnographer may encounter unfamiliar routines and cultural categories, and hence find it relatively easy to treat them as strange. Likewise, the anthropologist has proverbially been exposed to various forms of culture shock, whereby her or his familiar home culture no longer operates in the new setting(s). This is what Schütz (1971) described in his classic essay 'The Stranger', where the outsider or stranger is a model or metaphor for the phenomenologist. The stranger encounters others whose ways are not her own, and consequently finds that a kind of phenomenological bracketing occurs 'naturally'. But of course in and of itself, such ruptures would cause only directionless confusion were it not accompanied by much more directed observation and reflection.

Estrangement is not the sole preserve of the phenomenologist, nor indeed of the anthropologist. One of the protagonists of Russian formalist literary theory – Victor Shklovsy – worked with the idea of *ostranenie*, normally translated as estrangement, or occasionally as enstrangement (to preserve the odd spelling in the original Russian). As described by one of his translators and editors (Berlina 2017), ostranenie is 'arguably [Shklovsky's] most important contribution'. And she explains it as: '...the concept of ostranenie, of making the habitual strange in order to re-experience it' (p. 24). Shklovsky draws the contrast between *recognising* a thing, which is the product of habitual perception, and *seeing*, which is a feature of artistic practice. Of course, as Berlina recognises, such ideas were not wholly original or unique to Shklovsky. For instance, she quotes Coleridge in demonstrating the Romantic interest in defamiliarisation. Coleridge described poetry as:

> ...awakening the mind's attention from the lethargy of custom, and directing it to the loveliness and the wonders of the world before us; an inexhaustible treasure, but for which in consequence of the film of familiarity and selfish solicitude we have eyes, yet see not, ears that hear not, and hearts that neither feel nor understand.
>
> *(Coleridge 1840, p. 308)*

The 'film of familiarity' is precisely what estrangement seeks to challenge. The (temporary) position of the ethnographer is akin to the outsider or stranger, who confronts not just the unfamiliarity or oddness of everyday life, but, sometimes, its absurdity. In addition to being a methodological stance, it is a recurrent trope. The figure of the marginal or outsider, or of the naïve observer (simpleton or fool) is a recurrent literary device. For instance, as Fiedler (1973) demonstrates, the 'stranger' in Shakespeare is a recurrent and key type, whether it be the Woman, the Jew or the Savage. Caliban is the archetypical monstrous other, who simultaneously contrasts with and mirrors the behaviour of the Europeans. The fool, of course, has licence to comment on the action without reprisal (such as the fool in *Lear* or the simpleton in *Boris Godunov*). In a very different genre, the campus novel can satirise university people and culture by introducing a displaced stranger – an American in England, an Englishman in America for instance (Carter 1990)

The contrast between familiar and strange social settings can, however, be over-drawn, along with similar contrasts between anthropological and sociological inquiry. Most of the phenomena that the sociologist – or indeed the anthropologist 'at home' – studies are far from familiar in any meaningful sense. While some researchers undertake fieldwork among their 'own', and practitioner research exemplifies this most clearly, we should not assume that simply because a sociologist studies something physically near at hand that it is equally near to their own experience or expertise. The tensions between familiarity and strangeness pervade ethnographic exploration. As Delamont and Atkinson (2021) emphasise, ethnographers constantly need to question and confront the possibility of 'familiarity', lest their analytic imaginations can be blunted. They need to work on the 'strangeness' of everyday life. But, as they make equally clear, this goes well beyond the selection of a research site or topic. 'Strangeness' is not given to us simply by virtue of a lack of previous acquaintance, nor indeed is familiarity simply a property of prior exposure. Moreover, as we express it here, 'strangeness' goes far deeper than unfamiliarity. It means the cultivation of a radical ability to examine the 'whatness' and the 'howness' of anything and everything. It means the realisation that one must misrecognise phenomena, in order to comprehend how they are achieved, how they are put together, and with what skills social actors make such phenomena possible.

Between 'near and far' or between 'familiar and strange' lies a complex terrain of exploration, discovery and loss. A laboratory may be within walking distance of one's university office and may even be part of the same institution, but that does not make it a 'familiar' setting. Crudely stereotyped images of laboratory science circulate, which would poorly prepare any would-be fieldworker for the cramped surroundings, the apparent mess, or the tedious routines that are the environment for many workers in laboratory sciences. We may think we know what goes on in a hospital, but the technicalities of modern medicine, the daily and weekly cycle of rounds and conference, the ambiguities of clinical decision-making, the micro-politics of professional status – these and more are far from familiar. One can in fact take virtually any contemporary setting and recognise that many of its features are intrinsically unfamiliar to most ethnographic observers. And that is as it should be. PA's fieldwork with an international opera company is a case in point. The basic procedures of rehearsal in the world of music or theatre are not strange in themselves. But outsiders and newcomers cannot be expected to have a thorough working knowledge of how directors work hour by hour, day by day, how performers respond to direction and how productions are negotiated over a period of weeks.

Polarities of ethnography

One way of expressing some of these tensions is through the juxtaposition of the Romantic and the Classical (or perhaps the Formal). We find interpretative, qualitative work repeatedly oscillating between those two ideal-typical poles. In the Romantic vein, scholars celebrate the personal, the emotional, the local and the particular. The aim of the research is an empathetic re-creation of experience – experience of the social actors and the researcher. It is a sociology, more rarely anthropology, that is suffused with the subjective. It is, we must emphasise, a sociology of subjectivities, not necessarily subjective sociology. In some cases, it overlaps with a Postmodern style of thought. The formal, classical thought style, on the other hand, is more coolly detached, focusing on observable social action. The latter owes much more to the tenets of modern scholarship. It is, however, not necessarily positivist in style, and should not be equated with crude versions of science in its inspiration. The two styles are most clearly distinguishable in their stance towards language. For the romantics, spoken language – collected through dialogue with the observer – is the gateway to the interior life of the speaker. The collection of spoken language, by whatever means, is a way to gain access to the speaker's stock of knowledge, memories and biographically grounded experiences. It is a sociology of speaking subjects. For the formalists, spoken action displays the commonly shared motifs, tropes and resources of the speech community. Any personal or private matters are always refracted through idioms of expression that are held in common. Language is not an avenue to the persona, but a medium of performance.

From these points of view, phenomena like *narrative* occupy quite different positions. For the romantics, narratives unfold the personal, the autobiographical and the confessional. For the classically inclined, the narrative is a shared means of expression that can and should be analysed for its formal properties. The Romantics reproduce and celebrate personal narratives as providing uniquely privileged insight. For the Formalists, the narrative is no different in principle from any other culturally defined form of expressive performance. While the Romantics rail against the Classical approach for its lack of heart and coldly analytic stance, the Formalists criticise the Romantics for an overly sentimental model of the speaking subject and an unduly individualistic approach. The Romantics celebrate, and the Formalists analyse. Our point here is to suggest that this polarisation is but one way among many to try to capture the recurrent, and deeply entrenched, tensions and ambiguities of ethnographic engagement.

In fact, in our labelling, we do a disservice to at least some Romantics. Their celebrations of the natural world, for instance, were grounded in a close engagement with and observation of the natural world. It might have been greeted as representing the 'sublime', but it was grounded in a thorough grasp of the geology, flora and fauna that populated and shaped the landscape. Such Romanticism was not a matter of wallowing in sentiments alone. With some glee, we noticed the following extract from Goethe's letters (quoted by Auden and Mayer (1970, p. 8) in their translators' Introduction to Goethe's *Italian Journey*) where he comments on the work of a younger poet:

> Up till now he has limited himself to subjective modern poetry, so self-concerned and self-absorbed. He does very well with anything confined to inner experience, feelings, disposition and reflections on these; and he will deal successfully with any theme where they are treated. But he has not yet developed his powers in connexion with anything really objective. Like all young men, nowadays, he rather fights shy of reality....

We concur with Goethe that feelings alone are not sufficient, especially when they float free in a social or cultural vacuum, or when texts are narcissistic in their scrutiny of the self. In the absence of concrete observations, they are in themselves idle and self-indulgent. Goethe rather nicely identifies one of the recurrent issues in contemporary writing on 'qualitative inquiry': that in the absence of what I might call observational discipline, feelings become the main – even the sole – focus of interest.

Contemporary ethnographic practice can also find itself poised between cultural appropriation and cultural revelation. Anthropologists in particular have become increasingly uneasy concerning the manifest imbalances between their historically privileged position, mostly in Western academies, and that of the people whose lives they document, and whose hospitality they depend on. In a way that can be likened to the pillaging of artefacts that end up in museums or private collections, the Western anthropologist benefits from the relatively brief foray into the field, returning with precious forms of data that can be parlayed into academic credit and career success, through the production of a doctoral thesis and/or academic monograph and journal papers. The benefits to the host people are usually nugatory. On the other hand, one can represent the ethnographic impulse as one of the cultural celebrations. The twentieth century was the Age of Destruction: of habitats, languages and cultures. Multiple ways of life have been threatened and obliterated through colonial expropriation, but the interventions and interruptions of lone ethnographers have been minimally invasive. Moreover, they have often been celebratory and protective of marginalised cultures, being advocates for their fieldwork hosts, and adopting the perspective of the outsider, the underdog and the oppressed. In one famous contribution, Becker (1967) recommends adopting the point of view of the underdog. That has merit in disrupting taken-for-granted hierarchies of credibility. But wholesale adoption of any one perspective is clearly limiting. While the victim's experience may well estrange the observer from mainstream values, those are not fixed social positions. There is a clear risk of getting stuck in one orientation, rather than exercising the kind of intellectual mobility we ourselves advocate. There is no simple resolution. If there had been no ethnography, the mass obliteration of local cultures would have proceeded, and there would have been no systematic record.

Ethnography is not, however, stuck impotently between those and other polarities. Ethnographers work and live within these tensions and ambiguities. There is, moreover, a further polarity: between what is ideal and what is possible. While ethnographic fieldwork is the subject of virtually endless methodological advice and reflection, it remains stubbornly pragmatic. In the field, our work is determined as much by circumstance as by design, and by others as much as by our own plans and actions. We do not seek to emulate the criteria of other forms of research while trying to achieve the best ethnographic research that we can. We recognise the power of the ethnographer's creative imagination, without believing that it can be represented as a purely 'artistic' endeavour. We also strive for scholarly rigour, without endorsing the crudest caricatures of science. Throughout this book we address some of these tensions further, recognising that ethnographic research is more than just a method for data collection, and is always more complicated that can ever be captured in standard textbooks on research methods. It involves a distinctive personal commitment on the part of the researcher and is an intellectually risky business. There is no guarantee of success (however, that is counted), but it calls for acts of faith – steps into the unknown that absorb large amounts of time and energy. It represents a major disruption to the ordinary, daily life of the field researcher, while exposing her to the scrutiny and control of research hosts, dependent on their – often unpredictable – goodwill. It is a mode of biographical disruption that we shall explore in greater depth in Chapter 4.

We need to ask ourselves what lies behind the undoubtedly strong urges to undertake ethnographic work, notable among younger scholars and early-career researchers. Anyone who has taught a relevant research methods course will know that some topics – ethnographic fieldwork in particular – can give rise in some students to a distinctive kind of enthusiasm: excitement at the prospect of immersion in a social world, of embodied fieldwork, and of such direct engagement with others. Fieldwork promises the kind of biographical commitment that few other kinds of social science seem to offer. Student converts seek the opportunity for a kind of lyrical research – serendipitous, unknown, unpredictable. There is an openness to experience, a commitment to 'see things from the inside'. There is a set of desires that are not articulated through the maxims of 'research methods', and we explore some of them in more detail in Chapter 3. The personal commitments and exposures of research in the field also mean that ethnography demands one's embodied engagement, as explored in Chapter 5.

3

ETHNOGRAPHY'S DESIRE

Research desire

The autocorrect function on PA's computer changes the intended 'research design' to 'research desire'; on reflection, the latter seems equally, if not more, appropriate. Research and writing are not driven solely by rational plans and purposive actions. Our dispositions are more complex than that. Here, we write of ethnography's desires, not of ethnographers' desires. The topics we address are embedded in the tacit culture(s) of research; we do not want to imply that they lie in the psychology of individual anthropologists or sociologists. Even if we make use of some psychoanalytic ideas, we do not presume to analyse ethnographers themselves. It is, we repeat, a matter of research culture not of individual psychodynamics. So, we do not write of ethnographic desire through a possessive or pathological lens. Rather, we consider research desire as a way of thinking and as a kind of intelligence (Thrift 2004): as something productive, active and creative. Where Freud or Lacan see desire as uni-directional, with a point of focus, we see something fluid and open-ended. We explore desires that force, pull, compel, sustain and redirect us to action and creation. Moreover, we are not trying to diagnose the sources of desire: we try merely to suggest and map some of the ethnographic forces that work on and through us. In doing so we align desire with productive and creative impulses.

Our perspective is aligned with a number of feminist scholars, who have challenged the binary opposition of possession versus lack. Grosz (1994, p. 76) writes: '...as production desire does not provide blueprints, models, ideals, or goals. Rather, it experiments, it makes: it is fundamentally aleatory, inventive'. Probyn (1996) draws attention to desire as a movement, and how desire 'moves us at different times and in different ways to engage' (p. 151). Rather than thinking of objects or people or places as desirous – and therefore positioning the

DOI: 10.4324/9780429056802-3

ethnographer and her enterprise within an ontology of lack – we consider lines of desire that run through our ethnographic activities and encounters. In underscoring the productive and active force of ethnographic desire we seek to free it from connotations of individual psychology or implications of lack. Grosz's and Probyn's feminist reconfiguration places emphasis on desire as an energy that fuels our endeavours, breathes life into our analyses and sustains our writing and fieldwork relations.

Desire is, of course, relational. But unlike the psychoanalytic focus on a single point of lack, to be filled by the 'other', we see desire as produced by and productive of a multiplicity of relationships. On this, Gorton (2008, p. 23) writes that desire is:

> … something that produces connections and forges new bonds and as something that is destructive and annihilating. Desire is about the potential to cause all these things and is foremost an unsettling affect; it is characterized by its movement, its intensity and its ability to cause change.

In this vein, we regard ethnographic engagements as reflections of a constellation of desires, a shared range of forces that urge ethnographers into the field and beyond. Desire in its many guises permeates literary and ethnographic imaginations (Grande 2020).

Ethnographic fieldwork and writing are not driven primarily by research designs, if by that we mean that sort of design that is characteristic of so many methodological tracts: a linear plan, a timetable, distinct periods of data collection, analysis and writing, bespoke methods of investigation and highly specified sampling frames with strict criteria for inclusion or exclusion. We do not belittle such designs. Indeed, we suspect that very many social scientists aspire to designing and executing a 'perfect' piece of research that follows a brilliant blueprint from start to finish, and as a result generates unequivocal research findings. But ethnographic fieldwork is never driven or guided by such design or execution. Admittedly, we are often forced to create specifications that have that appearance, helping graduate students and early career researchers to formulate and justify their activities. We create plausible timetables for fieldwork, for the purposes of grant proposals. We specify sampling strategies for the perusal of ethics committees. Doctoral students and candidates for research posts demonstrate how research savvy they are by generating satisfactory designs for their own research. Those plans and others like them are not bogus, nor are they constructed entirely as matters of bad faith. Clearly any period of research involves some sense of plan and purpose, some general sense of timescale and other resources. But these remain strategic goals, rarely tactics, never set in stone. Departure from them in response to the contingencies of the field does not constitute research failings, and they certainly would not invalidate the envisaged research. If research is designed, then we must always be alert to the possibility of diversions and new directions, false starts and retracing our steps. As we write about elsewhere, we are repeatedly swithering between losing our way and finding ourselves once more. The ethnographic pendulum swings between a thoroughgoing commitment to the phenomena and an equal-but-different commitment to the development of conceptual frames. Anybody who stuck doggedly to a predetermined research design in the face of practical research would, at best, diminish the research itself.

We must also be alert to the fact that the ethnographer's work is based on an existential commitment and reflects 'desire' as much as design. Lundberg (2000) indeed suggests that desire reveals much about the work of anthropology. It is not, of course, confined to anthropology *per se*, though some of its salient features may be especially visible in that paradoxical discipline. Inspirations for this perspective include Hegel, Eliade and Butler amongst others. From Hegel and Butler, desire is for 'the other', but is in order to return to 'the self' (Butler 1987). Lundberg writes of the 'romance' of anthropology: 'the romantic's quest to journey to find self – an adventure that necessitates the stripping of the alleged artifice of the social' (p. 28). It is a journey that demands 'leaving', leaving home, 'Father' (supervisor/mentor) and the familiar every day. It is likened to a *rite de passage* in that the ethnographer in the field 'becomes a stranger to herself'. (We have already discussed the processes of estrangement.) This is, Lundberg suggests, a recurrent narrative of anthropology's shared culture.

> And one story that anthropology tells over and over again is that of the journey of desire. This is an archetypal story; it speaks of the journey to the centre – that sacred zone of absolute reality where truth and knowledge will be revealed. And the journey follows a 'difficult road' full of 'danger-ridden voyages'. These 'heroic expeditions' in search of knowledge and certainty are the story of the 'rite of passage from the profane to the sacred'.
>
> *(p. 29)*

The myth of the eternal return (Eliade 1954), for classic ethnography, implies a double or even triple dislocation (aspects of which we amplify in our discussion of Interrupted Lives in Chapter 4). It involves the 'voyage out', which nowadays may be symbolic rather than a matter of geographical distance, and it implies the return home. It is an intellectual and personal Odyssey, a period of social exploration and sometimes intellectual wandering. Eliade himself describes this myth journey as including the

> ...danger-ridden voyages of the heroic expeditions in search of the Golden Fleece, the Golden Apples, the Herb of Life; wanderings in labyrinths; difficulties of the seeker for the road to the self, to the 'center' of his [sic] being and so on.
>
> *(Eliade 1954, p. 18)*

These are cyclical journeys of discovery and self-discovery. The seeker passes through multiple tests and trials. It is akin to passing through the sacred flame, as immortalised by Ryder Haggard, in *She*, with all its attendant existential and physical dangers. It is the Masonic passage endured in *The Magic Flute*. It leads to enlightenment, which is more than simple acquisition of greater knowledge, as it implies the wisdom of self-understanding.

The return reintegrates the ethnographer back into the ordinary life of the office, of writing and of quotidian domestic obligations. For the sociologist or the anthropologist at home, self-evidently, the journey out is not one of great geographical distance. But in both cases, the journey out and back is symbolically potent. It implies a radical disjuncture in thinking and experience. The geographical distance of elsewhere is far less important than the cultural elsewhere of phenomenological strangeness. The desire of the eternal return is therefore to find a form of understanding others in a way that differs radically from virtually every other form of scientific and scholarly inquiry. It involves the personal, existential projection into the lives of others, in face-to-face engagements. It involves the virtual negation of the ethnographer's social status and her sapiential authority. The ethnographer is, metaphorically, stripped naked. Entry into the field recalls Erving Goffman's account of role-stripping and mortification. He of course described it as an attribute of the mental patient's moral career within the total institution (Goffman 1961a). But the obliteration of 'home' identity is similar in both cases. The ethnographer can of course escape in a way the asylum inmate could not. But she still finds herself in the same sort of vacuum, with the same experience of deracination. Eternal return is not just about the single return from there and back. For the ethnographer, the return is – if not exactly eternal – enduring. There are multiple returns to 'the field', not always in person but in the imagination. The initial period of fieldwork can yield multiple imagined visits, delivering material for many subsequent analyses, essays and reflections. It keeps giving, in a way reminiscent of mythical vessels such as magical pots of oil, flour and porridge. Yet, this is an ethnographic desire: to lose oneself within the unforeseeable contingencies of the field. It is an act of surrender, as we have already explored. As Lundberg also suggests, ethnography's desire can be glossed as: the journey out to the other in order to return to reconstitute the self. It is a desire for self-presence, hard-won from the exile of self-loss. It is a desire in turn for what Lundberg refers to as self-presence and a unified self. It is also a desire for origins, for the exotic and for strangeness.

Desire is more than, is different from, mere intention. For Barbaras (2006), desire is of fundamental phenomenological importance. It is also different from 'need':

> Desire has an important characteristic: the object that satisfied it intensifies it to the exact degree that it satisfies it, so that satisfaction signifies the reactivation of desire rather than its extinguishment.... Need refers to a definite lacking; it aims at restoring vital completion, which is why it is

> always a need for something determinate. Desire, on the other hand, is not based on a lacking and strictly speaking it does not lack anything. The aspiration that animates it is not the reverse side of an absence; it exceeds vital necessities and is pure overflowing.
>
> *(p. 110–111)*

The research desire of ethnography, therefore, is directed at apperception that is always elusive. Comprehension can never be complete: it is not satisfied by a single process of acquisition. Desire and eternal return mirror the cyclical nature of the ethnographic enterprise. The eternal returns of fieldwork can never exhaust the possibilities of cultural exploration and textual reconstruction. But eternal returns can also foreshadow the eternal journeys back – back to the fieldnotes and interviews, the photographs and the documents if not to the field itself.

Ethnography's desire for mastery lies in its ultimate impossibility. Others and their social worlds can be grasped only partially, and ultimately they elude full comprehension. Desire results in fragments of understanding, shafts of illumination, or shards of meaning, but the ethnographic aim of holism remains unfulfilled. Indeed, like much that is desired, it is born of hubris. The anthropologist commits months and even years to fieldwork 'among' people, and on that basis claims adequate knowledge to explain 'the culture' and 'social structure'. Yet no apprentice or novice would ever claim to have achieved mastery of such a complex subject on the basis of such a curtailed exposure, however immersive. So, desire is for encompassing mastery, and that desire is thwarted. It necessitates repair. The literary 'returns' often serve to remedy lacunae in a desired holism.

Girard's association of desire with Oedipus is pertinent in one specific sense. Anthropology, perhaps more than any other discipline, is conscious of its 'fathers' (some of whom were 'mothers') and their achievements. For Anglophone scholars, the founding figures (Bronislaw Malinowski, Franz Boas, Edward Evans-Pritchard, Margaret Mead, Ruth Benedict, Hortense Powdermaker, Clifford Geertz, Edmund Leach among them) cast long shadows. Subsequent generations display ambivalent attitudes towards them. They are revered, invoked and celebrated. But there is always the latent desire to overturn them, not merely to surpass their achievements, but to deny them their sacralised status as founding heroes. A controversial case is Freeman's fundamental criticism of Mead's ethnography (Freeman 1983). They feature in the origin myths of the discipline, and like some heroic figures, they must be denied in renewing the field and in achieving the independence of mastery. For ethnographers who follow the way of Sociology, ambivalence towards the founders – of urban ethnography, of deviance, of community and of institutions from Thomas Park, Ruth Shonle Cavan or W.I. Thomas in the First Chicago School to Everett Hughes, Virginia Olesen, Anselm Strauss or Howard Becker associated with the Second Chicago School – is equally manifested in an Oedipal relationship. The acolytes turn against their mentors, even in the act of paying them homage. The ethnographic desire is to surpass their achievements, through a constant renewal of methods and the creation of new problematics. The proliferation of innovations and paradigm changes signal the desire for renewal based on the denial of previous generations and the de-sacralisation of leading 'figures'. For instance, the expansion of 'post' moments and movements creates the impression of a kind of Futurist momentum of change (Atkinson, Coffey and Delamont 1999). On the widespread phenomenon of innovation without change, see Travers 2009. Revisionist texts reveal a recurrent desire to undermine the revered works of previous generations. The critique of Whyte's (1943) *Street Corner Society* is a case in point (see the special issue of *The Journal of Contemporary Ethnography*, 21, 1, 1992). We recognise of course that in the process heroes and heroines can be rediscovered and reinstated as intellectual history is reformulated: see for instance Chin (2014) on Katherine Dunham, or Boyd and Clinton (2003) on Zora Neale Hurston. The reinstatement of women scholars is a major achievement of recent years and reverses the neglect of pioneering 'mothers' of ethnographic desire.

Desire and personal transformation

Ethnographers are often driven by a distinctive enthusiasm. Students and early researchers can be moved by the prospect of an immersive research experience. The surrender that we outlined in Chapter 1 – and to which we return – can be anticipated as a total one, through which personal transformation is achieved by full identification with the research hosts. Far from seeking cultural appropriation, the desire is for cultural assimilation. The desiring ethnographic self wants to emerge from the fieldwork burdened and blessed with unique knowledge so much so that that a profound part of the self is forever altered. It is coupled with an enthusiasm for a kind of lyrical research – serendipitous, unknown, uncertain, messy, unpredictable. There is an inchoate desire to see things 'from the inside', or from the other's 'point of view'. In place of research schedules or protocols, there is the shadow and the fragment. Mess seems seductive rather than repulsive. Embracing the fleeting and the momentary over the meticulously planned, one's temporal horizons blur between the departure and the return. Even – or perhaps especially – accounts of mishaps, missteps and dangers can fuel the desire for intellectual excitement in a strange field site. For a pertinent account of faltering steps in the field, see Jackson (1986) on his fieldwork among the Kuranko of Sierra Leone.

Ethnographic desire is directed to a personal and moral transformation. The eternal return of fieldwork means that the ethnographer comes through fieldwork as through a trial by ordeal, and in the process goes through a form of ritual transfiguration. In Chapter 4, we shall explore this theme further. Here, we note the almost proverbial initiation, or rite of passage, that the conduct of fieldwork confers and confirms. 'Being changed' oneself (Young and Goulet 1994) and ethnography as a ceremonial of self-making is recurrent, if rarely articulated, Fieldwork, successfully completed and transformed from the base metal of everyday life into the sacred text of the monograph is a means of apotheosis. If not exactly a demi-god, the anthropologist has always been confirmed as a 'hero'. As Sontag (1966) pointed out many years ago, the 'anthropologist as hero' is a recurrent trope in anthropology's self-creation (Hartman 2007). For the sociologist, the journey out may well be less exotic, less distant. But similar tropes prevail. Understanding is hard-won and is achieved despite wrong turnings, roadblocks and other obstacles. Both disciplines' narratives include helpers and false friends. The latter are often well-meaning academic advisers who set the narrator in unproductive directions. Atkinson (1996) uses Vladimir Propp's analysis of the morphology of the folktale to analyse these narratives. He shows how closely they can conform to the archetype of the heroic 'quest' folk narrative; Delamont (2009a) generated a parallel morphology of autobiographical accounts of studies of neo-pagan Wicca (which included 'quests' for supernatural experiences). There is, as Atkinson argues, a tendency for the sociological ethnographer to present her/himself in a more self-deprecating way rather than straightforwardly as 'hero'. If the anthropologist is a hero of her own story, then the sociologist is more likely to be the 'schlemiel'.

We must, however, address the mythology of desire that informs ethnographic commitments. Hegel was not alone in emphasising the place of 'the other' in the formation and expression of desire. Self-realisation and fulfilment depend on the elusive comprehension of the other. To comprehend them is partly to possess them, and yet the others of desire must always escape full comprehension. Indeed, desire is to be located between the uncomprehending self and the inscrutable other. And the other can be a different world. As Girard (2004) suggests:

> Desire is not of this world. That is what Proust shows us at his best: it is in order to penetrate into *another world* that one desires.... Behind every closed door, every insurmountable barrier, the hero senses the presence of the absolute mastery that eludes him, the divine serenity of which he feels deprived.
>
> *(p. 1)*

Hence in Proust, Marcel's desire for Albertine is always expressed in terms of her absences, his painful and jealous need to know where she is, and who she is with. In that sense, his desire is never fulfilled, and when he and Albertine are together, living in his flat, he finds her insipid and boring. From this perspective, 'desire' derives from the unknowable other, and the search for a controlling comprehension. But such encompassing comprehension eludes the investigator. The ethnographer's desire is for holism, both in terms of comprehending the other, and in self-restitution – the wholeness of the ethnographic hero(ine). But both routinely elude her or him. The year of anthropological fieldwork, the cycle of absence and presence, shapes a trajectory of knowing and unknowing. The fieldworker must work her passage over the predestined period of being elsewhere, and she must commit herself to a fumblingly uncertain passage towards enlightenment.

Clough (2000) suggests that:

> The oedipal logic of realist narrativity that is operative in classical Hollywood cinema is easily recognized as being operative in ethnographic realism as well, there to stage the erotic fantasy of the ethnographer's penetration of the field and the final traumatic freeing of himself from immersion with the other in order to return home, a man and a hero, with a vision of the truth of reality.
>
> *(Clough 2000, pp. 164–165)*

But desire can never result in perfect fulfilment. The ideal of holistic understanding always eludes the fieldworker. She can carve out pockets of relative certainty (however provisional) but can never fully know the others. Surrender may be total, but then the catch of knowledge is very partial, as the ethnographer will lose the analytic cutting edge of estrangement. The desire for enchantment can always be disappointed by the stubborn realities of everyday life. The exotic can be revealed as mundane; the other as disappointingly ordinary. On the other hand, the ethnographer's self can be fully restored, displayed through self-revelation and celebrated through texts of 'confession'.

The eternal return from the ethnographer's journey is consummated in two forms of textual pleasure. S/he writes 'the ethnography' (usually a monograph) that captures and reconstructs 'the culture'. S/he also writes the 'confessions'. Through confession, the self is asserted and reaffirmed. In the course of fieldwork, the ethnographer becomes reticent, self-effacing. As a liminal participant, endowed only with provisional or fictive membership, the ethnographer's self must often remain muted. Once the return has been accomplished, there is a renewed exercise in self-discovery through writing. The catch of ethnographic comprehension is accompanied by a different catch – of self-discovery, or rather of self-reconstruction. Selfhood becomes in some cases the primary catch of all, through which the ethnographic journey is one of self-discovery as much as – or more than – an exercise in understanding others. The ethnographic confessional has been documented on repeated occasions, and as a genre, it has burgeoned under the rubric of *autoethnography*. Here, we shall not recapitulate all of the previous discussions, but some overview is desirable. Van Maanen (2011) identifies a small number of genres of ethnographic writing. When he first wrote his contribution in 1988, he identified the main genres that included 'realist' and 'confessional' writing. The distance between them, Van Maanen argued, partly allowed for the realist text – such as the main monograph – to remain unblemished by the personal aspects of fieldwork – especially the failures, the messiness and the personal. The confessional could then be a Janus-like document. It created the appearance of self-exposure, while simultaneously maintaining the purity of the 'real', which is realist, text. The revelatory could be consigned to an 'elsewhere' text, sequestered in such a way as to maintain a cordon sanitaire between the person of the ethnographer and the impersonal monograph.

But if we are to understand the ethnographic confessional and the desires it inscribes, then we need to look more deeply and more widely. We need to understand its place within broader cultural and historical currents, especially in American thought and literature. We also ought to pay attention to the wider historical landscape of confessional texts. Indeed, the construction and revelation of the self have been a recurrent theme in theology, philosophy, fiction and poetry. It has also been the topic of literary-critical and philosophical analysis. The confessional has been a mainstay of the Western Christian traditions but also of modern technologies of selfhood and subjectivity. Foucault, in his discussion of the history of sexuality, for instance, discusses the modern transformation of narrative and the emergence of the autobiographical:

> Whence a metamorphosis in literature: we have passed from a pleasure to be recounted and heard, centering on the heroic or marvellous narration of 'trials' or bravery or sainthood, to a literature ordered according to the infinite task of extracting from the depths of oneself, in between the words, a truth which the very form of confession holds out a shimmering mirage.
>
> *(Foucault 1981, p. 59)*

Foucault, therefore, suggests that the personal confession is a discursive technology in the process of individualisation. On a more compressed timescale, we can suggest that the implied narratives of ethnographic desire and fulfilment are transmuted from the modestly heroic to autobiographical confession.

The narration of the self and its revelation have multiple sources in modern culture. For instance, it is to be found in ecstatic, evangelical religion, in which personal testimony is evidence of grace and faith. Moody's account of African-American women (Moody 2003) provides one vivid example of such religiously inspired witnessing. More generally, there is a powerful tradition of confessional writing in American literature, in prose and poetry. Among the poets, Robert Lowell, Sylvia Plath and Anne Sexton have been widely identified as confessional in inspiration. Their lyric poetry 'firmly rooted in both the Romantic and modern traditions' (Hoffman 1978, p. 688) and its confessional sentiments are personally therapeutic in its poetic force (Gill 2004). The conventional term 'confession' here is inadequate to capture the genre(s) of poetry, and – as several authors have noted – it too closely aligns the subject matter of poems with the poet's own biography or psychological state. The genre does, however, reflect that wider cultural current, of which ethnographic self-realisation is itself a part.

The 'confessional' mode is to be found in late-twentieth-century poetry and narrative fiction, and Sontag (2001, p. 15) asked rhetorically, 'Is this frenetic reflectiveness distinctively American?'. To which a contemporary answer is that it is distinctively American, but not exclusively so. And in the context of ethnographic expressions of desire, its contemporary significance and pervasive visibility are indeed American in inspiration. It reflects and inscribes characteristically

American preoccupations: narratives of selfhood, self-revelation and authentic selfhood. As Sherwin (2011) notes in her survey of confessional writing,

> Robert Lowell's 1959 *Life Studies* marked the debut of a new a highly influential school of poetry and the emergence of a broader cultural moment, one in which nothing was too personal or too private to represent explicitly or to foreground self-consciously as a potential context of the author's own life.
>
> *(Sherwin 2011, p. 1)*

In a similar vein, Gregory (2006), discussing the confessional poets – Plath, Sexton, Berryman, Lowell and Ginsberg – focuses on their personal revelations concerning the body:

> All five of the poets ... employ the confessional mode to open up discussion of the power dynamics of poetry and the society it reflects and addresses. Gender politics supply the entrée to a range of linked issues of power. While these poets do not resolve the issues, they illuminate them brilliantly and expand the available options for speech.
>
> *(p. 41)*

Such poetry deployed the transformative possibilities of the personal lyric and its expression of personal experience: 'Confessing one's desires, one's pains, one's perceived "sins" against the world and others is a way to release the self from personal pain and bondage, thus creating a new self in the wake of trauma' (Harrod 2007, p. 4). Confession has its roots both in Catholic observance and in Puritan notions of cleansing and purging (cf. Bleakley 2000). It has distinctively Christian roots in European and American culture, but it is by no means confined to such contexts.

As anthropologists and sociologists, we should not assume that autobiographical writing is transparently revelatory of the author's subjective interiority. There are genres of autobiographical expression and confession that are specific to cultures and historical periods. If we must live in a time of self-writing on the part of ethnographers as well as by poets and other authors, then we need to cultivate an awareness of such culture-bound genres. It is a mistake to assume that autobiographical narratives are the exclusive preserve of Western literate cultures, as has sometimes been argued. Such a narrow perspective is clearly antithetical to the cultural sensitivity that informs the ethnographic imagination. A relevant case is provided by the multi-authored volume edited by Reynolds (2001), concerned with the Arabic tradition(s) of autobiographical writing. The authors challenge the view that Arabic literature has been virtually devoid of autobiographical texts. It is pointed out that the tone and content of the Arabic tradition is very different from any Christian counterpart. The Christian tradition required a confession of one's sins and shortcomings; early Arabic autobiographical followed a different imperative that included the presentation of one's life in terms of God's blessing and one's thankfulness, in accordance with the injunctions of the Qur'ān. Subsequently, Arabic autobiography developed multiple formal types, including more personal psychological accounts. The Arabic traditions are among many types of autobiographical writing, each constituted by distinctive literary forms and each inscribing what might 'count' as an appropriately shaped and narrative 'life'. Discussions of equivalent traditions include genres of Japanese life-writing (e.g. Miller 1985; Ames 1994), while the essays edited by Curran (2019) include discussions of self-writing in the Renaissance literature. See also Fallon (2019). The autoethnographic and biographical vein is not confined to current and recent Western writing after all.

There are, therefore, two directions in which ethnographic desire can lead. On the one hand, there is the desire to know the other(s), despite the manifest difficulties of such knowing and the limits of any such understanding. On the other hand, is the impulse to discover and uncover the workings of the self. The latter is manifested in the contemporary life-writing genre of autoethnography. In recent decades, autoethnography has elevated the personal to an unprecedented level among authors who regard themselves as ethnographers. It is the quintessence of a desire to transform one's self as one outcome of research and writing. Indeed, self-absorption and self-exploration cease to be a function of exploration of others' lives. One's own experiences become prime topics of interest. The balance slips from the twin lenses of self and others, to become a monological focus on the self. It is an ethnographic desire grown narcissistic, as Delamont (2009b) argues. Preoccupations with self-transformation always remain central to ethnographic desires, but in contemporary autoethnographic writing, they become a force for distortion. Like a hall of mirrors, autoethnographic texts only reflect back the self in multiple perspectives, with nothing visible beyond the mirror itself. Reflective writing in that vein results in the infinite regress of mirrors, with images of the self-disappearing into the distance.

Seductive analysis

Ethnography's desire is focused on uncovering its phenomena. Ethnography creates the objects of its interest out of the base materials of everyday life and transmutes them into something precious (Atkinson 2022). It means not just finding the phenomena, but losing oneself among them, following the phenomena and allowing oneself to be absorbed and even seduced by the objects of close attention. We are familiar with the notion of abductive reasoning, especially as it is applied to ethnographic research (cf. Timmermans and Tavory 2022). In essence, abductive reasoning demands of the researcher that, in the light of some observed phenomenon or regularity, she or he should ask: What underlying rule, pattern or process might give rise to such observations? It is clear, therefore, – as we have noted previously – that the typical question can be framed as: What might this be a case of? The initial question is one that invites provisional, even tentative, candidate answers. Especially in its initial formulations, any possible answer is speculative. Such speculation in turn implies and informs further inspection of possible examples of the same, or similar, patterning. Hence, there is an iterative process whereby observations (data) are inspected for possible categories or explanations, which in turn are further tested against more, other, observations. As that process of exploration and speculation proceeds, so the analytic categories – the possible modes of understanding – become thickened, or modified, confirmed or called into question. They may be abandoned in favour of alternatives, which of course become part of a further process of exploration. There is, therefore, a constant intellectual shuttling between ideas and observations. This is *not* a description of analysing a completed, inert body of data. The ethnography does not proceed blindly, devoid of any ideas, until the fieldwork has been completed. It is not (should not be) a matter of accumulating an unsorted heap of materials (observations, conversations, images, documents) and then trying to make sense of them from scratch. Such an image of ethnographic fieldwork and its outcomes does not do justice to the active intelligence of the ethnographer in the field and her or his intellectual commitments that lead to the conduct of fieldwork in the first place.

It is readily apparent that the speculative reasoning from first-hand observations (of all sorts) leads many commentators to overlook the tradition of abductive inference, labelling the analysis of ethnographic ('qualitative') materials as 'inductive'. But a purely inductive spirit does not pay sufficient attention to the significance of disciplinary ideas in the process of speculation and inference. Worse, it implicitly encourages the view that ethnography is conducted 'blind', without prior knowledge or guiding ideas. Such a view is empirically inaccurate: ethnographers are, or certainly should be, well-informed on the basis of theoretical and methodological ideas, and on the basis of previous investigations by themselves and others. Equally, a purely deductive approach runs into the sort of criticism routinely levelled against it. Namely, there is no obvious way of choosing *which* theories to test with empirical observations, if there is no space for prior observation and/or experience. A purely deductive approach, based on successive testing of hypotheses derived from existing theory, runs entirely counter to both the spirit and actual practice of any field research, in all disciplines. Any notion of exploration that involves the fundamental desire to discover 'what goes on here' will not depend solely on theory testing or theory confirmation. There *is* of course an important place for theory testing and theory amplification in ethnographic research. The careful selection of research sites, such as extreme or deviant cases, or the exploration of taken-for-granted routines, can lead to kinds of theory testing.

So much is well enough established in the methodological literature surrounding ethnographic fieldwork and analytic inference. Here, we wish to offer an additional idea – *seductive* analysis. Seductive thinking is the obverse of abduction. Abductive logic is based on *drawing out*: from initial observations, we draw out plausible explanatory patterns. Seductive reasoning is based on being *drawn in*. Seduction is a correlate of surrender, in Wolff's sense. We allow ourselves to be seduced in the sense that as ethnographers in the field, we become *absorbed* by and into the ordinary and extraordinary phenomena we encounter and the remarkable social actors who display their skilful performances. Like many actors in the course of their everyday work and domestic life, there are many moments when *nothing else matters*. Irrespective of the overall import of their activity, whether it be of great consequence or of passing interest, it demands fully focused attention. The teamwork of the operating theatre, the intensity of the rehearsal studio, the mutual attention of lovers and the absorption of the craft worker – these all compel engagement to the utmost degree. Through individual or shared concentration, there is created a domain – often very small and circumscribed – beyond which nothing impinges for the time being. It may be temporary, but while it lasts it corresponds to what Schütz called *paramount reality*. It is one of the most striking features of everyday life and works: what might appear to be trivial activities can command intense attention and strong feelings.

Seductive realities absorb their participants, and they absorb our attention too. We must emphasise that such seduction does not necessarily mean that we 'go native', by abandoning any analytic or critical reflection. Seduction and abduction go hand in hand. We are absorbed by the local action, and we draw out from that intense participation and observation the capacity to move to a level of greater generality. Seductive engagement and analysis is, therefore, a corollary of ethnographic surrender. There is a parallelism between the absorption of the everyday world and the sustained attention of ethnographic participation. When the fieldwork calls for genuine *participant* observation, or even for complete participation, the two domains of attention coincide. The field researcher who is totally engaged in a task in hand, or in learning some particular skill or routine, is simultaneously absorbed by the practicalities of making or learning, and by the demands of ethnographic attention itself (Atkinson 2022). O'Connor's apprenticeship in glass-blowing exemplifies that kind of full (literally hands-on) engagement (e.g. O'Connor 2005, 2006).

Seductive research desire leads us to enter into the phenomena. We witness not just 'from the inside' but also from multiple angles, especially from 'below'. This calls to mind Kathleen Jamie's essay on the *Hvalsalen* (Whale Hall) in the Bergen Natural History Museum:

> Then came the most prestigious room, the main hall. And there, entering through its double-height, double doors, I was taken aback. The architect must have intended a grand room – big enough to host a sizeable dance, or a city congregation – with thick wooden floors and cream-coloured pillars rising toward elaborate capitols, and arches, and arched windows, but the symmetry he intended was confounded because of the whales. The skeletons of whales. You walk through into the 'Hvalsalen' and, immediately above, side by side, like vast oxen yoked together to haul the most terrible plough, are the jaws of two great baleen whales. Not just the jaws – the entire skeletons,

> the ribcages, the great fans of the scapulas and fin-bones, at the sides the long receding trains of the spines. The bones are brown with age – and there are not one or two but twenty-four cetacean skeletons crowded under the ceiling.... The Hvalsalen. Whale Hall. What else could it be called?
>
> *(Jamie 2012, p. 96)*

The archive of desire

Ethnographic desire can include the impetus of the *collector* or the archivist. The culture of ethnography can encourage the search for ever more materials – 'data', memorabilia, documents and the like. Ethnographic researchers, in the search for completeness, embrace a plenitude of evidence. In the absence of quantitative estimates of coverage (sampling strategies, cumulative number of cases, distributions of events), there is an understandable desire to *accumulate*. Through multiple acts of acquisition and accumulation, the ethnographer endows with significance events and actions, from the most mundane to the most esoteric. It is in the open-ended and provisional nature of ethnographic fieldwork that the final significance of accumulated materials is unpredictable. Consequently, the ethnographer can create an archive-like accumulation into which she or he can 'dive', in a secondary act of immersion, after that initial immersion into 'the field'. This a theme that we shall return to in Chapter 7.

Collecting reminds us that ethnographic accumulation can sometimes take on the appearance of compulsion or obsession. There is nothing to suggest the extreme behaviour of the male protagonist and narrator of John Fowles's (1963) novel *The Collector*, who modifies his obsessive collecting of butterflies into the abduction of his female victim, Miranda, in the desperate hope that she will come to love him. (The film version was released in 1965, starring Terence Stamp and Samantha Eggar.) The act of 'collecting' another person is, of course, transgressive in the extreme; collecting in itself is not. But the creation of an archive, curated in the same spirit as that of the collector, is definitely an apt metaphor for at least some ethnographic accumulation.

The collection can consist of anything, irrespective of any aesthetic or use value. It is sometimes sufficiently significant for the enthusiast that it has been collected at all. Olivia Laing's memoir of loneliness in the city of New York (Laing 2016) and thoughts about some of its artists include a reflection on the life of the self-taught artist Henry Darger. As well as his achievements and quirks, he had an obsessive interest in string (pp. 264–265). Ordinary string or twine, that is, not the esoteric strings of string-theory physics. Strings provide powerful metaphors for belonging and comprehension. But they are also sources of frustration: their tangles and knots can drive one to fury. They are the ties that bind our mothers' apron strings. They can furnish a sense of belonging, although the tangles and unravelling can also evoke the loss of security or certainty. We string along others and sometimes ourselves. Our heartstrings oscillate with love and joy; they are snapped and broken. Ariadne's clue that led Theseus safely out of the labyrinth was a clue of thread. It led ultimately to her abandonment. The clue of thread that led to freedom became a web of entrapment. Social investigators like to talk of entanglements: their own entanglement with their research hosts and their mutual alignments. They find the phenomena of everyday life to be enmeshed and entangled one with another. They also like to disentangle the complex and multiple relations of implication in everyday life. In disentangling, they hope to pick up clues that they can follow and use as keys to decode local – often opaque – cultural conventions and interpersonal relations. And then re-weaving them into their ethnographic reports, reflections and recollections. We string together episodes, events or extracts into a continuous thread of narrative and exposition. So, metaphorically speaking, even an archive of string can trigger associations that could prove productive.

We glimpse the personal archive through various sources. Among them are Leiris' (2017) *Phantom Africa* (2017), his ethnographic record of the French expedition to Djibouti, and Walter Benjamin's *Arcades Project*, the amassed resources for an ultimately unrealised project of exploration and cultural history concerning the arcades of Paris (Benjamin 2002). In many ways Benjamin's archive of fragments has become even more iconic than the published monograph on those arcades ever would have been not least because the contemporary reader can lose herself within the archive and can trace multiple pathways through it, in a way that seems hypertextual *avant la lettre*. Wohlfarth (2006) identifies Benjamin's own obsessive collecting in terms of the *chiffonier,* the *Lumpensammler* or the rag-picker. These (near) synonyms partly capture Benjamin's collection of memorabilia – mostly textual – about a declining aspect of Paris's cityscapes. On the other hand, they also suggest a certain randomness. The rag-and-bone collector is not a 'collector' in terms of connoisseurship, whereas Benjamin's arcades collection was purposeful, in that it was focused on an intellectual project. The meaning of *Lumpensammler* as also indicating 'the last bus or tram', however, does resonate with Benjamin's, and the ethnographer's, interest in sweeping up the remnants of a given social or cultural milieu. The creation of the archive is also associated with the type of the *flâneur*, the idler who, sauntering in the city, observes its scenes, its characters and the passers-by (see Buck-Morss 2006). But although Benjamin refers to *flânerie*, this also seems too much dependent on happenstance to convey the obsessive preoccupations and desires of the ethnographer/archivist. Appositely, Abbas (1988) examines 'the collector' partly through the lens of Walter Benjamin's work. For Benjamin, the collector is a modern figure who stands in a paradoxical position *vis-à-vis* modernity. Benjamin argues that writers such as Flaubert, Conrad and Nietzsche examine the collector's dangerous passions:

> In Flaubert, it is the danger of classification that reduces the heterogeneity of experience; in Nietzsche, it is the threat of knowledge being increasingly reified and so losing its ability to 'serve life'; in Conrad, it is the ironic

> spectacle of the collector's object of desire producing a narrative of desire whose theme is the impossibility of desire being fulfilled.
>
> *(Abbas 1988, p. 225)*

It is perhaps Conrad's version that touches most closely on our own understanding: the ethnographic desire that cannot be completely fulfilled, as the collection always remains incomplete, the archive bounded and its exploration uncertain. The collector revels in the successes of acquisition and the chagrin of incompleteness. So too does the ethnographer. The personal archive, in the form of a material collection, can have virtually any contents, however, mundane: string, sealing wax, packaging and labels, matchboxes, beer mats and books of matches. The artefacts themselves may – unlike, say, fine-art collections – have no intrinsic value in themselves. Their significance derives precisely from the fact of *having been collected*. And by virtue of being placed within the archive, they gain significance by means of their place within the collection: they form parts of syntagmatic and paradigmatic relations. They can be parts of series, or sets, they can trace the development of an artefact over time or its geographical variations. The collection makes possible a multiplicity of arrangements and hence of associations. Any significance is created through the relations between the constituent elements.

Benjamin's Arcades Project is one of the most important personal archives in twentieth-century cultural studies. Like many other projects and artefacts – like an unfinished *pietà* by Michelangelo – the fascination of the arcades archive partly resides in the very fact of its unrealised state. Carefully, perhaps obsessively, collated by Benjamin over a long period of time, the huge number of fragments is open to multiple explorations by subsequent generations of readers and commentators. Dialectically, those Parisian arcades – a common architectural feature of nineteenth-century Paris already disappearing in the early decades of the twentieth – achieve cultural prominence by being documented and latterly by being restored. The published version available to us reflects Benjamin's own preliminary work in classifying his materials: it is an ethnographic analysis in embryo, frozen in time as the project, and ultimately Benjamin's own life, were cut short. This unrealised project parallels the bitter-sweet sense of impossibility that attends any attempt at an exhaustive, complete analysis. The cultures of ethnography always contrive to escape systematisation and remain only partially understood. It is the obsessive desire to collect and record that inspires the archive. As Sontag (2012) wrote in her diaries 'My library is an archive of longings'.

Leiris' fieldwork record is also a colossal, if ramshackle, document. *Phantom Africa* (2017) is his field journal, as he participated in the 1931–1933 trans-African Dakar-Djibouti expedition, organised by Marcel Griaule. The 'phantom' book stands proxy for the monograph that Leiris could or would have written. It is also peopled by what Leiris himself referred to as 'ghosts', rather than real human connections: '...little phantoms, in truth, which it would take less than a rooster's crow to dispel but which, despite their futility, remain awful, for they are a finger placed on a poorly concealed wound' (31 August 1932). Leiris' own reflections on his archive are partly illuminating: '... what emerges in close-up is no longer a fallacious attempt to *other* myself by taking a plunge – entirely symbolic, moreover – into a "primitive mentality" for which I was nostalgic, but instead a broadening and forgetting of the self...' (Leiris 2017, p. 64).

While undoubtedly of interest as an archive, *Phantom Africa* is also an enigma. For the reader, and probably for Leiris himself, it provides an extended series of *glimpses* of African life, many of which may strike the contemporary reader as inconsequential. Authors like Clifford (1988) have cited Leiris in the context of surrealist writing and aesthetics. And it is true that Leiris' oeuvre included surrealist work. But for the ordinary reader, what is really striking is just how banal most of the entries seem to be. Perhaps the 'surreal' sense is conveyed by the inconsequential character of so many of Leiris' observations. His apparent lack of comprehension of what he witnesses renders some of the events absurd (Absurd therefore rather than Surreal). For instance, an entry for 15 June reads:

> When most of the adult women had danced, the bearded griot [musician, oral poet, story-teller] performed the following number: while continuing to play his drum and shake his rattles with one hand, with the index finger of his right hand he traced patterns in the sand in time with the beat. They were magic Islamic squares and figures.... When the figures were done, he threw down the little stick he had been using earlier to beat the drum on occasion. The stick fell on one of the patterns and the griot pointed with his finger to show where it had fallen: an amazing pantomime of divination. A fusion of music, drawing, dance, magic.
>
> *(p. 93)*

The entry for the following day includes:

> The soothsayer griot, asked to explain his turn, declares that he does not know what the figures he is tracing mean, and that he does it to show that he plays the drum so well that he can do other things at the same time.
>
> *(p. 94)*

There are, of course, intriguing possibilities here. The contrast between the two entries is interesting. In the first, Leiris appears to have an outsider's view, though apparently knowledgeable enough to describe the sand drawings as 'Islamic' (or was it just guesswork?). The second entry just seems to undermine its self-assured descriptive fluency. But perhaps in describing the griot's performance as 'pantomime' Leiris is more knowing than naïve, as it first appears. Is the griot dissembling? We shall not know, and Leiris' own notes are frustratingly superficial. But the point here is not to try to conduct a secondary analysis or to read back later work on griot performers. What we allude to is the significance that the ethnographic archive can achieve, as a repository of challenges, regrets, turning points and revelations. It is their collation that renders them interesting at all. Neither Benjamin's archive project nor Leiris' African notes deserve to be sanctified as some sort of modernist 'collage' or 'montage'. But it is only by virtue of their being an identifiable archive that any such attribution is even possible. Vicariously, they provide partial fulfilment of the archivist's or the collector's desire. We suggest that though they be more humble and obscure, the archival desire is equally strong among virtually all ethnographers. The personal collection is a physical embodiment of one's heroic – if doomed – impulse towards the complete, exhaustive recording of a social world. The apparently inconsequential diary entries, and the memorabilia, so carefully rescued and curated, bear physical witness to the ethnographer's quest. We shall return to issues of collecting and archiving in more detail in Chapter 7.

The will for completeness is also reflected in the desire – often tacit – for *saturation*. Sometimes when we inquire into ethnographic desire(s), we need to look beyond the 'official' methodological literature, trying to intuit broader connotations of common usage. That seems to be true of the idea of saturation. The canonical use of that term is associated primarily with the orthodoxy of Grounded Theory. But what seems most revealing is the apparent misuse of it, when viewed from a narrow Grounded Theory perspective. The basics are, inevitably, outlined by Charmaz (2014) in one of her standard works on Grounded Theory. She points out that many authors treat saturation in an apparently naïve way, noting that it is often used to describe the sense that the researcher is not learning anything new, having witnessed or heard 'the same' things repeatedly. Hence, there is nothing further to be gained from further fieldwork or interviewing. Either the fieldwork is essentially finished, or it is time to move to another site. It thus becomes synonymous with the figure of repetition or a sense of completeness. Now Charmaz takes to task such researchers, insisting that such usage is not compatible with correct Grounded Theory. It is true that in such a context, saturation means something different, something more specific – at least according to strict Grounded Theory. After briefly reminding readers of the orthodox position according to Charmaz, we shall return to speculate on how and why the 'incorrect' versions might appeal to many ethnographers, in one version or another. Charmaz points out that the original meaning of saturation 'is not the same as witnessing repetition of the same events or stories…' (p. 213) and she quotes Glaser (2001):

> Saturation is not seeing the same pattern over and over again. It is the conceptualization of comparisons of these incidents which yield different properties of the pattern, until no new properties of the pattern emerge. This yields conceptual density that when integrated into hypotheses make up the body of the generated grounded theory with theoretical completeness
>
> *(p.191)*

In this 'orthodox' usage, saturation relates to issues of theoretical sampling and is aimed at achieving appropriate complexity. It is not intended to capture the accumulation of cases or collecting data to a vanishing point of novelty or conceptual insight.

Let us accept that Grounded Theory exponents have a sound argument here about the necessity of exploring and developing the dimensions and the range of variation within conceptual categories. But then let us explore the image of repetition and completion that is characteristic of others' usage in the context of ethnography. After all, some sense of completion is a powerful one for fieldworkers. The metaphor of saturation is suggestive. We can think of saturation in sensory terms. We speak of colour saturation, for instance, and that in turn suggests *intensity*. The saturation of colour also carries connotations of *depth*. So depth, intensity and repetition might be counted among the imaginaries of ethnographic ambition. The ethnographer's surrender to the phenomena of everyday life in all its variety and complexity can imply an openness – sometimes ambivalent – to being overwhelmed by the sensory and cognitive burden. Consequently, saturation is an ambivalent metaphor. On the one hand, it means a sense of fulfilment and a parallel sense of completion. Equally, it can feel like an overwhelming array of demands on one's personal and intellectual resources. As an ideal, saturation might also remind us of the almost inevitable incompleteness of our actual understandings. The rather stern injunctions of Charmaz or Glaser can seem all but impossible to live up to. The exhaustive exploration of all the possible dimensions and constellations of variation feels like a counsel of perfection. The goal of saturation contains its own negation – the impossibility of total analytic comprehension.

Similar observations might be made concerning an analogous ethnographic concept: *thick description*. Here again, we find a methodological term that has a specific meaning being stretched with much broader connotations. Once more we can attribute such a conceptual move to the generalised desire for *plenitude*, *completeness* and *concrete detail*. Geertz's (1973a) original formulation recognises the essential complexity of cultural forms and enactments (Leeds-Hurwitz 2021). There are multiple frames of reference that may be in play for any given activity and participants may bring to bear multiple interpretations. The idea thus encourages the ethnographer to explore the many layers and versions of interpretation. It encourages a sense of potentially partial, incomplete understandings. The relationship between the ethnographer and her or his hosts may be inhabited by misunderstandings, by competing interests, by errors of comprehension. The ethnographic text, Geertz argued, should take account of and reflect such complexity, including the possibility of incomplete comprehension. It was never an argument simply in favour of lots of detail or illustrative material. The broader – even vulgar – uses of thick description speak to another version of plenitude. Here, it connotes a descriptive rather than an analytic virtue. Thick descriptions are, it is claimed, replete with concrete detail and display the virtue of 'rich' data. The ethnographer can celebrate the accumulation of instances, and the detail of descriptive writing, or the dense population of social actors in the text. It sometimes accompanies the detailed and repetitious illustration of the argument with vignettes drawn from fieldnotes, or verbatim quotes culled from interviews. Plenitude and detail reflect the ethnographic goals of holism tempered with a sense of its impossibility, the tension between surrender to the overwhelming detail of everyday life and the imperfection of its capture. Whatever it can be made to mean, a thick description should not be used to imply that ethnographic quality is enhanced or guaranteed by the presence of lots of descriptive detail or data extracts. Thickness is not a matter of loading the ethnography with multiple accretions of examples. Thickness does not need to result in the turgid accumulation of descriptive or contextual material. If the thickness is to have any value for ethnographic work, it must surely lie in the recognition of multiple possibilities of significance that are to be found in any given social activity. In just the same way that Mills (1940) identified the possibility of multiple 'vocabularies of motive' that could account for any given action, orientation or value. Likewise, the thickness can reflect the multiple modalities of action and experience: linguistic, tactile, sensory and so on. Hence, the second item, 'description', also hints at a limitation. It reflects an interpretative approach to culture that treats it as analogous to a text that invites interpretation. A textual sensibility is an important aspect of ethnographic interpretation, and it is clear from the contents of this book that we favour approaches that draw inspiration from literary and critical sources. But it is clearly not the whole answer. Social action and social organisation are not 'texts' in even a metaphorical sense. Moreover, the emphasis on description implicitly under-values action, artefacts and embodied experience.

The impetus of the collector and the accumulation of the archive can also lead us towards the desire for ordering and re-ordering. If nature abhors a vacuum, then ethnography abhors a lack of order. While some authors may overtly celebrate 'messy' research and equally messy texts, there remains a deeply embedded desire for ordering. The archive, be it physical or conceptual, invites cataloguing and documenting. Whether it be books, compact discs, fieldnotes or transcripts, the collection provokes the act of indexing – of cross-referencing and categorising. Classic fieldwork was enshrined in notebooks and stored physically. They in turn could be indexed and the index created on three-by-five cards: just like the card index for an academic library. Cross-referencing included actors' names, places and key types of events. The physical archive and the accompanying indexing provided a simple way of navigating the fieldnotes, but they did more. They transformed a given social world into a tractable array of documentation that could be searched, cross-referenced and so rendered tractable. Such indexing was the physical manifestation of a desire to make things orderly and to bring a chosen social world into the narrow space of the office and the desk (migrating from the anthropologist's tent or other temporary accommodation).

In the contemporary world fieldnotes, interview transcripts and images can all be digital, and the parallel digital management of the archive is embodied in bespoke software. The relatively simple index can now be expanded and complicated. The software (CAQDAS) allows the ethnographer to identify segments of text in terms of what are now termed *codes*. Contemporary research methods in many qualitative disciplines advocate the dense coding of one's precious texts. Indeed, in many circles 'analysis' is treated as a distinct phase of the ethnographic process, and analysis is predicated on coding. There are multiple texts on the use of coding and the role of coding in computer-aided analysis. Like many such procedures, it is linked to Grounded Theory, in what has become a somewhat mechanical version of the original formulation. Likewise, the search for *themes* has become a textbook-based approach to the analysis of qualitative data. One can refer to textbooks devoted to codes and coding (e.g. Saldaña 2021). In practice, such contemporary versions are addressed more to 'qualitative' work based on transcribed interviews, rather than ethnography *per se*. Very few anthropologists invoke such procedures, although they have been foremost in the construction of personal archives (which can include material artefacts).

The search for themes, the manipulation of coded data, and similar manoeuvres, recall the collector's urge to catalogue and classify the collection, or the archivist's imperative to index. The researcher curates the personal accumulation of 'data' in order to sort through it, to retrieve instances and to create various orderings (such as recurrent 'themes') from them. The desire is to re-create order from the potentially inchoate doings of everyday life and the equally complex representations of what was observed and what the ethnographer participated in. Ethnographers look for the pattern in the carpet and seek out – or create – orderliness. They sort, classify and re-order in translating everyday life into ethnographic texts. In so doing they discipline the disorderliness of the ordinary, in the process making it extraordinary. We shall return to these observations in Chapter 7.

Escapes

Research desires can also encompass escape attempts. For the ethnographer, the sacred period of fieldwork can be 'time out'. The full commitment of time and energy devoted to immersion in a chosen social setting can be a relief from the mundane work of academic and domestic life. All research works are, or can be, immersive, of course. The laboratory scientist may never be happier than when at the lab bench; the historian may feel fully engaged only when dealing with primary sources; the archaeologist primarily when dealing with and documenting a 'dig'. Each of those kinds of activities might be regarded as the primary, paramount realities of the scholarly or scientific life. For the ethnographer, time in the field is precious. It can, as we know, be difficult and stressful. It can even be dangerous. It is often suffused with a sense of personal and intellectual insecurity. But the steps and the journey into the unpredictable can also be defining moments in one's biographical and intellectual career.

We shall explore some issues of biographical disruption and the construction of the ethnographic self in the following chapter. Here, we wish to mention that tacit desire to release oneself from ordinary, profane everyday life, in order to be granted an extraordinary or sacred period when surrender to the field means that for that period, nothing else matters. It is a period that can be marked by a sense of loss – loss of social status, of intellectual comfort, of certainty – from which there can be gains of intellectual renewal, of unique experience, of a new mode of knowing. For the ethnographer, that time away or time out also furnishes a store of knowledge and experience, that goes well beyond 'data' in the conventional sense, to which one can return symbolically through subsequent years of writing and talking. It is, or can be, a word-hoard (*wordhord* in Old English), as found in the poem of *Beowulf*, line 259 (see Heaney's modern translation, 1999; also Videen 2021). The word-hoard was, and remains, the stock of knowledge that the bard draws on in improvising compositions; the ethnographer also draws on her or his accumulated stock of knowledge in forming new versions of social life. We return to the ethnographic hoard – the collection – in Chapter 7 when we discuss the catch of Wolff's formula.

As we have explored already, time out can reflect the desire for self-discovery and transformation. It is also a precious time; and for the social researcher, time is a precious resource. Ethnography can rarely be accomplished in short bursts of activity in the field, although Atkinson (2022) has argued for the value of an aliquot of fieldwork, meaning a period of time and effort that is just enough for illustrative or exploratory purposes. Time out is vanishingly rare n many contemporary settings. The contemporary university department is subject to multiple external and institutional pressures. The imperatives of accountability and impact, the expectations of short-term productivity and the requirements for career advancement mean that extended periods of individual exploration and scholarship are increasingly hard to get and hard to justify. Regular year-long sabbaticals are things of the past for many, and time to prepare for research, or even teaching, is squeezed. Time out to conduct fieldwork may become little more than an explicit desire, something longed for and fondly remembered by older generations. For the conduct of ethnography that can constitute a threat. Of course, many fundamental studies have been conducted as doctoral projects, and the doctorate remains one period in an academic biography when time is explicitly allocated for personal research. The doctorate may be one of the last bastions for long-term fieldwork and the opportunity to take that precious time out. But even the PhD is being squeezed. It is increasingly seen as a training opportunity rather than a period of exploration and risk-taking. So, time in the field is a special opportunity that must be guarded and is increasingly under threat. In its place are more cost-effective and less time-consuming activities: a series of interviews or focus groups, an autoethnography or content analysis of public domain materials. We do not decry those and similar activities in themselves, but they are no substitute for fieldwork and all that it entails.

4

INTERRUPTED LIVES AND ETHNOGRAPHIC MOMENTS

The poem 'Interruption' (1900) by the Greek Poet C.P. Cavafy suggests that as mere mortals we are intruders, hasty and clumsy: *We interrupt the doings of the gods/We creatures of the moment, impatient and inept* (free translation by PA). Ethnographers are particularly given to interruptions: we interrupt the doings of others – our hosts – and our fieldwork also interrupts our own everyday lives. Criticisms and reservations concerning ethnographic research often include the trope that observed actors will act differently because of that observation: habitual social action will be disrupted, therefore. Collectively, we respond by pointing out that it would call for a Herculean effort of dramaturgy for whole organisations, networks, or villages to alter their behaviour over a protracted period of time. In practice, it is more likely to be the ethnographer who is changed by the experience of immersion in a research site – especially one that is relatively strange (cf. Goulet and Young 1994, p. 298). Sometimes, such changes are unforeseen; in other circumstances, they may be courted and celebrated. Some of those personal changes can be profound and have a lasting effect on the researcher. More profoundly, the intellectual and existential transformations of fieldwork can have far-reaching implications for anthropological or sociological comprehension. As we suggest throughout this book, there are many metaphors that can be applied to capture the ethnographic life. They include the images of border-crossings; of wandering and wayfaring; of drifting; and of engagement and disengagement. Here, we want to focus on one aspect of ethnography that relates in part to all other tropes. That is, ethnography as an interruption: the mutual interruption of ethnographic encounters and the biographical disruption of ethnographic absences. Such ruptures recall the phenomenological estrangement of the epoché. The personal commitments of fieldwork mean that the cognitive dislocations of strangeness are paralleled by the biographical ruptures of mutual interruption.

DOI: 10.4324/9780429056802-4

The existential commitments of ethnographic fieldwork always imply intense relationships with others; they have equally profound implications for ethnographers themselves. There is much emphasis in the methodological literature on rapport in the field and on the mutual alignment of lives and identities between the ethnographer and her research hosts. But we need to avoid any suggestion that ethnographic engagements are always about rapport, closeness and continuity. We need to think equally in terms of interruptions, turning points and ruptures. Ethnographic fieldwork can be a series of mutual interruptions, while the fieldwork itself can often be a period of biographical disruption for the ethnographer herself. We may need to move from a somewhat Romantic imagery of rapport to a more variegated assemblage of moments, encounters, puzzles and fragmentary togetherness. We should take account of damaged methods: damaged lives, broken relations and undertakings, fractured narratives and biographies of spoiled identities. One allusive image is that of the laboratory cloud chamber, which makes visible the path of otherwise invisible particles as they create traces through a cloud of vapour enclosed within a vessel. Rather than continuous and completely immersive alignment between the ethnographer and her field, often we just glimpse occasional and occasioned collisions of the researcher and her participants that create partial traces of intersubjectivity and the trajectories of encounters. That does not mean that all such interruptions are damaging. On the contrary, they can result in moments of discovery and self-realisation on the part of researchers. Ethnographic moments are embedded in the longer temporalities of fieldwork and reflection (Clift, Gore, Gustafsson, Bekker, Battle and Hatchard 2021).

In the course of this chapter, we shall discuss some aspects of biographical disruptions, conversions and epiphanies. They include ethnographers' reports of social incorporation and inclusion; of gaining and losing trust; of gaining access and leaving the field. We are especially dependent on ethnographers' own accounts of their field experiences and one must remain conscious of the fact that they are accounts. Ethnographers have a tendency towards self-centredness and self-importance and may exaggerate the significance of the mutual interruptions and dislocations they sometimes report. We have already outlined some of the tensions within and between ethnographic projects, identifying the poles of intimacy and estrangement that shape any and every series of ethnographic engagements. So too do the various tensions between 'insider' and 'outsider' positions. In the course of this chapter, therefore, we explore some features of the social relations of fieldwork. We do not take on trust the conventional categories. We do not assume that ethnographers can choose to adopt master roles or work from particular positions without change, disruption or ambiguity.

There can be no doubt that ethnographers (indeed, all researchers) are affected by their own identities and their biographies. Reyes (2020) provides a valuable overview of some important issues. In a discussion of 'reflexivity' (that is, reflection on one's personal and interpersonal influences) she suggests that attention needs to be paid to the complexities of intersectionality. What she calls the ethnographic toolkit consists of a multiplicity of personal traits and competencies that might help or hinder social relations in the field, and hence directly affect the kinds of results that might finally be published. While Reyes acknowledges the significance of cultural similarities and differences, there is currently too wide an assumption that cultural similarity is an aid to ethnographic fieldwork. But we wish to resist such mechanistic models of ethnographic biographies and identities. Irrespective of similarity or difference, disruption is – cognitively speaking – the basis for ethnographic comprehension. Such disruption can occur by virtue of immediate strangeness, or as the outcome of sustained intellectual work (bracketing). Either way, one should not be relying on biographical traits that appear to confer access and comprehension. As we have argued elsewhere (Whitaker and Atkinson 2021), 'reflexivity' in any case implies much greater epistemological complexity than just the researcher's identity and the capacity to reflect on her or his research practice.

We base our discussion on the figure of interrupted lives. In brief, ethnographers interrupt the lives of those they seek to study. At the same time, episodes of fieldwork interrupt the life of the ethnographer. These are not all-or-nothing states. We are not always 'in' the field or 'out of' the field. Even when physically present, we can fade in and out. Our attention wanders. We can try to switch off just as much as we try to focus intensely. So, our attention, our surrender, wanders and varies. Ethnographic attention is not a continuous process, but a variable one, even one that flickers in and out of focus. And so when we refer to interrupted lives, we are not just alluding to social relations with our research hosts; we are also thinking of our phenomenological attention. We cannot treat everything as strange all of the time. We cannot engage in reflective self-awareness on a constant basis. Hence interruption is an intellectual phenomenon as well as an interpersonal or biographical one. The social worlds that we study and the social worlds we otherwise inhabit interrupt and intersect with one another. Ontological and epistemological collisions can be disconcerting and troubling. But they can – and should – be productive too.

Our intention here is not to prescribe specific forms of relationship, nor to criticise the practices of other fieldworkers. Rather, we wish to explore some of the undoubted complexities of fieldwork relations in a nuanced fashion that helps us to avoid simplified and unwarrantably prescriptive terms. In doing so, we wish to undermine such dichotomies as 'insider'/'outsider', emphasising repeatedly the fluid and dynamic nature of social and intellectual engagements. We begin with one among several characterisations of the relationship between the ethnographer and her or his hosts. It has long been conventional to discuss field relations in ethnographic search in terms of rapport. A proper degree of rapport with one's research hosts has always been regarded as a 'good thing', while over-rapport has been regarded as a dangerous thing, threatening the objectivity of the research overall. We shall examine such phenomena more closely, and – amongst other things – ask ourselves why over-rapport endangers proper research while rapport does not. Indeed 'rapport', 'over-rapport', and 'no rapport' are all possibilities within the overall framework of ethnographic fieldwork, and rather than advocating one or another approach, we explore the existential and intellectual commitments that field relations imply. Further, we shall discuss some of the greater and lesser kinds of mutual interruption – between ethnographers and hosts – that follow from such biographical disruptions. We shall also discuss processes of personal transformation, including epiphanies and revelations, that ethnographers experience in the course of 'extraordinary' experiences in the field.

Biographical transformations and interruptions do not only inhabit the experiences of entering the field but also inflect the equivalent experiences of leaving the field (Smith and Delamont in press). While the former is frequently documented, the latter is infrequently so. But the loss of 'field' can be a disturbing one for ethnographers, with a fracture of interpersonal and intellectual ties to a chosen research setting. Those kinds of ruptures and interruptions have been particularly salient for anthropologists, especially when their chosen field has been physically and/or culturally distanced. But those general processes apply to sociologists (and others) working closer to home. Indeed, reflection on these phenomena throws into relief the problematic nature of fieldwork at home in any case. Where 'home' is to be found is not a simple thing. The relationships between places and personal relations are by no means simple. Intellectually speaking the ethnographer may need to be homeless for periods of her life and intellectually nomadic recurrently. Such dislocations need not be thought of as negative or traumatic. Indeed, they are productive in many ways, and they are among the sought-after outcomes of undertaking ethnographic fieldwork. Further, the process of leaving the field implies new challenges and new forms of strangeness. If one's research site becomes, over time, familiar, then the imperatives of 'writing it up' can become yet another cause of estrangement. Living, however vicariously, in a given cultural setting can become itself a taken-for-granted. The task of 'returning home' to the family, the university and the study, coupled with the task of transforming fieldnotes, documents, memories and images into novel text, can be a thoroughly alien one. Moving, intellectually and emotionally, from mundane experience to textual production can be as sharp a rupture as any other associated with ethnographic research. We discuss further the personal and intellectual ruptures of leaving the field later in this chapter.

As we mentioned in our introductory chapter, ethnography is conducted between the poles of social intimacy and social distance. Many ethnographic projects are defined not by one or the other, but by shifting relationships, driven by contingency, personal styles and intellectual commitments. Trust and commitment are interspersed with reserve and distance. Geographical distanciation is sometimes mirrored by social distance and isolation, while moments of intimacy can provide respite from a lonely presence in the field. Intimacy can even lead to romantic and sexual relationships in the field, and we shall also be touchy on such engagements below.

The interruptions and consolations of solitude

Ethnographic fieldwork is poised between sociability and solitude. Sociability is not necessarily pleasurable, and solitude is not always a source of loneliness. However, the effort to force oneself into the field, be co-present with relative strangers can be extreme. Ethnographic confessions and fictionalised accounts can capture the sense of reluctance, even of nausea, that can accompany fieldwork. To be in the presence of strangers brings existential threats, and we open ourselves to the critical scrutiny of all sorts. The single woman travelling alone can face close scrutiny as to why she is not accompanied, or is not married, or has no children. The single man who is alone can equally invite suspicion. Motives can be openly challenged (and not without reason). Field research is proverbially assumed to be evaluative, or even punitive, deriving from agencies of surveillance. More benignly, it can be intrusive and, in effect if not by intention, exploitative. The ethnographer extracts, as it were, surplus significance from her or his hosts and one is often conscious of the intrusion and its implications.

Solitude, while rewarding in many ways, can also be an existential penance. The lone researcher who is working 'away' can experience long periods when solitude turns to loneliness, and when fieldwork becomes something to be endured rather than celebrated and enjoyed. Even when one is working 'at home' (a misleading phrase), one can feel at least out of place: like matter out of place, a threat to the cosmic order of a given social setting. The ethnographer thus becomes a polluting intruder and is threatened in turn. It is not necessary for one's hosts to be overtly aggressive, or even just uncooperative to feel uncomfortable. There are often questions – spoken or tacit – as to what one is actually doing. Why are you here? What are you looking for? And when the ethnographer herself is none too sure of the answers (What are you hoping to prove?) then discomfort – at the least – can be the result. One proverbial way of describing social position of the ethnographer is that of the 'socially acceptable incompetent'. Now in practice, that phrase is potentially misleading: ethnographers do not cultivate incompetence in the sense of refusing or failing to learn social or technical skills. But it does capture the sometimes-fragile sense that marginal status can confer. Incompetence here refers not to ignorance *per se*, but to that loss of existential security that comes from losing 'normal' identity and status. It derives in part from that loss of control that is a necessary precondition for surrender in the field.

To move, however voluntarily, from familiar social and working relationships to a solitary and temporary position in the field constitutes a major biographical disruption. It is an enduring one. Without going native, it is a temporary state (though it may feel like a protracted one at the time). In terms of classical anthropological theory, it is a liminal state that is marked both by entry to and leaving the field. Liminality here refers to a temporary but special (even sacred) state experienced during a status passage or rite of passage. The initiate is symbolically and/or physically removed from mundane social life. Such liminality can be marked by extreme abstinence or a degree of license. For the ethnographer, that precious period in the field can be experienced as a special period of removal, while simultaneously one of profound immersion and personal change. Like many such transitions, the period of separation is limited, but it is an enduringly remembered experience. The disruption of fieldwork is rewarded with a career-long store of research experience. The 'ethnographic present' of written convention reflects and inscribes the lasting significance of fieldwork. It goes well beyond the tacit desire to deny history or to suppress social change. (See Fabian (1983) for the enunciation of that argument.) Torgovnick (1990) captures something of this:

> The anthropologist ages but remains tied, always, to the experience of youth, immortalized in a classic text of anthropology, Unlike the face and body of the anthropologist, this classic text – Malinowski's *Argonauts of the Eastern Pacific*, Mead's *Coming of Age in Samoa* – can never change, since anthropologists resist revision that might falsify original observations.
>
> *(p. 244)*

Needless to say, not every ethnographer will generate a classic monograph that remains central to the discipline for decades, but all fieldwork endures in the present tense. That 'long present' does not depend on a nostalgic view of the past of a given culture or social arrangement. But the fieldwork and its resulting texts *do*, like family photographs, fix the ethnographer at a period in her or his life which remains a special, even sacred, time of release from the demands of ordinary, profane responsibility and routine. Time and its passing are, paradoxically, enshrined in the ethnographic present. It can also elicit a certain chagrin, a sense of time lost. That is not just a regret for what might be a lost way of life but also the lost youth of the ethnographer, whose texts do not just create a present for the social setting that is described but also a search for lost time. (It is no accident that Marcel Proust is a most acute ethnographic observer of the social conventions and pretensions that surround him in the salon.)

The vivid ethnographic present is not just a mechanism for the erasure of history. The development of anthropology signalled a radical break with the diachronic narratives of evolutionary models. It served the anthropological programme of synchronic analysis, stressing the functional integrity of societies and cultures in the here-and-now. When we read classic ethnographies, we are not fooled into thinking that they represent a vision of eternity, but we can become absorbed in and by them in a way that would not be possible were they to use the distancing effect of the past tense. We do not believe that the Azande or the Nuer of South Sudan today live as they were described by Evans-Pritchard, that the life of contemporary Melanesians is still like Malinowski's accounts, or that the lives and organisation of the Bemba remain unchanged since they were written about by Audrey Richards. But the effect of reading such accounts in the present tense is akin to examining old photographs. Photographs allow us a form of vicarious witnessing: witnessing mediated by the camera and the photographic print. Anthropological or sociological monographs allow us to witness a different form of everyday living, mediated by the ethnographer and the mode of writing. We also read through a double witnessing. We 'see' the social actors in their cultural setting and their networks of relation. We also 'see' the ethnographer herself or himself, who is, like the actors described in the writing, simultaneously of that time and out of time.

Let us consider a sociological monograph that is less well known than the classics of the same period. Hortense Powdermaker is better known for her book *Stranger and Friend* (1966), which is about ethnographic fieldwork, than for her monograph on Hollywood filmmakers (Powdermaker 1950). But if we read the latter sympathetically, overlooking as always some sense of anachronism, then we find ourselves witnessing something of Hollywood in the immediate post-war period, in a manner that immediately calls to mind the classic movies of that era. We also see Hollywood through a temporal lens of Powdermaker's making. For us, it grates when we read of 'South Seas aborigines' when she draws some ironic contrasts with previous fieldwork experiences. But equally, we recognise – almost in black-and-white – the Hollywood of the day. It is a historical document precisely because it is in the present tense of 1949 or 1950. It is also, in some respects, thoroughly contemporary and prescient. Writing about the culture of Hollywood, she observes:

> In one community there is concentrated more pulchritude than probably in any other place in the world. Here are all the young girls who have won beauty contests in their home towns, and thousands of others with exceptionally good looks, with and without talent, all unswervingly intent on stardom. Only a very few out of the thousands can be successful and competition is keen. As in most industries, those in executive positions with decisive power are usually middle-aged or older men.
>
> *(p. 233)*

Powdermaker goes on to explain that the actual going-to-bed opportunities for starlets can be limited in number and outcome. But the vividly ethnographic present creates a potent testimony to the prevailing culture. The ethnographic present honours the immediacy of 'the field' while acknowledging its lasting significance. To read of people in the past tense – learning that they 'did' such-and-such, or that they 'believed' in something or other – is to create such distances between those actors, the text and the reader as to render the ethnography inert. Robbed of its immediacy, it is stripped of its significance.

For many of its practitioners, the rite of passage confers a lifelong identity and academic authority. The ethnographer becomes closely identified with the field site(s) that have been explored, sometimes more than with distinctive theories or concepts that they have developed on the basis of that field research. The periods of cultural separation and estrangement have often been described in terms of 'first days in the field', especially by sociologists working in the broadly interactionist tradition. It is acknowledged as simultaneously problematic and fruitful. Conceptually speaking, early field experiences can challenge the ethnographer's comprehension of the surroundings. It places her or him in the position of 'the stranger', who must suspend everyday assumptions in order to grasp novel phenomena or to treat phenomena *as if* they were strange. Interpersonally, the entry or entries into the field imply the creation of new social relationships, the establishment of trust and patterns of working.

Leaving the field

The notion of liminality has been over-used and has become something of a cliché. But it is appropriate in this context nonetheless. Liminal states imply processes and ceremonials of separation and reintegration during (often protracted) rites of passage. For the ethnographer, leaving the field can be a significant turning point. Reasons for leaving are various and sometimes complex. We do not need to review them all here. In general, exits are much less often written about than entries and processes of field adjustment (Delamont and Smith in press). As is so often the case, such accounts as do exist tend to reflect difficulties rather than straightforward exits: such is the nature of narrative and certain genres of autobiography.

Allan and Cole (in press) base their account on their fieldwork in contrasting schools in the UK., one an elite single-sex girls' school, the other a comprehensive school. Having left in less-than-ideal circumstances, they develop the metaphor of the labyrinth to try to capture some of the complexities of finding the 'right' way out: 'The labyrinth is commonly taken to symbolise a pathway or journey – one which is meandering (entailing complexities, detours and dad ends) but purposeful (always leading somewhere and with a pathway which does eventually lead outwards'. Of course, getting out of the Minoan labyrinth involved Ariadne's thread, and Theseus was the lucky one, as many had perished. Leaving the field is not normally quite so dark an experience.

Ethnographers have often written about gaining 'access' to their chosen field. It may be regarded as a stage or series of stages that move the ethnographer from the position of an outsider to that of 'researcher': Processes of access and early encounters can be thought of as liminal stages in a protracted *rite de passage*. But if we consider the general grammar of such status passages, then we also need to consider the processes whereby ethnographers leave the field in order to be re-integrated into whatever ordinary life they inhabit. In doing so, we recognise that leaving the field is not a simple or a single act. Moreover, the field does not always leave the ethnographer.

Changes – existential, intellectual and emotional – can persist. Field research has an abiding influence – sometimes persisting throughout a career: see Michailova, Piekkari, Plakoyiannaki, Ritvala, Mihailova and Salmi (2014), Iversen (2020) and Smith and Delamont (in press) for general overviews of relevant methods literature and examples of ethnographers' separation from their research fields – sometimes voluntarily, sometimes not.

Leaving the field provides yet another turning point at which lives become fractured and interrupted. Biographies are rewritten, while intellectual careers are prospectively and retrospectively defined in terms of such pivotal moments. Departure from the field can create its own kinds of existential and ethical pain. There is a repeated sense – on the part of some ethnographers at least – that fieldwork and subsequent departure constitutes an act (or a series of acts) of bad faith. Ethnographers sometimes report a sense of guilt. They feel guilty about their acts of betrayal. Periods of intimacy and shared living are transformed into academic texts, decontextualised and recontextualised away from the everyday lives and preoccupations of the actors described in ethnographies. As Brettell (1993) and others have observed, such a transformation can feel like a form of betrayal: everyday intimacies and routines are transformed into public knowledge. The rich complexity of actors' lives, culture and forms of social organisation can feel all too jejune when turned into the more linear narratives of anthropological or sociological analysis. Everyday life and textual forms mutually interrupt one another (an issue we return to in Chapter 6).

We can leave the field in numerous ways. Sociologists and anthropologists at home, of course, can leave the field on a daily basis, returning to their offices and homes. Their episodic engagements are, on the surface at least, quite different from those of the anthropologist who finds herself away from home on a long-term basis. For the classic anthropologist, 'backstage' periods of retreat from the field are hard to achieve and can provide brief respite from being on display and subject to scrutiny by research hosts. For the home researcher, retreats from the front-stage regions of self-presentation can be much easier to achieve. However, physical withdrawal or retreats to 'home' are only part of leaving the field.

Field researchers will sometimes admit to more existential or intellectual absences from their field research. It is not easy to sustain ethnographic engagement all of the time. After all, being physically present in that field is only a means to pay close and serious attention to interactions and actions. But sustained attention is not all that easy. Quite irrespective of research, everyday engagements with strangers, or prolonged concentration can be exhausting. Keeping up ordinary social interactions while trying to commit things to memory and pursuing research-led interests can be even harder. So, leaving the field can be a matter of 'switching off', over and above any physical departures. As Amanda Coffey (1999) expresses, leaving the field is not simply a pragmatic research decision. Critical of textbooks that reduce fieldwork 'exits' to practical procedures, she suggests that 'The ending of fieldwork and leaving the field usually represents the end of a particular phase of an ethnographer's life and career', so that 'fieldwork becomes, and is part of, who we are and will always be' (Coffey 2018, p. 74). Hence, we need to recognise multiple occasions and styles of leaving the field.

On a grander scale, leaving – or having left – the field can be a major juncture of intellectual and personal disruption. In the first instance, spending weeks, months or even years in the field is an extraordinary commitment. It is a prolonged engagement with a series of intellectual problems. It calls for repeated acts of social tact and felicity. It requires sustained intellectual curiosity. One can grow a little weary of intruding on other people's lives and activities. Constantly out of place and in the way, one can repeatedly feel clumsy and gauche. Leaving the field might therefore be experienced as a relief from the rigours of fieldwork itself. And in some cases, at least, that is true. Yet people also find that leaving the field is a wrench, a matter of regret and chagrin. That is often expressed in terms of the severed interpersonal ties and the relationships that are left behind. Leaving the field is also a return, just as entering the field implies absences. Indeed, presence and absence are always dialectically related. Fieldwork implies a degree of intimacy with others and a simultaneous absence from one's 'own', while the liminal experience of leaving the field implies that intimacy retreats into absence as the ethnographer is reintegrated into her or his life of academic normality and routine. The rhythms of everyday life and work are – or at least can be – radically transformed. The nature of work is, of course, equally transformed. The embodied, direct experience of the field as one's immediate surroundings (one's *Umwelt*) is replaced by the textually mediated engagement with 'data' – fieldnotes, recordings, or photographs – that are in themselves memorabilia denoting detachment from the field. Detachment is in itself productive, of course, and that source of absence is not in itself to be regretted. Indeed, absence and detachment can lead to an analytic estrangement. If entering the field can lead the ethnographer to encounter strangers and cultural strangeness, the work of analytic reflection can – and should – once more de-familiarise the field that has become familiar. It is an intellectual movement from the surrender to the catch.

There is, therefore, a constant movement between two domains – that of fieldwork and that of deskwork. The fieldwork itself is often experienced as unpredictable and frustrating and, even more often, incomplete. The same is surely true of the deskwork through which we try to make sense of the former. Both can be haunted by a sense of failure, or if not failure then at least a sense of unfinished business. However carefully planned and foreshadowed, fieldwork itself is unpredictable and we rarely feel that we have done full justice to that field, while writing imposes a set of logics and imperatives of its own that also fail to capture that field in its full richness. As Strathern (1999) writes:

> One kind of complexity lies, then, in the relationship between ethnography's double fields: each creates the other, but each also has its own dynamic or trajectory. The field ethnographer often learns the trajectory effect the hard way. What back at home had made sense as a filed proposal can lose its motivating force; the preoccupations of the people on the spot take over. Yet for all sorts of reasons, they cannot take over completely. The fieldworker has to manage and thus inhabit both fields at the same time: to recall the theoretical conditions under which the work was proposed, and thus the reasons for being there, while yielding to the flow of events and ideas which present themselves. To 'return from the field' means throwing those orientations into reverse.
>
> *(p. 2)*

But throwing them into reverse does not yield a perfect symmetry, like a palindrome of ethnographic expectations and achievements. We do not return to where we started. There are too many personal and intellectual interruptions along the way.

There is a parallel between ethnographic absence and what Roland Barthes writes in *A Lover's Discourse* (2018). In Barthes's own words: 'Amorous absence functions in a single direction, expressed by the one who stays, never by the one who: an always present *I* is constituted only by confrontation with an always absent *you*'. And in our words: Ethnography is always constituted by the alternations of presence and absence. When I am in the field, I am fully present, but the possibility of understanding comes eventually through my absence. My absence from the field is also my *return*. My return is flavoured always by absence and recollection. Barthes's lover might also share with the ethnographer the bitter-sweet chagrin of a lost intimacy that yields troubled memories but an unfulfilled desire for the reunion and renewed consummation. As O'Connor (in press) eloquently expresses it, leaving the field may even be a carnal disengagement, intertwined quite explicitly with erotic longing and loss.

Such a protracted rite of passage can endow the ethnographer with an ambiguous authority, based partly on the character-building process of solitude and absence, and equally on the basis of privileged firsthand witnessing. Kuklick (1997) expresses it in adroitly literary terms in a discussion of early anthropology and the development of other field sciences and investigation of field sites:

> That scientists had suffered the character-building rigors of fieldwork did not, however, suffice to confer presumptive plausibility on their reports. Like Ishmael in Melville's *Moby Dick*, they addressed their audiences from a peculiar position: they claimed the status of privileged witnesses to the phenomena they described. Of course, as the only survivor of the wreck of the *Pequod*, Ishmael can be our only source of information about the

> crew's experience. But fieldworkers reporting their observations to fellow scholars have assumed a similar role, since they have been obliged to impress audiences whose members cannot independently corroborate workers' accounts.
>
> *(p. 60)*

Conversions and epiphanies

Biographical disruptions take many forms. Some are deliberately sought and undergone, while others arise in unforeseen circumstances. The former include conversions and acts of enculturation. Ethnographers deliberately undergo rites of conversion and seek instruction and membership in an esoteric field of experience. (Religious conversion is an important motif in such ethnographies.) They can also experience unexpected conversions and similar events that change them and their identity. Indeed, being changed in the course of fieldwork is a recurrent theme – especially among anthropologists who may seek out or encounter otherwise unfamiliar forms of practice. Monographs and autobiographical texts contain many instances where the researcher – the anthropologist for the most part – has been initiated into a religious belief system. The anthropologist thus surrenders her/himself to the rites of passage and the observances that transform a postulant into an initiate. It is an altered condition of reality. Suspension of disbelief may be temporary, or may be enduring, but it cannot be done in bad faith without losing the phenomenon.

Such transformations and encounters are among the most significant of biographical, existential interruptions resulting from immersive fieldwork. Whether or not the anthropologist continues to practise the religion or belief system, remaining an observant convert, there is no doubt that such a juncture represents a considerable shift in experience and identity. Viewed from one perspective, it would seem an extreme case of 'going native'. Anthropologists – and to a certain extent sociologists – have fought shy of anything that smacked of such a trespass. Historically, anthropologists resisted any implication that they were aping the folkways of the peoples they studied. They were in that regard the antithesis of European travellers or settlers who deliberately adopted 'native' styles of dress, consumption and domestic arrangements: enthusiasts who adopted 'Arab', 'Indian' or 'Turkish' styles. T.E. Lawrence is a classic case in point. Such anxiety resonated with the ambiguities of an orientalist fascination with the exotic. While anthropologists sought out exotic peoples for study, they exerted an almost puritan avoidance of the taint of the exotic themselves. The Spartan discipline required to sustain adequate personal distance was one of the guarantees of the ethnography itself. The tent or the hut became more than just a physical domestic and personal space but also a symbol of separation in the field.

A number, indeed an increasing number, of anthropologists have reported extraordinary events that constitute epiphanies constructed within the cultural idiom of the culture they are working in. Marton (1994) argues that controversial though it was, Castaneda's published account of work with Don Juan, a Yaqui Indian sorcerer, created a discursive space in which experiential versions of anthropology could be explored and expressed (Castaneda 1968). The factual nature of Castaneda's account was called into question, and the work today is best thought of as a work of creative writing. It nonetheless prompts some intriguing insights: see Silverman (1975). Characteristically, anthropologists writing in this vein provide accounts of phenomena such as healing rituals and shamanic (or shamanic-like) dreaming. Paranormal events are reported as observed phenomena, encountered as consequences of cultural learning in the field. Marton also reports an extraordinary ('peculiar') apparition that coincided with his initiation into the Afro-Cuban religion of *santería*:

> After having been asleep for what seemed like several hours, I was awakened in the middle of the night by a light hovering over me directly in front of my field of vision. It was round and it glowed brightly (about the size of a tennis ball, I think). It was stationary, but somehow pulsing with the emission of the light and it contained what felt like an intelligent energy.
>
> *(p. 277)*

In the same collection of essays, other anthropologists also report similar extraordinary events. For instance, Swartz (1994) reports, in studying Native American Medicine:

> We laid [sic] back on the floor, forming a circle with our outstretched bodies, closed our eyes, and following the beat of the drum, descended, each to his/her own sacred space. During the first few minutes I found it difficult to visualize anything. Then, gradually I experienced a sensation of soaring above a wide, winding river. I continued my flight, searching for my spirit animal, but saw only the endlessly winding river.
>
> *(p. 213)*

In the same volume, Edith Turner (1994) recounts a dramatically extraordinary witnessing. Writing about fieldwork among the Ndembu, she describes a curing ritual, carried out on a middle-aged woman, Meru. At a dramatic climax to the procedure:

> Suddenly Meru raised her arm, stretched it in liberation, and I saw with my own eyes a giant thing emerging out of the flesh of her back. It was a large grey blob about six inches across, opaque and something between solid and smoke.
>
> *(p. 83)*

Dramatic accounts such as this are by no means rare; see for instance Grindal (1983) on witnessing the physical revival of a corpse. Such accounts can defy the reader's ordinary system of perception and belief, although belief in extraordinary events and observations is remarkably widespread: accounts of UFOs, angels and alien abductions are remarkably common in the United States and other 'developed' countries. But descriptions of healers extracting objects from the body of the afflicted defy normal understandings of visible bodies. Indeed, although it is not the main thrust of this chapter, it is noticeable that accounts like that of Turner and Marton – quoted above – are regularly at pains to stress the 'before my own eyes', or 'with my own eyes' trope. Witnessing is the key to ethnographic verisimilitude, but when it comes to extraordinary or supernatural events, then it really needs stressing. Authors can report such witnessing despite their own scepticism. For instance, in her account of the cult of John of God (Joao Texeira) in Brazil, Rocha (2016) describes the plausibility of his psychic surgery, which gained a widespread following. Sometimes the ethnographer feels a compulsion to believe the evidence of their own eyes, despite their deep-seated scepticism. We shall return to the specific topic of psychic or spiritist surgery later in the book when we discuss the textual possibilities of magical realism and the work of Greenfield (2008), who observed 'extraordinary' surgical interventions in Brazil.

Personal dislocations include hallucinatory experiences, such as those induced by the use of drugs. Taussig (1987) gives us just such an account, taken from his fieldnotes:

> ... My body is distorting and I'm very frightened, limbs stretch out and become detached, my body no longer belongs to me, then it does. I am an octopus, I condense into smallness. The candlelight creates shapes of a new world, animal forms and menacing. The lower half of my body disappears. I learn to use dissociation as an advantage as a way of escaping from the horror. I am not the person being got at; rather I am the disembodied face-presence calmly peering in and watching this other and unimportant me. I watch my other self, safely now. But then this second me, this objective and detached observer, succumbs too, and I have to dissociate into a third and then a fourth as the relation between my-selves breaks, creating an almost infinite series of fluttering mirrors of watching selves and feeling others.
>
> *(p. 141)*

Of course, such induced states are extreme in their consequences. But the general sense of disorientation, of observing one's self or selves, can be understood by all ethnographers who go through the disruptive suspension and interrogation of everyday realities.

Our point here is that such encounters and witnessing are extreme, remarkable cases of more ordinary and routine kinds of interruption that can be experienced by ethnographers in the field. Everyday perception and understanding are challenged and interrupted by much less florid events and reports. Surrender to another and different cultural milieu must challenge one's taken-for-granted realities. If we take seriously the social construction of reality, then a thoroughgoing relativism is unavoidable for any ethnographic exercise. It is not just what one sees. As exemplified in the passages above, it is not just a matter of observing something, but groping for the vocabulary to render it describable at all. Turner clearly does not know how to characterise that large, translucent grey blob, except in terms that leave it vague in the extreme. Marton's ball of energy is, likewise, elusive. But working in what appear to be much more mundane settings can radically alter one's perceptual categories. What is observed can never be unseen and ethnographic witnessing stays in the memory when other everyday occurrences can more rapidly fade.

Of course one could argue that any and all ethnographic encounters are exercises in the suspension of disbelief, given that this is the equivalent of a phenomenological bracketing. By definition, an ethnographic encounter with an unfamiliar (relatively speaking) social world requires a suspension of the ethnographer's taken-for-granted mundane knowledge. At the same time, any fieldwork in a setting that is already familiar requires the alienation effect of suspending belief. The suspension of thinking as usual thus implies a fundamental epistemological interruption. Fieldwork itself creates epistemic perturbations. We shall return to one aspect of such disturbances when we turn to consider conventions and genres of ethnographic writing in Chapter 6 and to issues of defamiliarisation in Chapter 7.

Transgressive intimacies?

We have already discussed the extent to which ethnographers have, over many years, expressed the dangers of 'going native'. Now quite apart from the historically and culturally loaded connotations of that term, we need to pause and interrogate quite what this might mean, and how it relates to our general theme. Here, we use the trope of going native in order to introduce the possibilities of personal transformation through intimate relations in the field. We suggest that the strictures against going native gloss a collective anxiety that is also expressed by our theme of surrender. Surrender has several connotations. In the absence of capture, it can imply surrendering – giving up – our critical faculty, leaving us only able to recapitulate and celebrate the cultural categories we have assimilated. When we surrender without due care and attention, then we transgress the boundaries between understanding and becoming.

The austere regime of the lone ethnographer in the field included chastity. At least, refraining from sexual contacts was a common injunction to novice field researchers. But erotic sentiments are by no means unknown in the canon of ethnographic research. (In)famous examples of erotic desire on the part of ethnographers are to be found in Malinowski's posthumously published diaries

(Malinowski 1967), where he acknowledged, privately, his sexual attraction to female Trobriand Islanders. Likewise, Michel Leiris's journal account of the Dakar-Djibouti expedition (Leiris 2017) includes his growing feelings for Emawayish, the daughter of Malkam Ayyahou, a local healer, possessed by potent spirits, in Gondar (in then Abyssinia). It seems to have gone no further than his personal reflections. Malinowski's and Leiris's personal accounts were private. But some ethnographers have quite explicitly rejected celibacy. As Kulick (1995) observes, there is no need to advocate sex in the field in order to acknowledge that 'if we focus on it and put it to work, the erotic subjectivity of the ethnographer *can* be epistemologically productive' (p. 23, emphasis in original). Ethnographic desire can include an explicitly erotic desire encompassing complex sentiments concerning self and others, intimacy and distance, appropriation, difference and power. Contrasting accounts include those of Dubish (1995), who describes relationships with men in the course of Greek fieldwork, or Blackwood (1995), who entered into a lesbian relationship with a woman in West Sumatra. What is significant in these and other descriptions of erotically charged encounters is the sense that sex in its many guises can contribute to a more generic process of destabilisation and reformulation of ethnographic identities and relationships, a renewed sense of the fluidity of self and others and sometimes a reaffirmation of the fieldworker's own identity. Erotic knowing can open up a range of sensitivities and sensibilities. As Altork (1995) suggests, in the context of her own erotic fieldwork experiences, elements of the erotic

> ... have a profound impact on what the ethnographer selectively learns in the field. This selective perception process also influences the ways in which a given land and its inhabitants are represented textually – the ripened fruit of the fieldwork process. These erotic elements include opening up to sensory possibilities, confronting sexual and emotional passion as elements of the field experience, and allowing a language of passion to permeate the construction of texts. By contextualizing sexuality in the fieldwork, anthropologists may add elegant tools to their scientific and intellectual tool boxes.
>
> *(p. 109)*

Sexual encounters between researchers and their hosts might seem transgressive in many contexts and are likely to be found questionable by contemporary ethics committees and review boards. A number of ethnographers have gone public on sexuality and sexual relationships in the field, however. Here, our interest lies not with the sexual nature of those relationships *per se* but with a more general issue. That is, the sense that ethnographic fieldwork is a liminal period – an interval – during which licence may be exercised. It can be a time not just of social exploration with others but also of self-exploration. There is, after all, a parallel between the cultural learning that constitutes ethnographic fieldwork, and the exploration of selfhood and identity on the part of the ethnographer him/herself. Hardly surprisingly, collective attitudes towards such encounters have displayed a double standard. Female ethnographers, such as Ruth Landes, who contracted personal relations with a man from the host society were disproportionately castigated for unprofessional or unseemly conduct.

Sexuality can be a focal point for expressions of selfhood and possible transformations of identity. The collection of autobiographical essays edited by Martin and Haller (2019) furnishes several pertinent examples. Susan Harper (2019) concludes her autobiographical account:

> I was no longer comfortable performing my bisexuality in a male-gaze-centred way, and steadily and ever more stridently refused to do so. This represented what was, I now realize, a very real challenge to my husband's unquestioned male heterosexual privilege, and his role as one of the "cool" NeoPagan men who "didn't mind" that their female partners were queer. Once he was taken out of the sexual equation when it came to my bisexuality, my husband had to grapple with the fact that he was, in fact, married to a queer woman – a vastly different proposition than being married to a woman who would occasionally have sexual flings with women, from which he benefited directly or voyeuristically. My shift from object to subject, to arbiter of my own sexual life, was one our marriage could not withstand.
>
> *(p. 112)*

This summarises a radical transformation in the course of fieldwork, including the end of a marriage and a radical shift in sexual identification. It arose in the context of fieldwork with NeoPaganism in the United States – which as Harper herself notes, is necessary to study sexuality, given the centrality of bodily experience, including sex – to NeoPagan practice and belief. NeoPagan values relate directly to sexual practice and expression, and as Harper (p. 105) observes, 'Many NeoPagan spaces are, in fact, highly sexually charged'. Having entered the field (in Texas) with a firm understanding of her own sexuality, the longer she stayed in the field, the more she was led to interrogate and re-evaluate her own sexuality and to re-frame past experiences of her own. Irrespective of the ethics of erotic encounters in the course of fieldwork, Hunter's frank account demonstrates the transformative potential of ethnographic fieldwork. In this case, it appears to have been a radical biographical shift and not merely a protracted episode of licence. More generically, sexual encounters in the field open up the possibilities of erotic knowing – which goes well beyond sexual relations – but makes the person more open to sensations, feelings and embodiment. As Lorde (1984) writes (specifically about women):

> The erotic functions for me in several ways, and the first is in providing the' power which comes from sharing deeply any pursuit with another person. The

> sharing of joy, whether physical, emotional, psychic, or intellectual, forms a bridge between the sharers which can be the basis for understanding much of what is not shared between them, and lessens the threat of difference. Another important way in which the erotic connection functions is the open and fearless underlining of my capacity for joy. In the way my body stretches to music and opens into response, hearkening to its deepest rhythms, so every level upon which I sense also open to the erotically satisfying experience, whether it is dancing, building a bookcase, writing a poem, examining an idea.
>
> *(p. 89)*

In other settings, the 'absence' that is associated with fieldwork, coupled with its intense presence 'elsewhere', means that personal exploration and experimentation are pursued. We have already outlined some of the more florid forms of epiphany and revelation, through a discussion of extraordinary encounters. But being 'away' from familiar surroundings can lead to personal transformations of less dramatic, but equally far-reaching, kinds. Doctoral and postdoctoral research are significant periods of enculturation for many, if not all, scholars. But the intense commitments of ethnographic fieldwork, coupled with the almost equally demanding tasks of 'analysis' and 'writing' (actually, two aspects of the work of reconstruction), mean that the ethnographer's experience of fieldwork constitutes a major biographical episode and period of *Bildung*.

When Delamont, Atkinson and Parry (2000) studied graduate students and their supervisors in a variety of disciplines, it was clear that when invited to summarise their academic careers the anthropologists – students and supervisors – provided the most elaborated and extended of accounts; in contrast, the natural scientists produced much shorter, unelaborated summaries. Within anthropologists' biographical narratives, the circumstances of fieldwork featured prominently. They included the place of the fieldwork and the supervisor. The latter is especially important in the academic trajectory, partly because her or his own fieldwork expertise is a major element in the transmission of craft knowledge, not least because it too has a bearing on the place of the fieldwork and of its intellectual flavour. The highly personalised nature of anthropologists' narratives also placed their fieldwork episodes in a lineage of influences and mentors' mentors. The episodic nature of fieldwork is endowed not just with personal and intellectual significance but is also inserted into a narrative that links disruption with a disciplinary *durée*. Similar observations could be made of sociological and other ethnographers: the ethnographic fieldwork represents an especially intense episode in one's personal and intellectual narrative.

Episodic surrender and catch

Our recurrent reflections on entering and leaving the field, coupled with an emphasis on long-term immersion can readily imply an unbroken stretch of ethnographic engagement with an equally undifferentiated stream of culture.

But the stream-of-consciousness image of participation and observation does not always do justice to the multiple interruptions and fragmentations of fieldwork. Ethnographic encounters and engagements can often be episodic. As researchers, we can 'dip into' episodes of that cultural stream. Our guiding image of such episodic experience is that of the *Shaduf*. PA writes autobiographically:

> Childhood. The basement of London's Science Museum, a regular treat. The children's gallery was devoted to displays that included early versions of interactive exploration.
>
> One of my favourites: a table-top display consisting of toy-sized models of ancient hydraulic engineering. It was made the more absorbing by the fact that each little model involved turning a handle to set it in motion. The models represented ancient mechanisms for shifting water. They included the Archimedes screw and the *shaduf* (the counter-weighted system for lifting skin buckets of water). They were among many child-scaled displays and dioramas: a series of small cases tracing the history of lighting, from reed lights in a cave to gaslight in a Victorian parlour, each of which was illuminated when you pressed a button also sticks in the memory.
>
> But the screw and the *shaduf* have left an impression that has lasted for over sixty years. Partly, of course, because they were engagingly toy-like, and turning the handle to activate the models (with real water!) was endlessly captivating. Had there not been competing attractions (knobs to press, other handles to turn) I might have spent even longer playing with those little models. No doubt modern science displays and museums have more sophisticated means of instruction and entertainment. But the little models had a potent charm. The Archimedes screw was, I recall, attached to a little figure who appeared to be turning the mechanism as I turned the handle. Where are they now? Have they been recorded or preserved?
>
> To return. What is evoked by memories of the *shaduf* and the screw? The mechanism draws water from river to land, from the water's natural course to the artificial channels that criss-cross and irrigate the land. And is this not what we do? As physical, emotional and existential labour? As ethnographers? Patiently, with effort, repetitiously we transfer from the streams of everyday life into ordered categories. We redistribute the flow of mundane occurrences into the classifications of our archives. The water remains the same, in its material being, but it is also translated from the undifferentiated mass into something given new shape, new form, purpose and direction. We channel metaphorically just as surely as the water is channelled materially. Both are accomplished through repetitious labour.
>
> The *shaduf* dips into the stream. The screw turns endlessly. The ethnographer and the *shaduf* dip and sample. Each moves (water, phenomena)

> from one level to another. Each ethnographic encounter is another dip of the *shaduf*, another sampling from the stream of the everyday, and in the process episodes, events and encounters are transferred from the stream of mundane life, into the episodic categories of ethnographic analysis. And do we not toil repetitiously, shifting instances from their original embeddedness in everyday life into new categories of analytic thought, sifting and sorting into new channels? In the process we endow them with new significance.

As we dip in and out of the stream of everyday life, our ethnographic understanding is often marked by episodic comprehension, rather than an all-encompassing, totalising gaze. Some of the most significant exemplars of ethnographic work are relatively fleeting episodes that are symbolically enlarged through textual elaboration. Cliché though it may be, Geertz's account of the Balinese cock-fight remains a key example (Geertz 1973b). This is a relatively short, self-contained episode in Geertz's fieldwork. Yet he treats it as displaying a synecdochal (part-for-whole) relationship with wider cultural and analytic themes. It, thus, becomes an *actual type* (Edmondson 1984; Atkinson 1990) transformed into an archetype.

Because we can rarely 'see' the totality of a social world or the full trajectory of a social process, and because we can never write enough to reconstruct fully that totality, we are bound only ever to 'glimpse' instances and traces. Indeed, it would be more accurate to acknowledge that there is no 'totality', no coherent social organisation, no single encompassing culture, and to acknowledge further that the glimpses, shards and traces of ethnographic observation are all that exist. A recent example, by one of the most famous ethnographic sociologists, is Elijah Andersons' monograph on African Americans' experiences of racism in America (Anderson 2022). It is not a 'traditional' ethnography of a single site or locale. Rather, Anderson's most general argument is sustained through a series of highly evocative episodes, each of which provides a lightning flash of illumination. The argument is cumulative, sustained by an unfolding series of episodes.

'Ethnographic moments' can arise from a variety of sources. Clearly, they can be episodes of heightened, dramatic activity on the part of the others (such as religious observances or moments of intense conflict, or indeed of celebration), or revelatory moments on the part of the ethnographer. Activities that are 'ordinary' for the participants can become 'extraordinary' for the anthropologist or sociologist, through a kind of intellectual or sensory Gestalt switch. Horsley (2012) provides two telling examples from her fieldwork with hospital pathologists. Looking through a microscope in the company of a senior pathologist, Horsley finds herself looking at a slide of tissue taken from a brain of a man whose autopsy she had attended previously. She describes how she was seized by the fascination of observing through the microscope, and how it evoked childhood memories of 'discovering the joys of the microscopic world' (p. 545). Such moments go beyond mere memory: '...I was also launched into a greater appreciation of the intellectual challenges that the science of pathology holds for its converts in pursuit of the causes of death' (ibid.). Likewise, she describes the revelatory fascination of observing autopsies, and especially of observing an empty skull that captures something of death and the body, absence and presence, person and object. Such moments can be sharply illuminating: flashes that briefly but luridly display phenomena in high relief and in hard contrast. The intellectual journey of the ethnographer can be one of the emotional and analytic interruptions and interventions. They are not encompassed by the simple accumulation of 'data'. Indeed, an obsession with volumes of observations, transcripts and images can prove stultifying by comparison.

These are 'ethnographic moments' *par excellence*. Of such moments, Strathern (1999) writes:

> We could say that the ethnographic moment works as an example of a relation which joins the understood (what is analysed at the moment of observation) to the need to understand (what is observed at the moment of analysis) ... any ethnographic moment, which is a moment of knowledge or insight, denotes a relation between immersion and movement.
>
> *(p. 6)*

In other words, ethnographic moments – sometimes brief episodes that gain iconic significance – interrupt one's natural attitude in the field, by prompting acts of transposition, from the ordinary to the remarkable and hence to the 'writable'. Strathern herself writes graphically on being 'dazzled' by such an ethnographic moment:

> ...I shall never forget my first sight of mounted pearl shells in Mt Hagen, in 1964, heavy in their resin boards, slung like pigs from a pole being carried between two men, who were hurrying with them because of the weight, a gift of some kind. It was only a glimpse; the men were half running and their path was almost out of my field of vision. But it belongs to a set of images which have mesmerised me ever since.
>
> *(p. 8)*

Many (all?) ethnographers can report such moments – that they will 'never forget', or that remain vivid 'even now'. Strathern's anthropological imagination was seized by that moment, to the extent that the focus of her fieldwork shifted, from a focus on 'sibling order and cash cropping success' to an exploration of 'prestations' or gift-exchanges (pp. 8–9).

The antinomies of biographical disruption also feed into the nature of our analytic, intellectual commitments. Ethnographies – as exercises in research and in writing – seem always poised between trust and betrayal; between searching for authenticity and traducing realities. These fluctuations and refractions connect directly to the authors' existential and intellectual disruptions. In everyday terms, we sometimes do not know 'where we stand', even when we strive to find and give voice to a 'standpoint'. Ethnographers can cultivate and express a sense of phenomenological nostalgia. They look back at their own rites of passage, recount their hardships bravely borne and celebrate the hard-won fruits of enhanced understanding. Such *nostalgie de la boue* enhances ethnographers' (mostly anthropologists') expressions of self-importance, even when the rhetoric seems to imply the opposite – personal reticence and intellectual modesty. Of course, as Haraway (2018) points out, the 'modesty' of the *modest witness* is a trope that obscures a multitude of immodest ends. The self-effacing *virtuoso* is a trope of realism, which affirms the validity of observations through the elision of the observer. So, the ethnographer can also be caught between the modesty of the witness and the self-importance of ethnography itself. For there is a whiff of self-centredness among ethnographers at large. Collectively, ethnographers like to create the impression that our presence in the field is not only of importance to us (which it is) but also significant for our hosts (which is not necessarily so). We do not mean to imply that the temporary interventions of ethnographic work are of no consequence, or that social relationships sustained there are spurious. Rather, we should recognise that fieldwork is not necessarily of such abiding interest to our hosts as we would sometimes like.

Undoubtedly *some* anthropologists and sociologists establish long-lasting relations with their hosts. Such enduring ties have been thoroughly documented. They can also be embedded in repeated returns to the field. But such returns can also emphasise how fleeting and impermanent many field relations really are. Briggs's (2013) study of crack-cocaine users in London, for instance, records his return to his research hosts. Expecting some sort of reunion, he finds that for some at least there was no recollection at all. What was a major commitment for one party can seem like a fleeting and half-remembered encounter for another. Briggs is not alone in reporting that research hosts can – quite honestly it would seem – deny any recollection of the ethnographer's presence: any intrusion or disruption was passing and of modest significance. That should not surprise us. It is, after all, a tenet of ethnographic fieldwork that we participate in and that observes the normal routines of everyday life. While actors may be conscious of our presence in the field, they are often far too busy getting on with that ordinary everyday life to pay undue heed to our presence. And on our departure ordinary life goes on as before. Ethnographic, episodic presence can soon be forgotten or at least relegated to the margins of memory. Perhaps a concern with our own presence and its lasting effect is an example of ethnographic self-importance. There is, after all, a degree of self-regard that leads field researchers to inflict themselves on their research hosts, sometimes apparently dragooning them into 'participating' in the research process rather than letting them get on with their normal life and everyday work.

There is also the related question: Does the field leave us? It is clear that whatever may be the processes of leaving the field, we do not simply turn our backs on it. In the first place, of course, we carry the field back to us. The field is not synonymous with the people and events that we happen to have encountered, witnessed and participated in. The field is not an inert temporal strip or spatial slice of life. The field is what we make it to be: through our acts of engagement, intervention and close attention, through our participation and our observation, we *make* fields. We inscribe them in our fieldnotes, transcripts, maps, photographs and the like. Having lived our time *in* the field, we then live *with* that transmogrified field. Our 'data' and our acts of composition repeatedly bring different aspects of the field to consciousness. Consequently, we do not really leave it behind but live through it in a different mode. Moreover, we can re-visit the field, not just through a physical return (although many do), but through repeated readings and re-readings of those treasured, hard-won materials.

The field thus becomes a site of memory, of re-lived experience. Memorialisation is a major source of biographical disruption. We constitute ourselves and our scholarly endeavour through what is memorable and what is forgotten. Indeed, the admixture of the two is what makes ordinary living manageable. If we remember nothing, or if we forget nothing, meanings are equally impossible to grasp. The 'mnemonist' studied by Luria (1987) who could, to all intents and purposes, recall everything is an extreme case, throwing into relief the selective nature of ordinary memory. Ethnographers train themselves to exercise their memory as fully as they can and to pay closer attention than would occur in the natural attitude of everyday life. But through actions of memorialisation (making fieldnotes, reading and indexing the notes, reviewing interview transcripts, making and viewing photographs and videos) the field' and its social contents are reconstituted. Analysis and writing – acts of retrieval and reconstruction – thus re-make the field on repeated occasions after we leave it physically. The afterlife of the field is a much more enduring presence than the ethnographer's original presence in the field. That afterlife and the reconstruction of its traces create the possibility of the catch, the counterpart of our surrender.

Conclusion

There is no single narrative to be pursued here: the trajectories are too diverse for that. But we conclude by emphasising that ethnographic fieldwork often constitutes a double interruption. We interrupt the doings of others, who consent to our temporary presence and our incursions into their everyday lives. Simultaneously, periods of fieldwork interrupt the lives of ethnographers themselves. The latter may be a sought-after period, but it frequently provides a mode of 'time out' that is simultaneously cherished and troubling. The personal solitude and intellectual disorientation are all but necessary in the great scheme of things. They can, however, be sources of disorientation. The alienation effect of estrangement is a vital resource in engaging with the new cultural setting, but it is also an existential challenge. We have, by no means originally, described the period of fieldwork as a liminal state. There is a process of disengagement from 'normal' social and academic life, and it is followed by processes of disengagement and reintegration. The vicissitudes of fieldwork can be celebrated as tokens of hard-won achievement and recollected with nostalgia in retrospect. In the meantime, periods of readjustment include the demands and disciplines of 'writing up'.

5

ETHNOGRAPHY INCARNATE

It is self-evident that participant observation and participation in the field are dependent on physical presence and also depend on the ethnographer's physical comportment. The fieldworker's self-presentation is a key aspect of adaptation to the social and cultural environment. Clothing is but one aspect of that. One does not have to dress in exactly the same way as the local actors, but clothing appropriately is a routine feature of the fieldwork enterprise. PA's fieldwork presence in a teaching hospital haematology service and subsequently in the rehearsal studios of an opera company called for different manners of dress, as did EMW's fieldwork among a team of social workers. But a physical appearance by no means exhausts the embodied work of ethnographic fieldwork. Standing, crouching, kneeling, dancing and walking – the entire repertoire of movement – are called for. Moreover, the physical accomplishment of attention and concentration are vital. It is a practical imperative to retain some degree of focus. Recall of events in concrete detail will be a vital resource in the compilation of fieldnotes. But attention and engagement go beyond that. It can demand all of one's faculties and senses. In the course of this chapter, therefore, we shall be considering the embodied nature of fieldwork in a way that is thoroughly attentive to a broad range of sensations. The chapter also deals with the ethnography of embodied skill through the socialisation of the body. Surrender to phenomena needs, therefore, to involve the ethnographer's embodied presence. The catch, it follows, is also a fully realised documentation of the sensory dimensions of a given social world.

Ethnographic work yields incarnate knowledge and fieldwork is thoroughly embodied. As the contributors to the collection of essays edited by Lawrence and Shapin (1998) point out, post-Enlightenment natural science was largely based on the trope of the disembodied, disengaged observer. Body and Mind parted company. This is also one of the themes of Michel Serres's contribution to a philosophy of the senses, where he argues that embodied sensory knowing

DOI: 10.4324/9780429056802-5

had been marginalised by scientific discourse (Serres 2016). Objectivity was warranted by pure cognition on the part of the scientist-observer, divorced from the person, and particularly from the male observer's body. As Marchand (2008) also observes in the context of craft apprenticeship, 'An Enlightenment pedestal to reason marginalised the body, and the pedagogy of formal schooling progressively confined embodied learning to regimes of disciplined training … and fitness' (p. xx). By contrast, in Judaic and Islamic traditions recitation is expressed physically in a way that expresses a thoroughly embodied relationship to the text and hence to learning itself (cf. Bullivant 1978; Eickelman 1978). Marchand goes on to argue that 'the body is a key site for investigating the expression, communication, negotiation and acquisition of knowledge' (ibid.). Marchand is drawing on his own work on building in Yemen and Mali and skilled woodworkers in England: studies that included 'deep participation' on his part as he undertook a practical apprenticeship. The ethnographer learns physically and seeks to learn about actors' physical activity. As Douny (2018) suggests, 'Through long periods of waiting, observing, imitating and practising repeatedly, the ethnographer experiences, adopts and so shares people's embodied perceptions of their everyday lives' (pp. 99–100).

The ethnographic study of work and science calls for a thoroughly embodied sense of what it takes actually to accomplish tasks and to work with materials, machines and devices (see Knorr-Cetina 1999). Krautwurst (2014) provides a concrete account of embodied work in a bioscience laboratory, leading him to reflect on 'how many elements of scientific practices maintain an artisanal or craft-like quality in which experienced body knowledge became entangled with formal scientific knowledge' (p. 15). Embodied knowledge and embodied ethnography can grant access to otherwise tacit knowledge, especially the kind of skill that Merleau-Ponty referred to as 'motor-intentional' in our physical engagement with things (see Gascoigne and Thornton 2013).

The acquisition of knowledge is not confined to studies of education or apprenticeship: it applies to all forms of ethnographic investigation. Ethnography that calls for full participation in the field, has – in the past especially – been implicitly represented as an exercise in disembodied observation. Corporeal experiences – like emotional responses – were historically relegated to autobiographical, confessional texts, where the ethnographer could recall feelings of discomfort and repugnance (see Van Maanen 2011). But the ethnographic project calls for multiple forms of perception and experience. It involves *observation*, and we need to distinguish between seeing, looking and observing. Participant observation is far more than an optic matter. It involves the full physical engagement with all that the field implies. Perception is thus an embodied activity, just as is participation. The phenomenology of seeing and observing implies the cultivation of embodied presence. It also calls for the acquisition of practical knowledge and expertise in the field, sometimes including active learning. There is thus a parallel between the craft of ethnography and the ethnography of craft. They are both forms of practical accomplishment that depend on physical engagement and embodied work (Atkinson 2022). Likewise, touch, smell and hearing all call for a fully embodied presence as a way of doing fieldwork. Ethnographers work *on* the body and they work *with* the body. Ethnography is always, in principle, incarnate knowledge. Surrender to the field is a physically embodied engagement. The phenomenology of perception requires practical expertise, tacit knowledge and embodied commitment. If surrender involves the body in all its senses, then the analytic Catch implies self-conscious attention to those sensory phenomena. If learning is embodied, then the Catch demands that we learn about how we learn (cf. Purser 2018). Furthermore, a recognition of the carnal basis of knowledge means that our critical, analytic reflection cannot be solely at the cognitive level. It calls for a response at a more visceral level too. It means 'bringing flesh to theory' (Lane 2016).

The fleshly, corporeal realisation of ethnographic knowledge was pioneered by Katherine Dunham, in her work on Jamaica and Haiti (e.g. Dunham 1969, 1983). In early recognition of the performative aspects of culture and the possibilities of performative ethnography, Dunham developed not only anthropological work on dance but also created dance itself. On both sides of that equation, she expressed a view of culture and of academic representation that was not just a matter of language and text but deeply embodied (Roberts 2014). Embodiment also evokes the pioneering work of Marcel Mauss, in particular his attention to the importance of *technique* (Mauss 2006/1935). Now Mauss's use of the term is familiar because his comments on *les techniques du corps* have received wide attention. That section of his work was one of the sources for the emergent sociology of the body, and it was translated and anthologised early in that process. That particular context, however, led to a distinctive emphasis on the socialised body and rather less emphasis on technique *per se*. And yet Mauss had things to say about the significance of technique much more broadly. Indeed, in his ethnology, technique is one of the pervasive concepts that runs through and links a number of different empirical domains. All techniques engage the body, through work, celebration, or interaction. Fieldwork addresses the multiple techniques of everyday living and therefore calls for a physical engagement with the everyday.

One consequence of physical participation and co-presence is a clearer sense of the rhythms of everyday life. The 'method' of *rhythmanalysis* (Lefebvre 2004)) has the air of a specialised, esoteric technique. In fact, it captures just one aspect of quotidian activity. The coordination of social actions, the interlocking and overlapping cycles of action are and should be a fundamental element of ethnographic analysis. Rhythms also imply pace and tempo. Physical engagement provides the field researcher with the opportunity to participate directly in the temporal flows, rhythms and cycles of everyday life. As Edensor (2010) points out, there are multiple perspectives on walking alone that all imply embodiment and rhythm and in turn can call for an embodied investigation, though not all studies depend on embodied or walking ethnography *per se*. Clearly, one can and should observe these phenomena anyway, but the embodiment of tempo, rhythm and pace gives an added insight into the interplay of time and bodies, at rest, in motion and at work. This is participation *with* and not just observations *of* phenomena. As Laplantine (2015) suggests:

> ...there do not exist bodily behaviors outside of experiences that are those of temporality. These may be extremely past-dependent (for example with tiredness) but also extended toward the future (in dread, fear, expectation, patience). There is no corporeality in itself but rather acts oscillating between slow and fast motion, acts prone to repeating themselves but also to being improvised in a singular manner at each occurrence. Such as the act of running.
>
> *(p. 15)*

One physical feature of fieldwork that deserves to be re-stated: It is tiring and physically demanding. One might at first blush think that surrender to and in the field implies some rapturous, languid form of relaxation. The contrary is true. Surrender to phenomena calls for alert, close attention. Surrender, in Wolff's terms, demands the suspension of one's everyday assumptions, being open to local phenomena. But it also demands the catch of sustained attention. It calls for the exercise of one's senses and of one's rained memory to capture phenomena in sufficient concrete detail. Without the catch, embodied presence in the field merely yields a sequence of experiences and impressions. When coupled with sustained attention, on the other hand, it generates observations. Physically, such a sustained attentive presence is tiring. Fieldworkers are acutely aware of the demands made upon them, as they stand, walk, crouch, kneel and concentrate for hours on end. Such effortful participation is not a handicap, it is not really one of the costs of fieldwork. It is a benefit, for it is through such physicality that we can learn about practical action in the material world. We learn of the significance of physical labour, of embodied repetition and of the specialised physical postures, gestures and movements that cultural conventions call for. Ethnographic learning is always effortful, and through such efforts we develop our embodied understanding.

Fieldwork can reveal phenomena through bodily encounters with the physical and social world. Löwstedt (2015) reports on a brief (four-week) period of fieldwork on a construction site. He encountered the site in two ways, from complementary perspectives: as an observer and as a worker. As he describes it, when working on the site, getting hurt was unavoidable:

> During those weeks I tripped on an electric cable on the floor and fell on to a metal bar hurting my elbow; I walked into an electric cabinet and hurt my knee; I somehow managed to stick my thumb into a hole in a wall and twist it; a large wooden beam hit my arm when sitting and measuring leaving me with a large bruise, which could easily have been much worse

> because it fell towards my neck and one of the workers screamed at me enabling me just barely to get my arm up in time to protect my neck .... By experiencing these events from a worker perspective it became very clear to me that just following established safety guidelines is not always enough to avoid incidents on the site.
>
> *(p. 411)*

The trope of the ethnographic klutz, a cultural dope and a physical misfit, is a common one, and Löwstedt exemplifies that perfectly. Sticking one's thumb into a hole is the sort of slapstick-like gaffe that ethnographers like to 'confess' to. But his account – although he does not really develop the point – does illustrate the way in which full participation can lead to physically embodied experiences. Löwstedt himself could well have gone further in his reflective analysis in thinking not just about the accidents and the near-misses but also in a more sustained way about the material circumstances of his work, the materials he was working with, the physical layout of the site, the movement of bodies within that environment and the movement of things in relation to bodies. His fieldwork experience does at least hint at an embodied ethnography on the social reality of construction. Sensory awareness also entails a thorough grasp of the materiality of a shared world: things, artefacts and their uses. It involves a comprehension of their 'thingness': the materials they are composed of, their surfaces, colours and textures. We shall elaborate on this theme later in the chapter.

Carnal ethnography, therefore, is not about sensory perception as an 'add-on', much less as a niche specialism. It involves us in enterprises that do not unduly privilege 'sight' (observation) or 'speech' (interviewing) as the primary modalities of understanding. As Kakavoulia (2008) suggests from the perspective of anthropology: 'Among the objectives of cross-cultural anthropological research is the exploration of the embedding of a "sensory" order in the social order of society. Sensorial anthropology studies various cultural systems of sensorial symbolism, contrasting Western perceptual models with orality and aurality in other cultures' (p. 215). As Papagaroufaki (2008) expresses it in terms of 'carnal hermeneutics':

> I use the metaphor *carnal* hermeneutics to suggest that the act of both ethnographic and native *interpretation* is not simply a 'mental' or 'cognitive' function but a sensory and emotional engagement in the world. This means that cultural interpretation (seen as either 'text reading' or 'conversing' or 'translating' or 'writing about') is not a conceptual re-presentation of experiences, understood as immediate and thus more real and prior to their representation.
>
> *(p. 115, emphases in original)*

The ethnography of charismatic Catholic healing by Csordas (1994) is an important case in point. His engagement with occasions of healing makes clear the significance of embodiment. The religious practices are performative and carnal, while the healer's practices are grounded in embodied perceptions (heat, pain, smell, vibration, as well as sight). The healers' olfactory sense distinguishes between 'evil' (sulphur) and 'good' (flowers). The latter reminds us also of Kenna's discussion of the sacredness of incense, based on her study of Orthodox practices on a Greek island (Kenna 2005). Whether or not phenomenology is explicitly appealed to, carnal ethnography is inescapably committed to exploring the bodily apperception of phenomena, including those of the Self and the Other in fieldwork and analysis. It rests on the embodied, trained sensitivity to one's physical, and social surroundings. It calls for a cultivated sense of place that recalls Shepherd's (2011) reflections on journeying in the Cairngorm mountains, of which she writes that the mountain-lover is more than a little 'fey' (a little mad):

> *Fey* may be too strong a term for that joyous release of body that is engendered by climbing: yet to the sober looker-on a man may seem to walk securely over dangerous places with the gay abandon that is said to be the mark of those who are doomed to death. How much of this gay security is the result of perfectly trained and co-ordinated body and mind, only climbers themselves realise....
>
> *(p. 6)*

The ethnographer is unlikely to achieve the kind of embodied facility as the 'fey' mountain-walker. Yet she or he aspires to that sense of sensory, incarnate belonging that makes observable the world of sensory phenomena.

Socialising the body

Presence in the field implies a distinctive way of physical being in the world. This is not just a matter of demurely self-effacing behaviour, or of mirroring one's hosts' bodily comportment, although those and similar actions can certainly be aspects of practical fieldwork. Rather it means that one must learn not just *about* the body but also *through* the body. It is exemplified by Preston (2016) in her ethnographic account of Japanese Noh theatre. The title of the monograph, *Learning to Kneel,* is evocative and precise:

> The first thing I learned about Noh performance technique was how much it hurt to kneel in *seiza*, with my legs folded beneath my body and my buns resting on my heels.... Having taken a quarter century of ballet and modern dance classes and endured the torture of pointe shoes and a few minor injuries I was shocked to discover that *being still* was the most challenging aspect of noh lessons. Maybe *seiza* was not painful for professional noh actors, who kneel while practicing, teaching and performing? I asked my teacher in Tokyo, Furukawa Mitsuru, about the position after attending

> several lessons and watching him kneel in the chorus (*jiutai*) for more than an hour during his group's production of *Kamo* .... He told me that *seiza* is painful for everyone but worse for beginners and foreigners, like me.
>
> *(p. 1, emphases in original)*

This is about more than an unaccustomed posture. The discipline and the effort involved provide the ethnographer with a phenomenological enactment of a cultural requirement that could be observable and the discomfort could be ascertained through conversations and interviews. But the embodiment of Noh conventions and observances permits an understanding of a different order. It is a form of surrender through the body. It opens up the fieldworker's physical and cognitive being to the requirements of being in the field. Preston acknowledges that she attempted to 'embrace' the Noh tradition embodied by her teacher, yielding to the tradition, 'suppressing my desire to add an original style or flair that would have been prized in my ballet and modern dance training' (p. 6). Submission to the physical discipline of *seiza* provides Preston not just with a way into her monograph but also a portal into a way of tradition and a way of life. Very similar observations could be made about the learning of martial arts (Jennings, Brown and Sparkes 2010): ethnographers learning South-East Asian martial arts also have to learn to re-discipline the body. In a parallel context, Downey (2005) writes about learning *capoeira*, the Afro-Brazilian martial art in terms of embodied skills and experiences. Students of *capoeira* have to re-discover and transform their physical habits and – more importantly perhaps – learn new ones:

> More than just a limited repertoire of skills added to previous proficiencies, then, capoeira ostensibly reforms how novices occupy their own bodies at a basic level. Like other forms of physical discipline, capoeira training reforms a person's habits to change the way the student lives in the world. Capoeira serves as a physical discipline for 'making a body'... and throws into high relief how changes in everyday behavior might bring self-transformation.
>
> *(p. 35)*

Just as Preston had to re-learn how to kneel, so students of martial arts need to re-learn how to fall. Both kinds of ordinary activity and posture are transformed into something consciously acquired as an embodied skill. Moreover, bodily performances of that sort, and many others like them, furnish enactments of authenticity – properly socialised bodies in Japanese or Brazilian style.

PA undertook lessons in Argentine tango and kept a fieldnote record of his learning. The adequate performance of tango calls for a fresh approach to bodily posture, in a way analogous to the embodiment of Brazil inscribed in the body of the *capoeirista*. The entire movement of the body must display an 'authentic' tango style. Moreover, the rhythmic demands of tango call for a distinctive approach to the dance itself and a thoroughly enculturated body that mirrors tango's subtle rhythms. The body is not merely disciplined, but also responsive to the music's pulse. As a male, with the responsibility of 'leading' ever-changing female partners PA acquired a clear sense of the physical expression of intentions on the dance-floor. Men lead with their chest, in a dance that is not rehearsed, but depends on an extremely close embrace between the couple. Of course, one can learn *about* that from instruction books and from watching lessons without participating. But dancing (or attempting to) gives a very different sense of posture, movement and rhythm. Learners of Brazilian *capoeira*, especially men from the Northern hemisphere, find that they have to cultivate a 'loose waist' in their martial-arts classes and in dancing samba (Delamont, Stephens and Campos 2017).

Participant observation demands a being-with-others. That includes sharing in the temporal rhythms of their everyday life, the choreography of their interactions, their physically embodied engagement with things and other social actors. It means sometimes doing things physically. A small example: When PA was observing rehearsals and performances at the Welsh National Opera company (Atkinson 2006), he rarely ventured onto the set in the rehearsal studio or onto the stage in the theatre. Those are spaces which, while by no means sacred, are really the preserve of the performers and the other members of the company, such as stage managers. Now in the rehearsal studio, the full set does not appear as it will when the opera is fully staged in the theatre, but the rehearsal version reproduces some crucial features of it. It is important that performers rehearse in a physical environment that models key features of the spaces they will encounter in the theatre. There are occasions when the studio is empty – before or after rehearsals or during a lunch-time break. From time to time PA would venture onto the mocked-up set. It gave a very different sense of the performing space than just observing it from behind the invisible fourth wall. As well as gaining a slightly different sense of scale and space, it (quite literally) offers a shift in perspective. Moreover, PA could gain a sense of what it was like to stand and move within that space. The Iannis Kokkos production of *Tristan und Isolde*, for instance, included a steep curving rake. One day PA walked onto that sweeping rake. He was startled. He had not altogether realised just how steep it was and why Tristan needed footholds to stop him from sliding down it. He could appreciate the steepness and the potential effort of walking up and down it while singing. Of course, that could have been observable from a distance, but the physical sense of precariousness and imbalance differed from that sense that was intuited alone. To 'feel with' others and their circumstances is not simply a matter of sympathy, but also sharing the physical constraints and opportunities that are shared in the immediate, physical lifeworld. There is a difference between seeing or even walking on a stage as a visitor (on a guided tour, for instance) and experiencing the physical *mise-en-scène* as a participant observer.

Physical presence in the field enables us to grasp the embodied sensations of time and place, of effort and experience. We know, rather than trying to understand vicariously, the sensation of tedium that is engendered by standing for hours waiting or working. We have the intense physical sense of concentrating on the matter in hand for hours on end. We move with others as they themselves move, and so mobility becomes something more than simply a rather fashionable sociological idea. Such embodied work also calls to mind the discipline of ethnographic fieldwork. We have to take ourselves physically into the field, to be with and work with other people, whether we 'feel like it' or not. We have to overcome, or at least live with, the fatigue that is born of protracted periods of intense fieldwork followed by equally intense periods of writing or dictating our fieldnotes. Early morning starts or late evenings or both mean that tiredness seeps into our bones and our brains. Studies of and in the city can involve footfall. Hall (2017) shared in the patrols of urban outreach workers, seeking out rough-sleeping homeless and other vulnerable people on the streets. Through that embodied socialisation, he derived an understanding of what 'searching' for signs of street-people might mean, stressing that searching is not simply seeing or even looking. One comes to understand the sensory work of searching and hence of finding:

> Experienced outreach workers hold and share an understanding of the ways in which the look of the city, as they encounter this out on patrol, might lead them towards the thing they are after; they know a good clue when they see one, and it is possible to list some such: the things that outreach workers see and consider a good indication. Many (not all) of these are ordinary enough objects, but it takes an outreach worker to see them for what they are in the context of outreach work, or even to see them at all. Who really sees a stained sheet of cardboard and a couple of cans in a doorway?
>
> *(p. 216)*

Hall's socialised and embodied sensibility allows him to 'search' through the eyes of an experienced outreach worker and hence to acquire that same perceptual competence, at least to a sufficient level to understand and report it.

Grasping reality

When we think of encounters with strange phenomena we seek to grasp their meaning. It implies an active consciousness reaching out to the surrounding world of material and symbolic phenomena. Grasping can also be a literal mode of comprehension. While the senses in general provide the resources for ethnographic fieldwork, there are specific aspects of touch – of haptic experience – that are especially pertinent. Here we consider the sense of touch that relates to embodied knowledge and skills, as acquired in the course of participant observation. The enculturation of the body, of the hand especially, can be a key aspect of participant observation and learning in a variety of settings. The alignment of the eye and the hand and the socialisation of the hand itself are fundamental aspects of skilled performance in a number of occupational and performative domains. We illustrate this with reference to PA's methodological exercises in participant observation. These have involved observation and physical participation in a number of craft studios. As well as general observation in studios, PA has taken practical classes in glassblowing, ceramics, jewellery-making and wood-working. These were all beginners' classes, and no claim is made here that he achieved anything beyond minimal competence in any of those disciplines. But well-documented participant observation in those studios allows us to reflect on the role of feel and touch in fieldwork (Atkinson 2022). There is a world of difference between observing an experienced craft-artist, such as a potter, and engaging directly with clay on a wheel, throwing and turning a pot of one's own – however clumsily. Both modes of being together with the potter yield significant insight, especially as the artist talks through what she or he is doing, or provides verbal as well as physical instruction. But they are qualitatively different: they offer the ethnographer different ways of being in the field and yield their own distinctive kinds of understanding. Learning how to throw a pot, for instance, necessarily involves getting a feel for the clay, its weight, thickness and texture. The learner needs to appreciate the kind of pressure that can be applied by the fingers to the outside of a pot in raising the clay: too little and nothing happens, too much and the clay can collapse into a messy heap. The same applies to applying support with the other hand from the interior.

The investigation of craft knowledge and the embodied skills of craft-workers provides perfect opportunities to explore haptic action and experience. Indeed, it is inescapable. PA's experience in a woodworking studio illustrates some aspects of manual discipline, of touch and grip. He needed to learn to let the tool do the work. Fieldnotes read:

> Each tool is the embodiment of a long process of development and evolution. The axe is, of course, the oldest human implement. (When a student of Archaeology I handled one from Olduvai Gorge). Likewise, the wood-working knives and chisels are perfectly adapted to perform specific kinds of task, to make possible certain kinds of action. Their weight, shape and sharpness are perfectly suited to those tasks. If used appropriately, then the tools make each stage in the making process predictable. But such use requires disciplined use. They must be held correctly. This is not just a matter of safety, significant though that is. The relationship between the tool, the body (not just the hand) and the wood has to be controlled. Hence the arrangement of the body itself is fundamentally important. Aching hands do not just reflect unaccustomed use, although all new activities find out little muscles that are not normally used in a sustained fashion. Aching thighs remind me that I do not normally kneel for any length of time. Simply put, we novices have a habit of simply gripping things too tightly and holding our bodies too tightly as well.

Similarly, in a glassblowing studio, PA's sensory engagement includes a 'feel' for the glass:

> There is the 'feel' of the glass on the pipe. It looks fairly straightforward to keep it turning and thus to keep the glass even. In practice, it is not so straightforward. With a lump of glass on the end of my iron, and heating it in the glory-hole, I am constantly aware of its potential to droop down. There are recurrent fears of it slipping off the pipe altogether and falling into the furnace. (What would happen then? Luckily it never occurred.) From time to time one stops twiddling in order to let the glass 'centre', but then it can start to droop almost immediately. The glass itself is at once responsive and malleable, yet hard to control, being highly plastic. Likewise, the heat is a resource, making the management of the glass a possibility, yet it creates a somewhat intimidating working environment. We novices are not accustomed to working in such an environment. One cannot simply reach out to touch the medium. The glass is always being manipulated at (literally) arm's length, except for when one is manipulating it directly with a tool, a block or one's hand through paper. But the direct touch of, say, clay is absent. One is also aware of the *weight* of the glass. When I was making my last piece (more on which below), which had a fairly chunky amount of glass encasing my blown glass interior, successive gathers meant that I ended up with a large amount of glass, which, given the length of the blowing pipe, was hard to control and to support at arm's length. In fact I had to confess to Layne that I was having difficulty managing the weight.
>
> Also, hands-on participation means that I was able to sense shaping the glass in my hand, with hand tools and also with a pad of newspaper. I can feel the resistance of the glass as it cools – it seems to go rapidly from being so soft it is in danger of slipping off the pipe altogether, to becoming quite stiff and intractable in a short space of time. It is, of course, for this reason, that it needs to go into the glory-hole repeatedly while one is working on it. Equally, there is something extremely satisfying in the weight of the glass as one works on it. It has a very considerable physical presence in its own right.

The following extracts are taken from a lesson in the studio of a jewellery-maker, where PA was learning to fashion a simple ring. At this point he was using copper – which is softer and therefore easier to work than silver, and of course a much cheaper material to learn on:

> It is now time for me to try to emulate what Ellie has done, still in copper. So she cuts me a length, and we take it over for annealing. I place the copper strip carefully, and cautiously turn on the flame. I am vividly reminded of just how much I recoiled from the heat in my schooldays. In the same

instant, of course, I also remind myself not to be such a wimp (something I often have to do when doing anything practical). I remember to apply heat round the copper strip and then to start heating it from one end. I try to ensure that the heat is applied at the inner cone of the flame. I realise that although it is easy to see the metal change colour, I do not have any feel for how long it should be heated, but I seem to get it more or less right, moving the heat fairly evenly along the strip of the metal. Being careful to do things safely, I turn off the burner, carefully pick up the copper strip in the tweezers and pop into the cold water. I remind myself aloud to do this, I feel it is too easy unthinkingly to reach out and pick things up in the fingers. I confess this to Ellie. She says she did so once, burning her hand very badly, burning her clothes, and – she points to a scar on the floor-boards – burning the floor.

After the pickle-pot I need to start shaping my ring on the mandrel. I try to emulate Ellie's mallet-taps. I try to give the copper two or three taps a time, angling downward, at a tangent to the curve of the mandrel. I am pleased to find that the copper is bending itself into a circle. Ellie makes an approving sound. I am immensely pleased with myself. I realise, however, that there is one issue I should need to concentrate on: it would be awfully easy to let the metal slide towards the thinnest end of the mandrel, and hence bending the metal into impossibly small, tight circles. However, I succeed in making a circle of metal that is more or less the right size (for my own finger). Self-satisfaction is short-lived. Now I have to saw through the two ends of the ring to make a perfect join. The ring needs to be held very firmly with the finger and thumb of my life hand while I saw with the right. I set off doing so. I don't seem to be getting it right, however. First, holding the ring perfectly still with my weak and unaccustomed fingers is harder than it really ought to be. Secondly, my sawing just isn't as smooth and regular as it should be, and certainly nothing like Ellie's. Thirdly, I realise I have no idea how my cut is progressing. All I know is that there is no satisfying cut through the first time, and the drop of the scrap metal, followed by the equivalent second cut. I ask Ellie for help. In the first place, she points out, I have the ring too far away, and so I am cutting into the wood rather than through the metal (why can't I feel that I wonder), Secondly, the ring has slipped – my grip was indeed poor – and so I have been making a double cut. In the event, I carry on a complete the second cut all the way through the two sections of copper. Surprisingly, the ends left by my second cut marry up adequately. Trying to keep the saw blade in a vertical plane, and sawing with a steady, regular motion is not easy. At times it sticks and I am conscious of the blade twisting. I say to Ellie that I am afraid of damaging her blade. She replies reassuringly that there are plenty of blades.

So, time to solder the ring. I apply the flux, conscious that I don't really know how much to apply or just how precise I need to be. I dab a bit on

> round the joint. Then I have to take out a pallion and place it and the ring on the ceramic tiles. As urged by Ellie, I try to apply heat evenly round the ring to begin with, rather than just at the joint to be soldered. I confess that, again, I could not really see with any certainty when the solder had been taken up. However, it seemed to be OK, so again it was quenched in the cold water, popped in the pickle-pot and taken over to the bench to be cleaned up. I worked round the ring, inside and out, with a file. I tried to make sure I was using the file in the same direction, following the curve of the metal, avoiding creating a flat-spot. Again, I wasn't sure I could actually see precisely what needed cleaning up, so my filing, and then papering, was perhaps rather ritualised rather than being purposeful. I then had a go at polishing the piece on the buffing wheels. I was glad I had put on safety goggles, as – rather as Ellie herself had warned – I lost concentration, relaxed my grip on the ring, and let it fly out of my fingers. Luckily it did not disappear under anything or between floorboards, and I was able to retrieve it, feeling a bit ashamed of such an elementary blunder. I also learned that one has to push the ring quite firmly into the brushes, keeping it moving all the time. One's finger-ends get quite a going-over at the same time. In any event, my copper ring is completed. It looks perfectly plausible. Working with the soft, warm-coloured copper seemed redolent of ancient metal-working, and I thought of Wayland the Smith as mythological prototype.

Here again we witness the embodied relationships between the eye and the hand, the tools and the raw materials. Technique (more or less successfully applied) implies the alignment of hand-work and the 'feel' for the materials. One can learn a lot from watching people at work. One can also learn a lot, some of it different, from actually trying out those practical activities for oneself. Embodiment generates its own modalities of understanding.

There are major studies that address, in different ways, the enculturation of the hand and the eye, and therefore address (not always explicitly) the significance of touch and grasp in the acquisition and use of esoteric, specialised competence. David Sudnow's study is a classic phenomenological description of an organised, co-ordinated activity (Sudnow 1978). He carefully traces his own performance of jazz piano. That requires a close coordination of the senses: the ear and the eye, the hands and the body. Posture and the management of the hand undergird such production. Bodily, incarnate knowledge includes a sense of places and distances: 'A grasp of the setting of the keyboard, and its dimensions relative to the hand's and arm's extension from the center of the body, develops. In time this skill becomes so elaborated that a precisely maintained alignment from the center point is itself unnecessary' (p. 13). This is not just a behaviourist description of the mechanics of musical performance, but it is a key example of a phenomenological attention to the hand and its engagement with material and symbolic means of expression. Felicitous performance is impossible without the adequate socialisation of touch (as well as sight and hearing). The way of the hand is not only about touch, it is also a matter of knowing or sensing where objects are available to one's reach and one's grasp. In a very similar reflective study, Chernoff (1979) learned African drumming in Northern Ghana. His remarkable monograph includes unusually detailed analyses of the aesthetics and techniques of drumming. He explains, *inter alia*, that African drumming – not preoccupied with the melody or harmony of 'Western' music – is based on counter-rhythms in conversation among several drums. He also shows the extent to which conventionally Western notions fail to capture the musical idioms of drumming. Here again, the way of the hand is implicated in a complex array of sensory phenomena – notably an acquired competence in following rhythmic and temporal patterns.

Paterson (2009) offers a valuable overview of the treatment of haptic knowledge in human geography and with wider significance beyond that particular discipline. He notes that 'the body' has been granted significance as a topic in a great deal of current social science, but writing *about* sensations of touch and feeling is less common, and is more difficult – not least in terms of finding appropriate language. Consequently, embodied fieldwork is actually rather under-developed. Visual culture continues to dominate, Paterson suggests. He echoes Crang (2003) who suggests that there is an absence of research undertaken on and with haptic pieces of knowledge. As Paterson makes clear, haptic knowing and the study of touch are necessarily embedded in complex orders of the senses and in sensory explorations (Stoller 1997). While touch has received some degree of attention in recent years (see Classen 2005), there remains a need and opportunity further to explore haptic aspects of embodied fieldwork in diverse settings. This needs always to be grounded in general ethnographic studies and not relegated to the margins as a subspecialty of sensory ethnography. Haptic knowledge – knowing through touch – introduces us to texture and weight; in the hand, we understand the heft of things and the manipulation of tools and equipment.

Many commentators have emphasised the extent to which the senses are intertwined in the formation of experience. Touch and feeling can be communicated visually, while vision, taste, smell and motion are all mutually implicated in everyday activities, such as walking (Taussig 1993; Pink, Hubbard, O'Neill and Radley 2010). The sensory experience of ordinary activities reflects their carnal, embodied character. That is most evident in a number of fields, such as the sociology of sport (Hockey 2006; Spinney 2006; Allen-Collinson and Hockey 2010). Dutkiewicz (2015) describes particularly clearly the embodied action of rock-climbing. This requires an engagement of the climber with the rock that is visual, kinaesthetic and haptic. The climber must grasp and cling to the rock as well as plotting a route. The climber does not merely touch the rock: he or she interacts physically with the rock and experiences it through the entire body. Haptic and, more generally, carnal ethnography is reflected in a number of monographs on embodied sport, such as Wacquant (2005) on boxing, which displays the fully embodied nature of *participant* observation. It is carnal ethnography in its most fully developed sense.

Embodiment in sport or dance can be expressive of more than just physical competence. Bailey (2013) conducted an embodied ethnography of ballroom dancing among LGBT Black Americans, focusing on one category – the 'butch queen'. For Bailey's hosts, ballroom dancing and participating in dance events is a medium for expressing particular forms of identity. It articulates what the members described in terms of 'realness' in an environment where they could enact their preferred identities in the community of dancers while demonstrating that they had what it takes to fit into the 'real world'. Likewise, Hancock (2013, 2018) drew on his own embodied participation in Lindy Hop dance in the United States – by becoming a learner – in drawing out an analysis of race:

> Only through an embodied ethnographic approach could I have come to understand the anxiety and tension that Lindy Hop dancers undertake consciously or unconsciously and the ways that race gets refracted through culture in learning how to dance. Focusing on the embodiment of dance allowed me to see the ways embodiment becomes a tool for interpreting and understanding the world.
>
> *(2018, p. 158)*

It is in this sense that 'feeling' has multiple valencies for ethnographic research. As we have seen, feeling for and feeling with one's fellow women and men is an unavoidable – indeed welcome – aspect of our ethnographic encounters. But feeling in a far more literal, concrete sense is also part of our experience in the field. When we have hands-on engagements with the material world around us, we use our embodied competence to comprehend textures, surfaces, softness or hardness, responsiveness and consistency. Learning to feel (in that latter constellation of meanings) is often a key part of occupational enculturation. The specialist learns to feel in specialised ways and to ascribe significance to what is felt. She or he also learns a vocabulary of terms to capture such haptic phenomena. The multiple valences of feeling are nicely captured by Underman (2020). She writes about the medical pelvic examination from a unique standpoint, as she works as a gynaecological teaching associate (GTA) in medical school, and undertook field research at three American medical schools. GTAs are well-trained expert female laypersons and instructors. Rather than learning and practising on hospital patients, or relying on simulations, medical students learn to examine the female pelvis with (rather than 'on') professional women. The GTAs not only make their body available for internal and external examination, but they can also guide the – often nervous and clumsy – student on the basis of what they themselves can feel and what they understand about their own anatomy. So GTAs' embodied expertise involves learning to sense their own organs, while the medical students also learn to feel those organs, often guided by the GTA. The double semiotic of feeling is clear enough: medical novices have to cope with their emotional responses to the pelvic examination, while simultaneously gaining the haptic knowledge of anatomy. Underman's is simultaneously the work of an insider-practitioner and an ethnographer, focusing on the phenomenology of 'feeling with' – which 'attends to the ways in which the physicians' and patients' bodies co-produce one another in the clinical encounter…' (p. 143). Equally, she suggests that: 'The expertise that physicians produce and the authority they deploy in the clinic are *fundamentally a part of* their own embodiment and the embodiment of their patients' (p. 165, emphasis in original). The work of the GTA thus involves what she feels, what the medical trainee can feel, and how the GTA herself can feel the student's exploratory feeling.

Engaging the senses

Embodiment addresses the use of the senses in ethnography. They are not perfectly synonymous. As Hancock (2018) succinctly puts it:

> Sensuous scholarship shares one of the aims of carnal sociology in that they both seek to move beyond treating the body as a text to be deciphered and instead incorporate the sensing body – the smells, tastes, textures, and sensations of the agent – into scholarly practices, representations, and description. However, sensuous scholarship remains an outsider perspective on the issue of embodiment.
>
> *(p. 157)*

Sensory ethnography has become a prominent and fashionable topic in contemporary discussions of ethnographic practice. In one way sensory ethnography is not new. In the field anthropologists and sociologists have always relied on their own senses to participate in and understand the life-world around them. Members of society do so all the time. Ethnographers use their senses in much the same way. While the language of observation can imply an emphasis on the scopic (the sense of vision), participation is impossible without the full use of one's sensory competence. The difference – insofar as there is any – lies in the prominence granted to sensory work and the intellectual effort to bring that to consciousness. What were once taken-for-granted resources are now more likely to be foregrounded, as researchers in the field become more analytically aware of the multiple channels of communication and interpretation. Consequently, a phenomenological attention to the phenomena in the field requires a thoroughly self-conscious use of a range of sensory resources. As Stoller (1997) puts it in linking bodies and sensations explicitly:

> The full presence of the ethnographer's body in the field also demands a fuller sensual awareness of the smells, taste, sounds and textures of life among the others.... For ethnographers embodiment is more than the realization that our bodily experience gives metaphorical meaning to our

> experience; it is rather the realization that … ethnographic things capture us through our bodies, that profound lessons are learned when sharp pains streak up our legs in the middle of the night.
>
> *(p. 23)*

Those sharp pains are associated with sorcery in this case, but there can be many sources of pain and discomfort, just as there can be sharp sensations of desire, pleasure and joy. Fieldworkers must have been aware of the smells of the field in many, if not all, contexts. Food and cooking, animal and human bodies, waste of all sorts, vegetation and flowers, industrial and artisan processes, perfumes – these all have their distinctive odours and must have impinged, in their context-specific ways, on generations of fieldworkers. That is to say nothing about the distinctive sounds and noises – and indeed silences – that help to define the practical and symbolic modalities of a given social environment. But such sensory modalities were not always attended to systematically and self-consciously. We should not, therefore, get too seduced by 'sensory ethnography' *per se*. A thorough grasp of our modalities of experience and the sensory bases of our interpretations should be incorporated into all and any fieldwork, as appropriate and relevant. Surrender and catch must imply a full awareness of the senses, of the impressions they form, of the actions they permit. The catch of analysis demands that we cultivate a self-conscious awareness of sensory phenomena. We must attend to the *analytic* implications of sensory awareness. Moreover, our ethnographic surrender enjoins an openness to the *sensual*. It is noticeable that standard texts on sensory ethnography can be drained of anything sensuous, let alone sensual, either in their subject-matter or their textual style.

Authors celebrated as pioneers of sensory ethnography can have their blind spots. Stoller's path-breaking book contains a specific episode that relates to perfume (Stoller 1989). He was instructed to bring perfume when visiting a female informant. He did so, having bought Bint al Hadash. Later that phial of perfume is discovered to have been dismissed and smashed. He should have bought Bint El Sudan, it transpires. But Stoller, for all his commitment to the senses, shows remarkably little interest in the perfumes themselves. What, for instance, was so special about Bint El Sudan? What was it? Where did it come from? In fact, minimal research would have shown that Bint al Sudan was manufactured in Kano, Northern Nigeria, by an English company for the African market. It thus inscribes a rich colonial as well as olfactory history. Why did it acquire such currency among African users? What indeed were its ingredients? What did it smell like? Stoller is silent on those matters. A simple sensory phenomenon (a perfume) could bring in its wake a variety of histories and narratives.

Even works committed to sensory ethnography can thus fall short of a thorough engagement with the world of the senses. Too often, the 'sensory' collapses back into an almost purely visual observation, whereas embodied, sensory fieldwork calls for actively engaged and trained sensibility. The inclusion of the senses is not a matter of passively absorbed 'sensations'. The senses – like observation –

demand active focus. Stoller's relative 'failure' we have just identified leads us to a complementary study of the olfactory sense. In the first place, we can find phenomena like smells to be among those barely attended to background features. It is all very well to point out that aromas can be evocative, conjuring up memories of persons and places, or even of specific occurrences. But sensory ethnography calls for thorough phenomenological attention to such phenomena. It is not enough merely to respond to aromas at a personal level, or to write evocatively about them. It calls for disciplined attention. If in the field we may surrender to the phenomena of the senses, then the catch calls for something more. This is intellectually and personally demanding, not least because: 'Aroma signs do not have the same logically semantic structure as linguistic signs because smells are traces that, unlike words, only partially detach themselves from the world of objects to which they refer' (Rasmussen 1999, p. 69). Consequently, as Moeran (2007) observes: '...smell itself can, like the Cheshire cat, fade away ...because we tend to talk around the subject, rather than tackle it head on' (p. 154). This in turn reflects the confusion of descriptive categories that actors use to characterise aromas. Moeran continues: 'I have heard *neroli* oil – which I personally regard as a rather soft and pleasant scent taken from orange flowers – likened to grapefruit, flower water, cologne, a not classy perfume, plain wood, parsley, *retsina*, nail varnish, toilet cleaner, Vicks vapour rub, creosote and (by a nine-year-old girl) frogs and bats' (p. 157).

There is no etic system for scent, but highly context-dependent, cultural categories for its classifications, connotations and descriptions. The 'nose' can be trained by parfumiers, and professionals have their own well-developed descriptive and craft practices that can be transmitted through formal training (cf. Muniesa and Trébuchet-Breitwiller 2010). Latour (2004) uses olfactory sense as an exemplar of a wider discussion of embodiment and his discussion is derived substantially from the ethnographic work of Teil (1998), who undertook a short course in olfaction (associated with food rather than perfumes). She describes a specific, highly structured, training programme that was aimed at the inculcation of a vocabulary of aromas: 'In order to represent the olfactory sensation, and also to communicate it, it is necessary to learn a language of description of the sensation' (p. 510). The point here is *not* that sensory ethnography depends on the acquisition of expertise in the description of scents. But it is the case that foregrounding sensory phenomena, as part of an incarnate ethnography, does call for a great deal more than the passive reception of impressions, or evocative writing about personal responses.

From this point of view, 'thick description' demands an adequate representation of sensory codes, conventions and actions. Without concrete, detailed description and analysis, the sensory remains unexamined background sensation – local colour at best. Embodied ethnography therefore does call for some degree of close attention to the means of observation and description. It is disciplined and analytic work. Ethnographic surrender does not mean abandoning the analytic in favour of the impressionistic, nor does it mean acting as a passive recipient of experiences and sensations. It means being open to phenomena in all their complexity and their potential significance. A phenomenological bracketing of sensations means enrolling the body of the ethnographer not just as an occasion for emotions and personal response, but as the site for sustained, attentive engagement.

Conclusion

We do not argue that every ethnographer can or should engage in fully embodied participation. Clearly, there are many settings where it would be impossible or inappropriate. It is not necessary for every period of participant observation to include practical, hands-on activities. We do, however, reiterate that thoroughly participant observation calls for an embodied phenomenology, through which the physical and sensory aspects of social action are grasped. And we do insist that talk alone – through conversations and interviews – is not in itself sufficient to do the job. Needless to say, talk is important. When we are attempting to make sense of any practical actions, then a commentary can help us to make sense of what is going on. When working with craft-artists, PA found their talk-in-activity (talking through what they were doing and how) and the conversation while they were making something far more revealing than any more contrived 'interview' could be. Talk is necessary in most circumstances, but it is certainly not always sufficient. It is, we emphasise, important to encompass more forms of activity, more modes of signification and more types of action. Speech is action and speech acts are important kinds of activity. But they are not the be-all and end-all of ethnographic fieldwork.

It is, we have stressed, important not to let 'sensory' ethnography to become almost synonymous with visual analysis. Moreover, it is equally important not to let embodied ethnography become equated simply with sensory work. As we have argued and illustrated, much field research depends on the ethnographer's embodied presence. The ethnographer is no mere 'observer', but it fully co-present with her or his hosts. Together they physically inhabit the same social spaces, and they participate in the same temporal flows and rhythms. They grow tired together. They can share the physical sensations of ecstasy, possession, dread and desire. The social worlds we investigate are not just 'meaningful' but also carnal.

If we return to the ideas of surrender-and-catch, then it is clear that surrender to the phenomena of social life must include surrender through the body and therefore through the senses. The nature of things and occasions is not captured through visual observation or listening alone. Participant observation certainly demands close watching and listening, but the world of sensations is much more densely layered than that. Our embodied competence is needed if we are to learn how to be in a given social world and how to conduct ourselves. We need to participate in the physical expressiveness of any given cultural field. When we listen, it is not just to what an informant is telling us, but to the world of sound that surrounds us and our fellow men and women. Understanding the soundscapes of music requires separate treatment (DeNora 2000) and is beyond the scope of this chapter, but there are many settings when the rhythms of everyday life include the rhythms and melodies of music-making and music-sharing. The catch of fieldwork therefore needs to encompass close attention to the full range of visual, auditory and haptic possibilities that are in turn dependent on carnal knowing.

6

FAILED MODERNISM?

WRITING AND THE GRAIN OF EVERYDAY LIFE

Against the grain

In this chapter, we reflect on some aspects of ethnographic writing. Our opening metaphor, recapitulating our thoughts on surrender and catch, concerns the grain of writing and the grain of social life. When we cut wood or butcher meat we can go with or against the grain. If we cut (or otherwise engage with it) *with* the grain, then we are working in the same direction as the material's natural texture and the fibrous products of its growth. Against or across the grain, clean cuts create the surfaces of joints and slices. Each direction, each cut gives us a different relationship to the material, each reveals a different composition and each enables a different orientation to the wood or to the flesh. Here, therefore, we reflect on the multiple grains of everyday life and, in particular, on the possibilities of ethnographic writing with and against the grain. When we work with the grain, we follow the temporal, narrative flow of events and actions. Against the grain, we interrupt and transgress that 'natural' flow. With and against, we surrender to the flows of everyday action, and we interrupt others and ourselves to trouble those flows and their narratives. Each cut reveals a distinctive grain, a different formation, a new orientation. Each calls for a distinctive discipline, a particular style. It is not the case that one way is easier than the other, or inherently more faithful to everyday life than the other. Each approach frames analytic possibilities and limitations. Like all such conventions, each genre of ethnographic writing is productive and imposes constraints: see, for instance, the essays edited by Archetti (1994).

There is no ethnography until it is written or shaped into some other kind of representation (film, photography or artwork). Here, we focus on written texts and their literary antecedents. We consider some of the ways in which ethnographic texts get done, and what their possibilities are. In particular, we reflect

DOI: 10.4324/9780429056802-6

on how ethnographic texts embody some of the issues we have already outlined. We examine what we identify as *textual surrender*, as the written counterpart to surrender to the phenomena. It is writing with the grain, while writing against the grain implies an attempt to de-familiarise the social world, by means of textual and rhetorical styles that interrupt the taken-for-granted and comfortable forms of narrative.

The ethnographic imagination implies a commitment to a textual form of life. Our existential and ethical commitments to a way of life as a way of research, in turn, lead us to a way of writing; or rather, to *ways* of writing, as there are of necessity multiple ways of reconstructing a form of life (our own and that of others). A comprehensive review is impossible, as the awareness of 'metaethnography' has grown and the mutual relations between ethnography and literature have become ever more overt (Anagnostou 2006). Indeed, we wish only to identify a number of themes that relate to recurrent concerns in this book.

Ethnographic aesthetics

There are multiple histories of ethnographic writing and aesthetic models and there are multiple paths through those histories. That multiplicity reflects differences in discipline (anthropology and sociology), in nationality (American versus Anglo-Saxon versus European traditions) and choices in periodisation. They also reflect different choices in the selection of literary and other aesthetic parallels. In a way that departs somewhat from earlier attempts (Atkinson 1990, 2020) we pick our own way through those many differences in order to construct our own version(s) of affinities and differences, fashions and amnesias, discoveries and rediscoveries. Throughout, we refer to styles of avant-garde writing and visual art, with a recurrent motif of Modernism. A brief comment on terminology is relevant here. By Modernism (capitalised) we refer to an – admittedly loosely defined – series of movements in literary and other arts, characteristic of the early decades of the twentieth century. When we refer to 'modern' anthropology or sociology, by contrast, we refer to work that is by no means Modernist, but characteristic of a period in both anthropology and sociology when taken-for-granted conventions of realism marked a certain maturity in ethnographic writing, that can be glossed as realist in style. Would that these things were all cut and dried, but they are not. Likewise, when we write of aesthetic and literary styles, artists or authors, and their relation to ethnography, we are not necessarily attributing direct influence in either direction. There are in some cases. But more generally we need to think in terms of affinities that reflect cultural currents, periods of experimentation, periods of professionalisation and so on. Elective affinities, as suggested by Goethe and Weber, are in many ways more potent, and certainly more suggestive, than direct influences between protagonists in different artistic and scientific fields.

Affinities between ethnography and literary Modernism have been explored by numerous commentators, each of whom identifies different varieties of ethnography and equally different literary sources. For instance, Heuston (2011) finds ethnographic influence and inspiration in four modern poets: Yeats, Frost, Warren and Heaney. Yeats, for instance, found nationalist authenticity in his explorations of Irish peasantry and folklore, effectively doing 'fieldwork' in the last two decades of the nineteenth century, while Frost identified himself with the 'native people' of New England: 'Frost...acts in his poems as both participant-observer and native informant, effectively feeding his own opinions and interpretations into the ongoing polyphonic discourse of the characters' (p. 57). More directly a number of authors have argued that Modernism inhabits the early days of anthropological ethnography. Edwin Ardener (1985), for instance, argues that the fieldwork monograph, as developed by Malinowski, was 'the form that Modernism took at its developmental stage in social anthropology' (p. 49) and he accompanies that with a throwaway comparison with James Joyce: *'Joyce's "Bloomsday" in 1904 is of the same substance, intellectually, as Malinowski's Trobriands'* (p. 57, italics in the original).

In a similar vein, Peppis (2014) places the emergence of the anthropological monograph within the broader cultural context of Modern disciplines, especially 'the newer, modernizing "human" sciences of ethnography, sexology, and psychology' (p. 4). Rather than Malinowski's *Argonauts of the Western Pacific* (1922) Peppis's anthropological point of departure is Haddon's *Head-Hunters: Black, White, and Brown* (1901): 'I read Haddon's text at the intersection of Victorian popular literature, modern anthropology, and literary modernism; it reveals in lively detail lively traffic between these competing discourses and disciplines at a formative moment for modernism in literature and anthropology' (p. 20). He also suggests that Haddon's characterisation of 'savagery' contrasted with modernity's contradictions, 'struck by the disorienting cohabitation in the presence of artefacts and activities both "modern" and "primitive", "civilised" and "savage", he confronts the radical implications of intersubjective time' (p. 27).

Literary Modernism embraced an 'ethnographic' sensibility (Manganaro 1990). Snyder (2008) observes that British authors – Conrad, Woolf, Lawrence, Forster – set some of their fiction in exotic elsewheres where characters encountered people from other cultures, and simultaneously reflected back on the oddities of British culture. Comparing Malinowski and Woolf: 'There is a surprising kinship ... between the persona of the modern ethnographer and the modern novelist, engaged in parallel "adventures" that entail imaginatively inhabiting foreign identities' (p. 19). Virginia Woolf's *The Voyage Out* is one of Snyder's key examples here. On their trip (by sea) to South America, British travellers reflect ironically on British culture, viewed from a distance. One character reflects that in London it would be the hour of a reception at Buckingham Palace and that the Mall would be busy with carriages, each of which would reflect with great precision the status of the occupants, including the permitted number of footmen. The exact calculus of rank and precedence seems startlingly absurd. In a parallel vein, Snyder identifies 'bewilderment' as a recurrent sensibility in the writings of Mary Kingsley, Joseph Conrad and H.G. Wells. For example, writing on Kingsley's travels in Africa, 'Kingsley's articulation of a flexible, chameleon model of ethnographic subjectivity is given … expression in [a] passage from *Travels*. Here, she describes the ethnographic collector's mind as a 'disorganized vessel, containing a conglomeration of discordant ideas, facts, and observations …' (p. 75). Nineteenth-century fiction displayed an 'autoethnographic' attempt to represent authors' home culture from a fresh perspective of estrangement (Buzard 2005).

Modernism and ethnography together created an awareness of cultural description and of the distance between home and elsewhere and reflected back on the home culture. The anthropology contained an elegiac element too. Haddon's was 'salvage' ethnography and the early modern monographs also conveyed a sense of pristine but waning cultures. It was one facet of anthropological ethnography that owed more to Romanticism than to Modernism. Romanticism and adventure writing – such as the African fiction of Haggard (*King Solomon's Mines*, or *She*) – combined in conveying a sense of strangeness, of adventure, of distance. Romantic imagery enhanced that sense of the lone venturing explorer, seeking out remoteness and strangeness, whether it be Maria Czaplicka (1914) making her way to Siberia to be with shamans, Katherine Routledge (1919) to Easter Island or, a little later, Reo Fortune to be with the *Sorcerers of Dobu* (1932), on yet another tiny, distant island. The thrill of adventure and discovery was strongly coloured by a sense of the extreme strangeness, even weirdness and of exotic cultures: magic, shamanism, witchcraft and sorcery.

Romanticism and Modernism converged in a heightened sense of myth and ritual. Eliot's Modernism included a strong sense of myth, as did Joyce's, most overtly in *Ulysses*. Ethnographic reports inspired people like the Cambridge Hellenists, of whom Jane Harrison was a most influential figure, writing about ritual and myth (Carpentier 1994; Beard 2000). From anthropological ethnography as well as from classical sources the Hellenists celebrated myth and ritual. Early anthropology and Nietzsche's work on Greek tragedy brought to the fore the significance of myth, magic and ritual. The orgiastic, ecstatic, or Dionysian elements of Greek celebration were retrieved from beyond the Olympian gods of classical literature. And beyond that, there was the Mother Goddess, a primal representation of the essential female, a chthonic force. She could be identified in the iconography of the pre-classical Mediterranean, such as the statuary of the Minoan and Cycladic cultures, that archaeology was uncovering. The influence of Minoan culture on modernist aesthetics is explored by Gere (2009).

We shall suggest that modern anthropological ethnography lost the Modernist and the Romantic spirit until recent decades when – under the rubric of postmodernism – some of that inspiration was reignited (though with very little acknowledgement of possible literary antecedents). After the flourishes of Modernist experimentation, that sense of ritual and magic became 'flattened' by repeated appeals to common rationality. Evans-Pritchard's treatment of Azande is a classic case in point. More generally, the promotion of universal rationality (if based on culturally different premises) and the social functions of ritual tended towards a demystification of the world, and a symbolic assimilation of 'other' cultures to a generalised human reason. An ethnography that remained faithful to the extraordinary, the supernatural and the weird could explore a 'magical' genre beyond the flat realism of classic modern ethnographic texts. We shall return to these topics later. For now, we return to the more general problems of representation and textual forms.

The textual basis of ethnographic observation

It is a fundamental tenet of ethnographic work that we should translate what we observe and participate in into texts: fieldnotes, that is. The fieldnote is the bedrock of traditional ethnography. We enjoin our students to note everything down and to do so as quickly after the event as possible, lest memories fade and details be lost. While it is obvious at one level, it needs repeating: fieldnotes are not unmediated representations. It is meaningless to say whether they are or are not 'data', as all data are mediated by the apparatus of measurement and recording. Any and every observation or measurement is mediated by the kind of instrumentation that is used to make that observation. That is true whether we are making a direct observation of a physical object or event, or whether we are using imaging devices such as CT scans or microscopes. Without some technology of observation and recording, there is no phenomenon. But one crucial difference is this: the ethnographer is much less naïve about the nature of recording than others might be. We know that in making written records of what we do, say, hear and observe we are engaged in the first of many processes of transmutation. We also know our fieldnotes for what they are – transitional texts. As Delamont (2018), amongst others, suggests, fieldnotes are liminal or boundary objects and are 'precarious' constructions, standing as they do between the field, the ethnographer and the written ethnography – that final text that is never truly finalised (Jackson 1990).

Textual self-awareness derives from a number of sources. Some can be traced to the styles of literary criticism characteristic of the second half of the twentieth century. Varieties of structuralism, with its roots firmly in French literary and cultural disciplines, directed attention to the formal properties of text, reviving interest in earlier semiotic and formalist modes of analysis. It emphasised the essentially conventional nature of the sign, a perspective that could be applied not only to the objects of semiotic study but also to higher and more complex textual forms, such as myths and literary texts. For the study of ethnographic writing, the legacy of semiotic analysis includes the point that there is no 'natural' mode of representation. What literary history recognises as Realism does share features with ordinary interaction and action. Its representation of dialogue has a family resemblance to everyday conversation, for instance, and descriptions of places and events correspond – to an extent – to ordinary modes of expression, But attention to semiotic codes and literary genres also affirms that such realism is itself dependent on writers' and readers' conventions. It is important to point out that to say they are conventional is not to imply that they are arbitrary in the everyday sense: they are not whimsically generated out of thin air, and they are not lacking in referential value. If anything, it is a recognition of how fruitful textual conventions are in constructing and reconstructing social worlds.

What we call Realism, of course, can take many forms. The realism of nineteenth-century European fiction is quite different from, say, that of mid-twentieth-century American fiction. Representations of social conditions and characterisation in, say, Dickens and Steinbeck, are quite different while being recognisably based on the realism of a sort. Equally, there are many kinds of reality that can be constructed on the basis of starkly different kinds of textual practice. One need only contrast representations of a love affair by Hemingway (*Across the River*) and by Proust (*The Prisoner*). Hemingway's spare, laconic prose is in stark contrast to the extended, introspective and neurasthenic narrative of Proust's first-person Marcel. Both texts create a plausibly realised version of reality, but their literary effects are produced from radically different standpoints.

The point of these observations is merely to remind us that there is never any single best or most natural style in which we can aspire to reconstruct social realities. We shall not intend this observation to grant us all licence to write whatever and however we want, irrespective of the evidence, without regard for what we have actually observed and participated in. Indeed, the translation of lived social life into some sort of text is fundamental to the ethnographic enterprise. In the first instance, therefore, we move from participant observation to fieldnotes. As Visweswaran (2015) suggests: 'Fieldnoting is the process through which the field itself – its scenes and analytics – is denoted or defined, tracked through a field of proliferating associations but also a network of blockages and apprehensions. Any field, and our perception of it, shifts over time. It is both structured by the processes of accretion, sifting and assemblage and attentive to those same processes' (p. 209). So, they are also provisional, tentative, and full of hesitations and incompletions.

Fieldnotes are selective. It is more or less impossible to observe and record everything, and indeed it is far from clear what 'everything' would possibly mean in any concrete situation. We like to encourage fieldnotes that are as thorough as possible and as concrete as possible, preserving a record of persons, events and actions. But we do not fool ourselves. We cannot consult them as definitive records of those happenings. Moreover, as all ethnographers are aware, we know more than we can read in so many words in the written notes: sometimes 'head notes' are invoked as supplements, although the term does not do justice to the complex memories, sensations and embodied experiences that contribute to the ethnographer's comprehension. So, although we all do so by way of shorthand, we really should not think of fieldnotes in terms of 'data', as if they were just like any other corpus of observations or measurements. Likewise, talk of analysing those 'data' can create quite the wrong impression, suggesting that the body of fieldnotes is an otherwise inert accumulation of measurements that can be aggregated, manipulated and sorted in ways analogous to the management of survey or laboratory data.

Fieldnotes are materials to think with. They are not pure fiction any more than they are pure fact. They are unavoidably shaped by the ethnographer's attention, in turn reflecting her or his interests, determined by powers of recall and of expression. By virtue of being ordinary-language texts, they are always subject to the possibilities and limitations of the ethnographer's linguistic and literary competence. In our recording of a social world, therefore, we are creating the equivalent of preliminary drafts for our textual reconstructions. They are always, in principle, provisional texts. What our notes can help us to do, both as we write and as we read them on subsequent occasions, is to bring (back) to consciousness the phenomena of our attention in the field. Making fieldnotes, therefore, is an important element in our essentially phenomenological work of observation. As we have made clear already, in the course of our fieldwork we interpolate ourselves into the flow of everyday events and activities. These are exercises in interruption. Our own lives are interrupted, as are the lives and doings of our research participants.

In the course of those repeated interruptions, we make selected phenomena visible or legible. We can thus transform them from events in a stream of events into phenomena that we can make the objects of reflection and scrutiny. If it is the case that there are no phenomena without an apparatus for their observation, then our fieldnotes are among the resources available to us to conjure up phenomena of the field. Of course, the fundamental apparatus is our own capacity to interact with others, to take the role of the other, and to observe and to reflect on ourselves and others – indeed, the whole range of socialised competences that interactionist sociologists have identified and celebrated. The act of writing helps us to undertake such work in an explicitly self-conscious manner. Hence everyday life is no longer experienced as an unbroken flow, but as a series of social phenomena. The acts of recording are unavoidably selective. But their value lies in that very selectivity. The fact that they are partial and episodic allows us to detach events and observations from the matrix of everyday life and having done so we can then treat them as objects of scrutiny.

The construction of fieldnotes, therefore, mediates between the stream of social events and the identification of sociological or anthropologically significant topics. They bridge from mundane and undifferentiated life to selective analytic perspectives. The raw fieldnotes follow the flow of life. To that extent, they are written *with* the grain. We cut against the grain when we mirror our interruptions by selecting episodes, cases and types, in order to shape our analytic work. The temporal flow of fieldwork and its fieldnote narratives corresponds to the *syntagmatic* axis of organisation. Events are linked by their sequencing, by the continuity of their personnel and by the passage of time. By contrast, the episodes we record and then select to reproduce correspond to the *paradigmatic* axis. Syntagmatic relations go with the grain, while the paradigmatic cuts across it. We deal, as ethnographic researchers and authors, simultaneously with those two dimensions. Narratives and analytic themes are, in practice, intertwined in our field data and in our analytic imaginations. But it is important to maintain a sense of how they intersect. There is a repeated dialectic between narrative flow and episodic or conceptual interruption.

Genres

We have already suggested that ethnographers may write with or against the grain of ordinary assumptions about texts and everyday life. Put simply, it depends on the extent to which ethnographers challenge ordinary attitudes through the textual forms they deploy. It rests on the realist literary conventions used to reconstruct social worlds or 'alternative' textual genres that overtly challenge taken-for-granted forms. For the purposes of our argument, we perhaps exaggerate that contrast, but it is one of the recurrent tensions and interruptions that we explore in the course of this entire book. Realist fiction has several characteristics that – on the whole – render it a problematic model for ethnographic writing. To begin with, let us consider two such aspects – narrative structure and characterisation. Realist fiction and its conventions can readily imply a sense of direction in its narrative and a sense of an ending, denouement or reconciliation. But everyday life is not like that, and the ethnographer is not likely to uncover such a direction. Rather than a teleological sense of narrative closure, the ethnography is more likely to revolve around repeated, cyclical patterns of routine activity. Indeed, one might suggest that the act of writing ethnography transmutes mundane everyday life into a quasi-mythical, idealised realm of cyclical returns.

Realist fiction characteristically achieves or even imposes a degree of coherence. Realist ethnography also constructs a coherence which, though by no means spurious, can certainly be exaggerated. By constructing our descriptions and narratives of social worlds and events we can convey a sense of order that exceeds the overall orderliness of observed everyday realities. If that sounds paradoxical, it is meant to be. After all, it is our sociological or anthropological task to demonstrate and to be faithful to social organisation and shared culture wherever it is to be found. And in accordance with both classical and modern theory, we are committed to the ubiquity of the moral and interactional order. Since the contributions of the interactionists, of Goffman and of the ethnomethodologists, we seek out the interaction order in all its densely patterned complexity. Our point here is not to deny the orderliness of conduct. But rather to place in brackets – to suspend belief in – an over-arching narrative or an orderliness that imposes itself as a fully coherent, functional framework both for our analysis and for everyday life itself. We must allow for the possibility of more fractured orders, of kaleidoscopic arrangements and of multiple realities in simultaneous existence (Clifford 1988).

In the same way, the realism of realist fiction can rest on a certain approach to 'character'. The classic realist text is grounded in a relatively stable portrayal of persons and of character. That is not to say that characters do not 'develop', but the classic *Bildungsroman* is predicated on the teleological development of the central character – a Studs Lonigan for instance. But such fictions operate towards the revelation of the person's 'true' character (for better or worse). A character can be deceptive or treacherous but retains an underlying moral self that can be displayed and revealed through his or her actions and relationships. The world of realist fiction is thus furnished with a strong sense of coherence, stability and order. Appearances are often deceptive, but behind or beyond appearance is a recognisably predictable world. In contrast, the interactionist, phenomenological or anthropological inspiration that informs the ethnographic enterprise calls into question such taken-for-granted certainties. An apparently stable reality and an equally stable self are the outcomes of sustained work by social actors, and of interpretations and fragile negotiations. It cannot be taken on trust by ethnographers or other analysts, and we should not therefore rely on unexamined, taken-for-granted modes of textual reconstruction. 'Alternative' means of expression and reconstruction, however, should not be deployed willy-nilly with no thought for their implications – their constraints as well as their possibilities. We need to guard against excessive experimentation without a clear analytic pay-off. George Marcus, himself a notable contributor to debates on anthropology's textual practices, has observed an 'involution' of writing styles that can be coloured by 'a mannerist or even a baroque form' and 'a desire to surprise by tropes of unusual juxtaposition' (Marcus 2015, p. 36).

Nonetheless, we might write against the grain of realist narrative and its apparent order. If we challenge the appearances of over-simplified realist texts, then we also challenge the surfaces of our representations. We can free ourselves to explore contradictions, fissures, irrationalities. In practice that can mean several things. In contrast to the surface appearances of order, reason and predictable selves, anthropologists and sociologists have explored the implications of surrealism. A surrealist sensibility is not 'the answer' – there is no answer – but it can help to free up our imagination, allowing us as ethnographers to capture some of the ambiguities and irrationalities of everyday life.

Another way of thinking about this: Surrender in the field is never total. There is, or should be, resistance as well. Without some degree of reserve, some critical self-consciousness and a sense of phenomenological *epoché*, the catch is jejune. Consequently, our textual adventures can hold up phenomena for scrutiny rather than endorsing a common-sense perspective. In doing so we need – provisionally – to empty the social world of 'meaning'. We need, therefore, to allow for an Absurd view of the social world, a world where the texts of Samuel Beckett are as relevant as any more conventionally realist textual forms. A great deal of everyday conduct has the inconsequential character of a Theatre of the Absurd. Observation of everyday talk in workplaces or in families suggests that actors can fill stretches of interaction 'discussing' things with seemingly little purpose. If we are committed to constructing orderliness and meaning, then we can far too freely discard the inconsequential by simply omitting it from our accounts or impose a spurious degree of rationality and purpose. Rather than suppressing the absurdity of everyday life, perhaps we should allow some texts to be more faithful to those phenomena. In other words, we recommend two things. First, in conducting and thinking about our fieldwork, we need to work with the grain of everyday life. But sometimes we need to write against the grain. Just as our fieldwork can be thought of as a series of interruptions, so we might think of our writing as a disruptive incursion into everyday common sense. In recognising opportunities such as the Absurd, we can find ways of suspending assumptions about the nature(s) of social reality.

Closely akin to some version of Absurdism is the hyper-reality of concrete descriptions of persons, places and events. The seemingly endless proliferation of concrete details – in the manner, say, of Alain Robbe-Grillet – can have a thoroughly alienating effect (in the Brechtian sense). It recalls the seemingly endless long shots in some of the films of Andy Warhol, who was also adept at turning the mundane into the elemental. There is an intriguing relationship between narration and the *durée* of events. A great many realist descriptions last a lot less than those events actually take in real time when written, although we conventionally regard them as realistic in themselves. An evening in, say *The Great Gatsby* takes far less to time to read than the original evening would. In contrast, Proust's description of a musical evening at the Verdurins in *The Prisoner* from *A la recherche du temps perdu* takes far longer to read (by normal standards) than an evening of a few hours. Consequently, there are some intriguing issues of scale in the writing of ethnographic accounts. The more detailed the description the less realistic it can seem. Proust, to continue with the allusion, seems so very detailed as to be *un*realistic. *Ulysses*, in its monumentally epic style, covers twenty-four hours.

Scale and *durée* remind us that, as we suggested in Chapter 4, much of our ethnographic work – like realist fiction – actually consists of 'moments' or 'episodes'. Precisely because we cannot reconstruct and recapitulate all that happens chronologically, we must report it through incomplete concrete detail. Consequently, our insights and our writing tend to be couched in terms of specific events, such as encounters, that our acts of writing endow with particular significance. In practice, this corresponds to some key methodological commitments, at least on the part of some sociologists and others: that the fundamental units of analysis are situations, relationships, or networks. They are quintessentially revealed through concrete episodes (just as Proust's vast novel is composed of a surprisingly small number of very extended episodes). In English-language fiction, a multi-volume work like Powell's *A Dance to the Music of Time*, which spans seven decades of the twentieth century, is artfully contrived through a series of episodes, often social gatherings, that bring together recurrent characters. The flow of time and narrative direction are implied through a string of incursions or interruptions.

Textually speaking, therefore, we need to think about what moments might mean. To begin with they imply a very close reading that results in *close writing*. Together they are reminiscent of Gilbert White's *Natural History of Selbourne*

(1789/1977): the eighteenth-century vicar and naturalist advocated and practised paying very close attention to, and giving very detailed descriptions of, natural phenomena. In doing so, he was able to recreate a world of natural species from his own garden. For readers then and since (the book has been in print continuously) it is a gem of observational writing, that still captures our intellect whether or not we have any interest in birds, earthworms or bats. White *makes* them all interesting precisely by virtue of the concentrated power of his observation and equally precise writing. Our moments, the glimpses that they offer, gain significance – like White's natural-history observations – through the quality and detail of the original observations and precision of the writing. Things and circumstances gain significance partly through the simple fact of being visible and susceptible to description. The very earliest years of cinema demonstrated that fact. The Lumière brothers, for instance, in the 1890s trained their cameras on such mundane events as workers leaving the factory gates, or workmen demolishing a wall. Nothing 'happens' in such brief sequences, except the event in itself, made noteworthy by the observability of bodies in purposeful, sequential action.

This close observation, born of surrender and fidelity to the phenomenon can even lead to what Rutherford (2015) refers to as a reclaimed commitment to the empirical.: 'An empiricism that admits that one never gets to the bottom of things yet also accepts and even celebrates the disavowals required of us given a world that forces us to act' (p. 105). Perhaps one should modify the first part of that statement to read: 'An empiricism that accepts that there is no "bottom" of things to be reached…'. According to Rutherford, however, this is *not* an empiricism of the traditional flavour: it is 'kinky like a slinky, twisting back on itself but also kinky like S and M and other queer elaborations of established scenarios, relationships, and things' (p. 105). Perhaps one might add that, like S and M, fetishistic desire and gratification are grounded in an intensely concrete aesthetic, obsessively and intensely focused on surfaces and textures, visual imagery, clothing, scents and touch. In its own ways, the ethnographic gaze mirrors the fetishistic gaze, revelling in the pleasures and pains of the concrete. We can also relate our emphasis on episodes and moments to what Rutherford invokes in terms of 'circumstance':

> Circumstances consist of the patterned distribution of happenings that makes it more or less probable that a certain person will have certain experiences. Circumstances shape the expectations that lead particular people to read a particular cause or effect of a particular event.
>
> *(Rutherford 2015, p. 110)*

Moments, episodes and circumstances capture aspects of social organisation and social action that transcend their local specificities.

Examples from anthropological and sociological texts are numerous and are among the most memorable, most cited examples from the literature. Among the almost cliché examples is Geertz's classic account of the Balinese cock-fight. It is worth remembering something of its rhetorical force and function. Cock-fighting is not memorable for us because it occupies a prominent part of everyday life and excitement for Balinese social actors. Rather, it acquires its significance precisely because Geertz writes it and describes it in a particular way. First, he offers a vivid, graphic eyewitness account that includes himself as both the observer and the participant. Secondly, he uses it to demonstrate 'bigger' aspects of culture. Thirdly, he uses it to demonstrate the principles of interpretivist anthropology. He not only presents the textual episode itself but also establishes through his own hermeneutic exercise its methodological significance as a microcosm. Among the sociological classics, Whyte's *Street Corner Society* (1943), set in Boston's North End, includes a description of bowling among the Italian-American male friendship group. Again, the author, in providing a concrete description of the episode, uses it as a microcosmic 'moment' that is laden with significance for an understanding of social relations, status and masculinity. The episode is *made* to tell readers about key aspects of local culture and social organisation. [Bowling is, of course, itself an icon of American sociality – witness the symbolic significance of Putnam's *Bowling Alone* (2000)]. Such moments can become iconic, standing for an entire ethnography, or indeed an entire culture.

The close, descriptive observation of moments and situations is mirrored in textual realisations of *place*. While places and spaces have become significant topics of ethnographic and similar research in recent years, the strong sense of locality has been a major feature of ethnographic writing from much earlier. Recent and contemporary sociological writing on place parallels other genres, such as autofiction, memoir or psychogeography. Here, by way of examples, are comparable extracts from two authors, one of whom is a social scientist and the other a poet:

> On the morning of the floods many people in Hebden Bridge went down to the edge of the waters and stood in shocked silence, bearing witness in a kind of collective agitation on this Boxing Day holiday morning. Water that should have been two or three metres below bridges was crashing over the tops of them, and car and building alarms were sounding in a mad frenzy as the town's electrics became submerged beneath them. The town centre was a series of deep lakes, creating wide expanses that were impassable and looked so much wider than the familiar network of criss-crossing streets and pavements that were submerged beneath them.
>
> *(Mason 2018, p. 155)*

> We can't see the fjord walls, only cloud. Very soon, the ship's decks and rails and superstructure are under snow, the vessel becomes a frail, white-rigged thing, despite its metal and modernity and ice-strengthened hull.... When the snow lands on the water, it doesn't melt away. Instead it coheres

into soft patches, little discrete clumps, until the water all around looks like an animal's pelt, lifting in the swell, breathing.

(Jamie 2012, p. 18)

Apart from their watery subject matter, the two passages differ, of course. But they also share some features. There is in both an emphasis on graphic, concrete detail, even to the point of being gratuitous. The specificity of place and the topographical descriptions contribute to the immediacy of the moment as well as its transcendent significance.

Alternations and mutual interruptions of the here-and-now and the generic, of the concrete and the abstract, are characteristic of virtually all current and recent ethnographic writing. Often they alternate graphically on the page. As Edmondson (1984) and Atkinson (1990) have suggested, the empirical exemplars, the extracts and the glimpses of everyday life are not just 'illustrations', nor does the common designation of vignettes quite capture their significance. They are described as actual types, by analogy with and contrast with Weberian ideal types. They inscribe key features of the generic phenomenon under discussion. They are anchors to the wider discourse, trig points in the topography of ethnographic gazing. The voice of fieldwork and the authority of experience alternates with the voice of disciplinary learning. Each without the other is jejune. Together they form the basis of an antiphonal whole.

Fictions and the grain of ethnographic writing

There is another sense in which we can explore writing with or against the grain. That is, the creation of texts that reflect or transgress the main conventions of academic writing itself, through the creation of ethnographic fiction(s). There is a long tradition of ethnographic fiction but it is not a single genre. Much of it is couched in terms of 'realist' novels or short stories, while some others explore different kinds of writing in order to explore and reconstruct social realities. Again, these are not hard-and-fast contrasts, but they do capture – in an ideal-typical way – further tensions within the field of ethnographic representation. We are not arguing for or against any particular textual practices, although we shall suggest that realist ethnographic fictions can miss significant opportunities for textual complexity. Without trying to transform the discipline into a branch of applied literary criticism, we shall suggest that realist fictions can be unduly neglectful of the reflexive construction of cultural and social phenomena, and equally neglectful of the sheer diversity of fictional precedents.

It might be thought that ethnographic fiction is a recent phenomenon, given the contemporary emphasis on arts-based research and alternative forms of writing for qualitative research. But ethnographic fiction has a history virtually as long as the conduct of sustained ethnographic research itself. We have made reference to the work of Balandier elsewhere (Atkinson 2020) and will not recapitulate it here, other than to point out that Balandier's novel *The Delight Makers* was published in 1890 (see Babcock 1982). It derived from Balandier's anthropological fieldwork at the Tehua pueblo of San Juan and the Queres pueblo of Cochití in the Southwest of the United States. Balandier made clear that his fiction incorporated his firsthand ethnographic knowledge. The anthropology of Native Americans was also the basis of other works of fiction. Among early examples is *Waterlily*, by Ella Cara Deloria (1988). Deloria (1889–1971) was a pioneering figure in several ways. She was an early example of Indigenous Research, being a Dakota Sioux and a member of one the best-known Indigenous intellectual families. Without formal qualifications in anthropology, she was mentored by Boas and Benedict, who found her an ideal insider/outsider field researcher. Her work was neglected in her lifetime, and her major work on the Dakota remained largely unpublished. *Waterlily* itself was only published after her death, some forty years after its composition (1990). Deloria included a great deal of ethnological insight in the narrative, mostly based on accounts garnered from older women, describing everyday life among earlier generations. *Waterlily* itself can be accused of being too sentimental, too sweet, but the literary quality is not its most important aspect. The narrative is doubly significant. The Sioux way of life is marginalised from hegemonic American culture and the perspective is that of women. In its double dislocation, it is a subaltern account (Spivak 1988) constructed before that was a fashionable term, exploring the lives of a muted group, before that too became current in anthropology (E. Ardener 1972; S. Ardener 1975). The reader is introduced to and guided through aspects of Sioux culture through the instruction received by Blue Bird, an outsider taken into a Lakota camp circle, together with her grandmother. Deloria's book parallels the much better-known stories of Zora Neale Hurston, who based her fiction – such as *Their Eyes Were Watching God* (Hurston 1937) – on her fieldwork among Black Americans in the South.

There have now been many works of fiction by anthropologists based on their ethnographic knowledge. The novel allows the ethnographer to create a particular kind of narrative format that shapes the ethnography in ways less demanding than the conventional monograph. The genre allows the ethnographer to create characters and dramatic episodes that encapsulate key features of the relevant social setting. In some ways, it runs against the grain of academic writing. On the other hand, the narrative style of realist fiction – which is the style of ethnographic fiction – does little or nothing to disrupt the surfaces of taken-for-granted assumptions. Much ethnographic fiction, together with a great deal of autoethnographic writing, displays *expressive realism* (Belsey 2002). Of the latter, Belsey writes that it is a style of fiction that purports to reflect the reality of the experience of characters and to express that reality in a way that others can interpret as real or true. It is, therefore, literature that inscribes stable characters who inhabit an equally stable social world. It is the style of a great deal of recent and contemporary fiction: so much so that we might readily take it for granted as the obvious mode of expression. Virtually the same could be said about the great majority of 'alternative' ethnographic texts. Atkinson (2012) describes a great deal of contemporary ethnographic fiction and autoethnography in terms of *sentimental realism*, also intended to capture an emphasis on feelings and emotions, treated within a framework of realist literary conventions.

In some keyways, therefore, much ethnographic fiction is paradoxical. It breaks with the conventions of academic reportage. The novel can be based on fieldwork knowledge, but it can dispense with the apparatus of the anthropological monograph. It can give voice to actors – often composites of real social actors – and endow them with feelings and emotions that are not directly apparent to the dispassionate observer. To that extent, such fictional writing can run counter to the academic canon. On the other hand, it displays what Atkinson (2012) calls a 'failure of nerve', remaining as it does within the conventions of realism. When Josipovici (2010) asked rhetorically 'Whatever happened to modernism?' he addressed contemporary realist fiction, expressive realism in Belsey's terms. He draws attention to the alternative history, an imagined history that reflects the genre(s) of Modernism from the early twentieth century. Modernism is disruptive. It interrupts the even flow of narrative time. It explores the use of language that is not semiotically transparent. Characters can be unstable, situations fluid, ambiguous or just uninterpretable. Modernism can revel in the flow of language for its own sake and can recognise that language – written and spoken – is itself a 'thick' medium: it can conceal as much as reveal, and it can construct a world of riddles and puzzles. We therefore turn to consider the possibilities that a Modernist turn might have taken in the past and its continuing relevance today.

Between modernism and romanticism?

The intersections of ethnography, aesthetics and literature are multiple. The notion of so-called 'blurred genres' is, in terms of the history of the human disciplines, relatively recent. But mutual influences across and between genres are not a recent, postmodern phenomenon. The period of high modernism, in the early decades of the twentieth century, was marked by experimentation and cross-genre engagements. Late romanticism also contributed to the heady mix of ethnography and literature. By the turn of the century, 'professional' ethnography in anthropology or sociology was barely nascent. There was little difference, textually speaking, between academic, amateur and literary 'ethnography'. Cross-cultural encounters informed literary developments, while anthropological ethnography was among the emergent disciplines of modernity, together with psychoanalysis (with which it also had affinities in the early years).

The realist novel – ethnographic or otherwise – stands in complete contrast to the almost submerged strands of Modernism in the history of anthropological fieldwork. From its earliest years, ethnographic fieldwork held the possibility of a modernist intellectual undertaking. The radical break with 'armchair theorising' and the development of firsthand ethnographic exploration could have signalled a rupture in style and substance: a break with the genre of reportage redolent of travel and biographical writing. The dispassionate observer could well have been replaced by an engaged author. The authorial hand might well have been more self-consciously evident. Writing against the grain of narrative realism would have or could have given greater impetus to an anthropology that reflected the fragmentary surfaces of everyday life, which rendered the temporal flow more problematic and created more problematic characters. Such a Modernist undertaking would not have voiced the self-assured author such as, say Edward Evans-Pritchard and might have followed the more fragmented text of the monograph *Naven* (Bateson 1936).

Naven is, admittedly, a classic case. When anthropologists or writers about anthropology cite monographs that depart from the normal conventions, *Naven* is likely to be mentioned. There is a good reason for that, as it stands in contrast to so many monographs of its period. It is not marked by their authorial certainty and self-assurance but has a more open, even tentative, spirit. The topic of *Naven* is a ceremonial observance by the Iatmul of New Guinea. Bateson quite deliberately develops multiple perspectives in ordering his text. He is torn between an impressionistic interpretation of Iatmul cultural values – what he calls their *ethos* – in his reading of specific ritual aspects, and the dry empiricism of his descriptions of Iatmul social and cultural organisation. Bateson explicitly acknowledges his own hesitancy, in a reflective Epilogue to the 1936 edition that discusses his own intellectual and authorial dilemmas. His honesty is refreshing and stands in contrast with the standard texts of the time:

> My fieldwork was scrappy and disconnected – perhaps more so than that of other anthropologists. After all, we set out to do the impossible, to collect an exceedingly complex and entirely foreign culture in a few months, and every sincere anthropologist when he comes back to England [sic] discovers shocking gaps in his [sic] fieldwork. But my case was somewhat worse. The average anthropologist has some definite interest in some one aspect of the culture he is studying, whether it be in historical reconstruction, in material culture, in economics, or in functional analysis, and he will at least collect an adequate supply of material for a book permeated by his particular point of view.
>
> *(p. 257, page no's second edition, 1958).*

Confronted by his own lack of conceptual certainty or empirical focus, Bateson cuts into his field materials, including his photographs, to focus on the *naven* ceremony. As Marcus (1985) summarises it:

> … to understand *Naven* as a text we must understand that it originates in a self-conscious predicament of arbitrary choice of beginning. Bateson cut into his material by what grabbed his attention, and this turned out to be the ornately exotic behavior of mother's brother-sister's son relationships, particularly as they are exhibited in the celebratory ritual naven in which the maternal uncle congratulates the nephew for committing some notable

> deed like homicide. The transvestism, the exaggerated agonistic displays, odd utterances, the rubbing of buttocks on shins all become the details Bateson seeks to explain by systematically contextualizing them in the descriptions of broader features of Iatmul culture.
>
> *(p. 69)*

In doing so, Bateson shifts perspective, quite explicitly, through the text. Like many ethnographic accounts, it shifts from generalities about local social organisation and culture and the graphic detail of ceremonies themselves. In effect, his monograph inscribes the completeness of his understanding and of his fieldwork, and displays how he cut against the grain by composing a multi-perspective text, while also writing episodically and against the grain of mundane, everyday life.

We should not celebrate *Naven* beyond reason. It is too easy to see it as a pioneering 'messy text' long before its time. It is, however, salutary to remind oneself that analytic self-consciousness and textual variation were possible even in the 1930s. It is therefore tempting to locate *Naven* within a different genealogy – not as a precursor to postmodern texts, but as an example of the modernism that ethnography could have embraced. Anthropological fieldwork and urban ethnography share their birth in the years of the late nineteenth and early twentieth centuries, and with modernism in art and literature. It was also a time of rapid changes in technology and saw the birth of distinctively modern disciplines. Modernism cuts against the grain of mundane narrative, fragmenting temporal flow so that time can be compressed, extended or reversed, shifting place and point of view. It thus contains within it modes of phenomenological or anthropological estrangement.

The birth of ethnography also shares time with the earliest years of film, and they have commonalities in what was possible and what was lost in the rise of realism and documentaries. A visual digression is thus in order before we return to textual forms. Grimshaw (2001) uses the work of W.H.R. Rivers to suggest a short-lived parallelism between Modernist ways of seeing and anthropological vision. Rivers was a significant figure in two ways. First, he was a member of the pioneering Torres Straits expedition, and later he was centrally involved in the treatment of WWI veterans at Craiglockhart Hospital, made famous by Pat Barker's trilogy of novels that begins with *Regeneration* (1991). Rivers's anthropological imagination stressed networks or structures of relations (realised through the kinship diagram) and Grimshaw finds an affinity with the structural vision of Cubism. Early and avant-garde cinema also suggests a number of exemplars: the restless camera of D.W. Griffiths (e.g. *Intolerance*), or the experimental films of Vertov (e.g. *Man with a Movie Camera*). Grimshaw writes:

> I like to imagine *A Man With A Movie Camera* as the cinematic expression of Rivers' project. It embraces the movement and complexity of modern society, offering no single, privileged vantage point upon fluid contemporary realities, only a series of overlapping perspectives, shifting view-points

> in which seeing involves a discovery of the self as inseparable from the discovery of the world. The camera eye searches, questions, and interrogates. It is both human and mechanical, at once an observer and a participant. Vertov's vision is profoundly subversive of the conventional ways of seeing and knowing the world.
>
> *(pp. 42–43)*

Avant-garde cinema used a number of techniques to disrupt the viewer's 'seeing as usual'. They included the techniques of super-impression and rapid montage. In his major silent works such as *Napoléon* or *La roue* (The Wheel), Abel Gance deployed such techniques on an epic scale. His cinematic method did not supplant narrative but enhanced narrative through heightened visual effects (King 1984, p. 180). Some sequences in *Napoléon* are constructed through rapidly shifting montage. King describes one such scene, the snowball fight that the young Bonaparte takes part in, a prescient glimpse of his military prowess:

> … as the snowball fight intensifies the narrative look becomes increasingly inadequate as the action escapes a narrative control. Hand-held cameras may for a moment create an impression of involvement in the action, but the overall effect is that of a camera so close to the action that it is unable to make sense of what is going on. Excitement is again constructed at the surface of the image, and intensified by rapid montage: the climax accelerates rhythmically from shots of twenty-two frames of the main action intercut with inserts of the young Napoleon of half that length down, in stages, to single frames.
>
> *(p. 206)*

The Modernist cinema could have furnished inspiration for anthropological texts. Early cinema was, after all, by no means realist in its visual styles: Modernist, Expressionist and Symbolist aesthetics were all important. But as Grimshaw points out, a brief period in which that was possible was quickly superseded by the Romanticism and literary style of Malinowski and in turn by the yet more impersonally scientific style of Radcliffe-Brown and his followers. Our interest here is not primarily in photography, film and visual ethnography *per se*, but rather in the latent possibilities of filmic effects, such as montage, for ethnographic representation more widely (cf. Marcus 1990; MacDougall 2019).

Modernism therefore offered new topics for inquiry and novel ways of exploring them. Malinowski's ethnography was not exactly a contribution to Modernism, although the subject matter of his *Sexual Life of Savages* was congruent with the sexology that Peppis identifies as one of the sciences of modernism, represented by the figure of Havelock Ellis. Malinowski also engaged with the new discipline of psychoanalysis, using his knowledge of non-Western kinship to challenge the universality of the Oedipus complex. Among the Trobriand Islanders and other matrilineal cultures, the line of authority, and hence of potential fracture is between a son and his mother's brother. (This was also the line of cleavage expressed in the *naven* ceremony, as discussed by Bateson.) Such cultural reversals could challenge taken-for-granted European categories and assumptions while engaging directly with some of the sciences of modernity.

Women were among the pioneering spirits of Modernism and of anthropological fieldwork. Their contributions have been overlooked in many cases and have only recently been restored to the canon. The lesbian protagonists of Modernist literature Djuna Barnes and Gertrude Stein are among the 'remembered' (e.g. Field 1985; Souhami 2021). First published in 1936, Djuna Barnes's *Nightwood* is a text that defies reading-as-usual, sometimes leaving the reader disoriented (Barnes 2007). At its heart is a monologue in the mouth of a character, Dr Matthew O'Connor, of which Jeanette Winterson writes in a preface to *Nightwood*:

> The doctor is wearing full make-up, a nightgown and a woman's wig – he had been expecting someone else, but he begins his speech, as good as Molly Bloom's soliloquy in *Ulysses*, and this episode is a linguistic, artistic and emotional triumph. It matters that it is emotional. *Nightwood* is not afraid of feeling. It is not a glittering high-wire act; its pearls are deep-dived, and then dissolved into the language.
>
> *(Winterson 2007, p. xiii)*

It is not easy to excavate all of the possible intersections between pioneering women ethnographers and women modernists in fiction and verse, not least because they have been neglected and only brought to collective awareness in relatively recent times. For early anthropological ethnographers, see Larson (2021) on Katherine Routledge, Barbara Freire-Marreco, Maria Czaplicka and Winfred Blackman, or Mann (2012) on four American modernists: Lola Ridge, Evelyn Scott, Charlotte Wilder and Kay Boyle.

Nobody is suggesting that ethnographies in the early decades of the last century should have been couched in the language of Modernist fiction. But the spirit of Modernism, in addition to disrupting and fracturing temporal and narrative structure, treated language as a 'thick' medium. Realism in fiction and in factual reportage implies that language is transparent in representing persons and circumstances. Modernism confronts the reader with language that is dense and problematic, with a life of its own. Allusions can abound. The overall effect can be a vertiginous tumble of virtuoso composition. Here, is a brief flavour of Dr O'Connor's soliloquy on the topic of Night:

> To think of the acorn it is necessary to become the tree. And the tree of night is the hardest tree to mount, the dourest tree to scale, the most

> difficult to branch, the most febrile to the touch, and sweats a resin and drips a pitch against the palm that computation has not gambled. Gurus, who, I trust you know are Indian teachers, expect you to contemplate the acorn ten years at a stretch, and if, in that time, you're no wiser about the nut, you are not very bright, and that may be the only certainty with which you will come away, which is a post-graduate melancholy – for no man can find a greater truth than his kidney will allow. Do I, doctor Matthew Mighty O'Connor, ask you to think of the night the day long, and of the day the night through, or at some reprieve of the brain it will come upon you heavily – an engine stalling itself upon your chest, halting its wheels against your heart; unless you have made a roadway for it.
>
> *(p. 75)*

Clashing imagery and densely allusive language characteristically create an opaque, if glittering, surface. Such written style stands diametrically opposed to Belsey's 'expressive realism', or Atkinson's 'sentimental realism'. Action, identities, time and place are all destabilised. At the very least Modernism challenges the reader's practices of reading and comprehension. It challenges conventional readings through processes of estrangement. Ethnography could also challenge cherished but taken-for-granted cultural assumptions, confronting educated Western readers with strangely exotic practices that were then rendered comprehensible through the attribution of function and rationality. To that extent, therefore, we are not convinced by appeals to postmodernism or other 'posts' in the context of textual variation and experimentation. As we have suggested, *Modernism* in its literary and artistic inspirations, already suggested challenging and disorienting styles of representation.

In the course of its development in anthropology and sociology, ethnographic writing lost its Modernist flavour. Anthropologists like Radcliffe-Brown or Evans-Pritchard established canonical work that was inscribed in monographs that did not disrupt the author's relative certainty, nor did they challenge the taken-for-granted styles of reportage (though the cross-cultural content could certainly challenge readers' cherished ideas). Hence the professionalisation of the social sciences in the academy was accompanied by a loss of Modernist sensibilities. Recent innovations have not necessarily re-traced those modernist contours, as contemporary authors have embraced versions of sentimental realism and the autobiographical essay. But there are other perceptible possibilities and submerged currents. When we surrender to phenomena and when we observe the minutiae of everyday life, then we may find ourselves in the realm of the *nouveau roman*. The painstaking, sometimes almost painful, observation of detailed activity, emptied of extraneous interpretation or imposed 'meaning' is in some ways a perfect model for the close description of everyday life, however inconsequential. Indeed, it finds the fleeting and the ordinary pregnant with possibility, however understated. Consider one of the early classics of the genre, Sarraute's tiny but highly important *Tropismes* (Sarraute 2015, orig. 1957). It consists of a series of brief episodes, not self-evidently linked, with no characters, only the cool observation of actions and events. The text succeeds, however, in evoking the human comedy that might be found in more overtly Realist works of fiction, or in more elaborately developed ethnographic texts. Sarraute does so through minimalist means, a series of momentary glimpses, often ironically observed, such as:

> They could be seen walking in front of the shop windows, the upper part of their bodies very erect, slightly thrust forward, their stiff legs a bit apart, and their small feet, arched above their very high heels, knocking hard against the pavement.
>
> With their handbags under their arms, their gauntlet gloves, their little regulation "bibis" at just the right angle on their heads, their long stiff lashes set in bulging lids, their hard eyes, they trotted along in front of the shop windows, stopped all of a sudden, ferreted about with an avid, knowing look.
>
> *(p. 29)*

Such lapidary writing makes the detail of everyday comportment legible and simultaneously mysterious, and it does so in such a way that would escape purely mechanical recording, which would in turn need to be translated into textual forms of representation. We do not need to emulate such a style in its entirety to learn from it. It is one of the limiting cases of literary precedent.

In a similar, more overtly 'ethnographic' vein is Perec's exercise in observation (Perec 2010, orig. 1975). In one of his 'attempts' (one meaning of 'essay' of course) Perec located himself in cafés on the Place Saint-Sulpice and over a three-day period in 1974 he wrote down what he observed in the square. He notices what he calls the *infraordinary*. He notices the signs and symbols, the lettering, the numbers and destination of buses, as well as the comings and goings of people. Through the dry inscriptions of what he sees, Perec manages to convey a slightly eery sense of an Absurdist parade. The sparse descriptions of such mundane scenes, elevate the mundane to a surrealist artefact. The exercise is, as Sheringham (2006) makes clear, one episode not just in Perec's work, but in a wider strand of French writing, in which the literary and the ethnographic converge. In collective attention to the everyday (*quotidien*) authors such as Queneau, de Certeau, Barthes and Lefebvre turn their attention on the otherwise unremarked aspects of modern life, and in so doing elevate them to the remarkable.

The genre of Magical Realism might complement such a sensibility. A great deal of everyday life, in all documented cultures, is – in the broadest sense – magical. The ethnographic search for the order can readily lead to an over-emphasis on rational action. Anthropologically and sociologically, there is a long tendency – often epistemologically and analytically correct –

to treat rationality in a relative way. Hence, anthropologists traditionally analysed what appeared to be irrational beliefs – such as witchcraft beliefs – in such a way as to render them reasonable. The differences between Western and non-Western systems of thought rested on different premises and different chains of explanation, rather than primitive mentality. The classic, now clichéd, case was Evans-Pritchard's exploration of witchcraft, oracles and magic among the Azande of the Sudan (Evans-Pritchard 1937). He demonstrated that witchcraft interpolated a human agency in an otherwise unremarkable causal chain, in such a way as to explain the particularities of a given misfortune. The appeal to witchcraft answered the implicit questions: Why me? Why now? The logic of the explanation as well as the logic of Azande's belief is impeccable. But in general, such explanatory models seem to 'flatten' belief and action, so that everything can be described and understood in the same terms: actors are pragmatic and exercise reason and judgement. The contrast with Western systems of thought now seems oddly misplaced. Perhaps an Oxford don might exercise judicious, rational thought (although there must always have been plenty of counter-examples). But Western thought currently encompasses very large numbers of people who have been abducted, sometimes sexually assaulted, by aliens; people who have personal relationships with angels; people who express their religious faith through snake-handling; people who prepare for the imminent Rapture. Martyrs of all faiths harbour strong beliefs concerning rewards in an afterlife. The Enlightenment has never fully touched such belief systems. We under-analyse such cultural elements if we explain them away by simply relativising rationality or expunging any appeals to irrational beliefs.

If we are not to flatten cultures and if we are not to relativise phenomena out of existence, we may need a different mode of expression. Rather than the implicit structural-functional mode of expression, we might explore other means: genres of representation that express the enchantment and strangeness of social worlds. In other words, the everyday world of many people has been and is one of Magical Realism. While authors like Schütz (1967) explored the natural attitude and its associated common sense, they did so in terms that reflected the taken-for-granted categories of a European practical actor. Their paramount reality was disenchanted and flattened into a landscape of pragmatic reason. But as we have hinted, anthropology and sociology are replete with examples of cultural milieux wherein the 'supernatural' attitude exists alongside the 'natural' attitude and the irrational co-exists with reason. Reporting them is not just a matter of debunking various belief systems but describing them in terms that do justice to the fabric of the social world. Surrender to the phenomena – which does not preclude the catch – calls for textual practice that mirrors it. It is writing that follows the cultural grain of actors' everyday realities while cutting across the grain of ordinary expectations. It simultaneously challenges mundane reason and the conventions of realist writing.

Classics of anthropology, such as Fortune's *The Sorcerers of Dobu* (1932), document cultures that are pervaded by sorcery and magic. But the attribution of such terms can readily imply an abiding distinction between the ordinary and the extraordinary. A culture in which one's yams can be stolen from a distance and induced to walk themselves to another's garden makes no such distinction. It is a culture that calls for magical realism in its textual treatment: if not for an entire monograph, at least as one authorial resource among several. Ironic distinctions between 'our' taken-for-granted understandings of human and yam behaviour and those of Dobuans need to be suspended, just as we need to elide equally uncritical, if implicit, contrasts between Western and other systems of thought. While various ethnographic accounts *do* take seriously the uncanny and the supernatural (such as experiencing shamanic trance, or possession), they have in the past often been framed as 'fictionalised', so that the texts become extra-ordinary as well as inscribing extraordinary experiences on the part of the ethnographer. Much more recently, McLean (2017) has attempted to address some of the intellectual and textual tensions within anthropology's treatment of the extraordinary. Treating extraordinary phenomena as 'symbols' or 'metaphors' or 'discourse' maintains the implicit distinction between the 'real' and the 'symbolic', whereas a thoroughly Magical Realism dissolves it in a cultural domain in which, say, sorcery and practical medicine can alternate (McLean 2017, pp. 88–95).

Latour's thesis that 'we have never been modern' deals with a very particular set of ideas, grounded in a discussion of the history and sociology of science (Latour 1993), but its general spirit could be extended. If contemporary issues, which he calls 'hybrids', call into question the radical distinction between the natural and the social, cultural or political, then the vast range of everyday beliefs and practices do so more fundamentally still. Everyday thought that celebrates, say, the liquefaction of the blood of San Gennaro in Naples does not reflect the primary tenets of 'modern' thought or of 'science' as conventionally understood in the Western canon. Likewise, some of the extreme 'theories' proposed in the time of the pandemic and against vaccination strongly suggest that modernity, rationality and the rule of science do not prevail unopposed in contemporary society. The same is true for many urban legends (Fine, Campion-Vincent and Heath 2005) and encounters with extra-terrestrial life (Roth, Samuels and Lepselter 2006), or with ghosts (Waskul and Waskul 2016).

Ethnographic sensibility is to be found paralleled in one of the foundational, canonical texts of Magical Realism. *The Kingdom of this World*, by Alejo Carpentier (1957) explores the cultural rupture between the powerful and the enslaved – a generic characteristic of much of the genre – and juxtaposes two versions of a witnessed event (an execution): for the alternation between competing realities, see Todorov (1970). An equally canonical text, *One Hundred Years of Solitude*, by Marquez (2000) inserts alternative realities into the narrative, disrupting any common-sense view of 'paramount reality' (see Hart 2003). Susan Lepselter (2005), writing of 'extra-terrestrial culture' and the 'uncanny' more generally, suggests:

> Uncanny and fantastic narrative dismantles conventions of realism and replaces them with irreducible uncertainty. But at the same time, when told outside the bounds of fiction, it usually demands to be read as *real*, as true, that is, to some ambiguous but felt and embodied experience. When the uncanny is encountered as part of an ethnographic relationship, therefore, the emotional force of its stories compels the listener to attend to the teller with the same openness demanded by the genres of ordinary personal narrative.
>
> *(p. 144, emphasis in original)*

In his multi-layered account of magic, colonialism and resistance Taussig (1987) also touches on the possibilities of magical realism in representing both the ordinary and the extraordinary in the history and anthropology of indigenous Colombians. The conventions of magical realism in representing extraordinary or paranormal phenomena call into question any easy reliance on a sense of the ordinary. We have made reference already to social phenomenology, and authors like Schütz (1967) describe 'thinking as usual' as an everyday mode of thought that constitutes the actor's sense of paramount reality. The general sense of that, as an analytic device is clear. But it must not pass unquestioned. When magical realism is a reasonable representation of belief systems and practices, then handy distinctions between the ordinary and the extraordinary start to break down. In many contexts, it is not the case that people inhabit a secular and practical world that is occasionally interrupted by extraordinary happenings. For many cultural environments, what 'we' might regard as paranormal is 'normal' in the sense of being an integral part of everyday life. If one believes implicitly in the incursions of 'aliens', then that is part and parcel of the everyday, however improbable it may appear to others. Raëlians, for instance, believe that life on Earth was created by advanced alien scientists (in contrast to other, mostly Christian-fundamentalist creationists), but there is for the members no sharp contrast between such a belief and more widely held beliefs – a view that can be reinforced by the contemporary biological science of cloning and genetic engineering (Battaglia 2005a; Chryssides 2003). What Battaglia (2005b) describes as ET culture is widespread. If witchcraft is a pervasive aspect of everyday culture, then simple distinctions between the ordinary and the extraordinary do not hold (Favret-Saada 1980).

Greenfield's observations of spiritist healing in Brazil could be key exemplars of descriptive accounts in a Magical Realist manner (Greenfield 2008). The descriptions of surgery are graphic; it is performed without anaesthetic and without aseptic procedures. One semi-literate surgeon (a bricklayer) used everyday tools to operate on his patients. In one case this involved opening up the patient's back with a circular saw, having first made a deep incision with a pair of scissors:

> Antonio returned to his motionless patient, turned on the saw, and inserted its spinning blade at the base of the open wound. A carpenter of the flesh, he noisily enlarged the split in skin and muscle alongside the spinal column. Blood spurted up. The roadside chorus of onlookers gasped and muttered. The young man from São Paulo remained absolutely still, as if indeed only a board.
>
> *(p. 51)*

When he practices, this healer is possessed by the spirit of Dr Ricardo Stams, from a century before. The treatments, an apparent absence of pain and recoveries from interventions like this are inexplicable in standard medical or scientific terms and are in effect Magical Realism in action.

Our purpose here is not to review all of the extensive literature on Magical Realism, still less to examine all the potentially relevant texts (of which there are many). Rather, we wish once more to draw attention to the relatively limited nature of ethnographic writing in the 'postmodern' vein when compared with the far richer and more extensive array of genres and exemplars offered by modernist and expressionist literary models. That is especially true when one extends the 'literary' gaze beyond English-language fiction. For an overview of Magical Realism itself, see the collection edited by Hart and Ouyang (2005.) Again, this is not an argument that contemporary ethnographic writing should embrace magical realism as a model. Rather, it is a recognition that our more conventional ways of writing are not the only way to represent social worlds in which our rationality does not prevail, and where categories of the natural, the supernatural and the human are implicitly called into question. Representing the uncanny is in itself a tricky business (Goslinga 2012).

Conclusion

In the course of this chapter, we have allowed ourselves to range over a number of literary genres and their relevance for ethnographic texts. We have suggested that much of classic, modern ethnographic writing has rested on a failed modernism. The exciting conjunctions of anthropology, sociology and literary modernism could have given birth to a rich variety of representations and reconstructions. They could have presented and explored a multiverse of meanings and significance, of phenomena and puzzles. Instead, we have witnessed several varieties of failure. Whatever happened to Modernism? we echo. Classic ethnographies had a centripetal tendency, reconstructing cultures towards a 'standard model' of function and rationality. As we have suggested, they flattened the variegated contours of culture into a homogenised style, characterised by literary Realism. By contrast, contemporary attempts at alternative modes of writing, sometimes justified in terms of postmodernism, celebrate a different kind of realism, offering narratives of sentimental realism. The burden of our argument is that we could do with less postmodernism, and more high Modernism, Absurdism, Magical Realism and indeed other genres that go against the grain. In the same vein, we could probably do with less sentimental realism and a greater sense of destablisation.

7

THE CATCH AND THE COLLECTOR

The catch

So far, we have addressed constellations of ethnographic desire, the ambiguities and fractures of fieldwork, some demands of the body and varieties of the text. Earlier in this book, we invoked the ideas of surrender-and-catch, in order to capture key aspects of an ethnographic attitude. For the most part, we have returned to surrender as a leading motif, stressing ethnographic openness to the phenomena, the extent to which the conduct of ethnography rests on close and sustained observation in the field, and on the social relationships that make that work possible. Participant observation is not just a convenient alternative term for fieldwork but points to a set of intellectual and personal commitments. Here, it is appropriate to return to the catch, the second aspect of Wolff's formulation (Wolff 1976). Catch refers to the analytic sensibilities we bring to bear on the everyday life we have shared and observed. The phenomenological bracketing that helps us address phenomena does not mean that pure surrender is ever sufficient. It must meet the intellectual resistance of conceptual thought and theory. If surrender means going with the grain of everyday happenings and doings, then the catch leads us to think also against the grain. We interrupt the flow of events, narratives and memories to construct categories of analytic significance that transcend those original observations.

We shall not be discussing in any detail all of the how-to-do-it accounts of 'analysing qualitative data' (e.g. Coffey and Atkinson 1996; Corbin and Strauss 1998; Charmaz 2014), although we shall have things to say about some such approaches. As we shall make clear from just a few examples, we think that many contemporary orthodoxies of 'analysis' are wrongheaded and inimical to ethnographic conduct and thought. So having looked at some of the moments of embodied, engaged ethnographic fieldwork, here we concern ourselves with

DOI: 10.4324/9780429056802-7

ideas: how we can tend to them, lift them and cultivate them. It is perhaps easier to begin with what the catch is not. As shall explain, Wolff's catch is not 'data' in any conventional sense: the catch can happen at any point in the life of an ethnographic project and indeed in its afterlife. The catch is not 'analysing the data' in the sense of a separate, parcelled-out process. Rather, it resides in ideas about the phenomena and about the project in hand. We mean the intellectual and existential outcome of Surrender. It is its yield and the harvest. It is a waking and seeing afresh. The catch is the beginning (*Anfang*) of a new way of conceiving, of new ideas or a renewal of established ones. What is caught, what is comprehended, conceived and seen, cannot be anticipated. Nor is it guaranteed by procedures and protocols. But we can pay good care and attention to setting the conditions for its generation, and we address some of the issues involved in the course of this chapter. In its most formalised and public form, the catch is conceptualisation-in-writing towards the ethnographic monograph or paper. Yet the catch does not have to be so formal and so final. Indeed, the catch must precede the final writing, for the catch really amounts to the ideas, the revelations and insights that we should have about the project, the participants and the field. As Wolff writes of the catch, 'it is a new conceiving, a new concept, a new beginning, a new being-in-the-world'. The catches can happen at any stage of a research study, but we seek the catch most visibly in the hinterland between active fieldwork and 'writing up'.

The catch is less a metaphor for watching and waiting, albeit with the right tools in the right place, like a fisherman; it is a yield, being something that is cultivated and tended. The horticultural allusion to tending is appropriate, as the catch grows, far from haphazardly, rooted in the exploration of everyday life. Such curating is not confined to ethnographic research, of course. Laboratory scientists, for instance, must needs tend their laboratory animals (such as mice and rats) or their cell lines and cultures. Lab scientists and technicians need 'green fingers' (again, the horticultural trope is appropriate). See Meskus (2018) for a discussion of craft and curating of stem cells, where she concludes that the strict protocols of laboratory procedure do not correspond to the 'experiences of doing the stuff' in the laboratory (p. 138). Getting cell lines 'growing nicely' calls for the hands-on experience of the practicalities of laboratory work. For a parallel discussion of cell lines, see Stephens, Glasner and Atkinson (2011). On the management and curating of laboratory animals, see Lewis, Featherstone and Atkinson (2013). We do not intend a whimsical approach to data here. The laboratory, the animal-house or the garden all imply lengthy attention and hard work. Likewise, harvests do not just happen. They demand all our faculties, our work, our local knowledge and an alertness to changing conditions. One is reminded of Malinowski's *Coral Gardens and their Magic* (1935) and its descriptions of practical horticultural management and cultural belief systems. Achieving the catch needs patience, agency, care and work. We tend to our participants, our projects and our peers; we care for the work and the relationships, while we repair missteps and misunderstandings. Later in the chapter, we shall expand on how we like to develop ideas. But for now, we note that productive ideas that constitute the catch are the outcome of intellectual *work*, however and whenever they come to us. Ideas do not 'emerge' by magic. They are crafted, created, managed. The catch is invention, but not just good fortune.

Many share the experience of supporting bright, committed students or early-career researchers, who have notebooks packed with observations, but who feel lost and morose. Often it is the result of what PA calls with his students the 'penny plain, tuppence coloured' syndrome. An explanation is in order. The terms derive from the printed sheets of characters that were once sold for toy theatres. The sheets, that might contain pantomime or fairy-tale characters, could be bought in black-and-white outline for a penny, to be coloured in at home, or could be bought printed in colour for two pennies. It is a common phenomenon that students embark on their fieldwork with excitement and enthusiasm and it seems brightly coloured. But when they come to 'analyse' and 'write up', the project dims, becoming monochrome, and feels dull., The students lose focus and they lose enthusiasm. They are more than 'saturated' with 'data', but have little insight, and few ways of conceiving how to think with it all. This is independent of the subject matter of the fieldwork itself. Some potentially thrilling fieldwork experiences fail to materialise into texts that go beyond bland descriptions or dull content-analyses. Equally some of the most mundane of settings can generate the best developed and moving insights. Indeed, the tough intellectual work involved in making the ordinary into something special is a rewarding challenge for all researchers who are prepared to think beyond the obvious, and who can establish sufficient analytic distance from mundane, even boringly routine activities (Delamont and Atkinson 2021). Sometimes we can challenge others, including students, and ourselves to select just any event, or fieldnote passage, or segment of interview transcript – more or less at random – and find something, anything, productive to say and write about. After all, if we endorse that mantra of ethnography, that 'nothing never happens', there ought to be 'something' there. It can be a salutary exercise in identifying phenomena through mundane activity. It is a useful exercise in prompting people to make something out of a small amount of data rather than boiling down a lot of information into nothing much at all.

We also recommend to students that they 'read something else' or remind themselves of the inspiration(s) that originally informed their choice of fieldwork. We encourage them to distance themselves from the data or indeed from the field. We thus recognise that for ideas to develop, it may be necessary to create distance, temporal or imaginative. Wolff knew this too. His field research in Loma was conducted in the early 1940s but he was still generating ideas about what it could mean three decades later (Wolff 1976). Paul Rabinow (1977), in his *Reflections on Fieldwork in Morocco*, includes in his analysis the important role of both time and change. Rabinow clarifies his rethinking and repositioning during and after fieldwork, noting that he needed a long time to come to an understanding of a variety of aspects of the Moroccan way of life. It is, of course, his own changing perspective that is at the core of his analysis. Revisiting one's field materials can help to generate different analytic insights, sometimes in the light of changing methodological understandings. PA realised that he could have a quite different approach to reading and working with his fieldnotes. He had materials from his fieldwork in the early 1970s on medical students' first exposure to surgery, having based nearly all of his doctoral thesis and subsequent publications on his observations of general medicine (such as his monograph, published in 1981). His re-examination was not based primarily on the contrasts in subject matter (general medicine versus surgery) but was grounded in a different approach to reading the materials altogether (Atkinson 1992). His earlier treatment of the notes from medicine had reflected what he called 'the culture of fragmentation': taking small extracts of data from their original contexts and grouping them with similar gobbets of fieldnotes. When he came to revisit the notebooks and their contents, nearly twenty years after they were first collected, and ten years after the monograph appeared, he adopted a different strategy of reading them. Rather than fragmenting the materials, he tried to use them to reconstruct much more extended passages of interaction, that allowed him – however imperfectly – to capture something of the ceremonial and performative nature of the action. The exercise contributed to the continuing critique of fragmenting and coding that we touch on below.

It is not simply elapsed time in itself that matters. It is the opportunity it provides for fresh perspectives, from the interpellation of subsequent ideas and experiences. Newer perspectives can feed back into earlier fieldwork and that can be cast in entirely new light. Retrospective reflection can also be coloured by persisting senses of regret and chagrin: of opportunities missed or foregone. It is what Annette Leibing (2007) describes as a 'lifting out', stemming from a critical confrontation of interruptions and contradictions in time and space. When past notions become incongruent with more recent perceptions, they are recontextualised: the past is reconsidered through the lenses of the present. In other words, the fieldwork is always in the past, though expressed in the ethnographic present, and its significance is always shaped by memory and retrospection, in turn shaped by ideas that can have evolved in the time since the fieldwork was completed. Newer ideas can always suggest different ways of addressing our collection of field materials and recasting our key ideas. There is a constant dialogue between 'data', ideas and the work of other authors. Holding space for the catch requires repositioning, flexibility towards classifications and an openness to changing one's mind. It is reflexivity that holds the key to insight.

The catch is reflexive in a way that we have outlined elsewhere (Whitaker and Atkinson 2021). Ethnography is reflexive in multiple ways (Whitaker and Atkinson 2022). To an inescapable degree, there is a range of tacit assumptions that frame our research and the help to shape the phenomena we identify. They include taken-for-granted features of academic disciplines, national traditions, schools of thought, methodological preferences and personal or biographical characteristics. Notwithstanding widespread use to the contrary, reflexivity does not mean simply 'reflection' (however critical) on one's own research practice. Reflection is always necessary, but it is not sufficient. The essential reflexivity of research does call for acknowledgement that we frame and define the topics of our observations in the light of our disciplinary knowledge – as sociologists, anthropologists, geographers and so on – and through the research methods we bring to bear. It also demands an awareness that such disciplinary knowledge and methodological experience, however well-formed and sophisticated, cannot exhaust all the possibilities. We can never arrive at a final and definitive version of potential analyses. We cannot be certain of what we feel sure of. What we thought at the time can be subject to revision. Sometimes we need to look at things askance, not remain with a fixed gaze. We can devise alternative perspectives, deliberately suspending fixed ideas and forcing ourselves to think about things afresh. This is the kind of advice that we try to give our students – graduate students in particular – when we urge them to establish some sort of intellectual distance and propose alternative perspectives. Together we need to nourish ethnographies with ideas from different traditions, about different places, couched in different forms. This is not easy and of course it can be time-consuming. It may point towards a bit less time spent actually conducting the fieldwork and more time establishing distance and testing out possibilities. We shall develop these reflections later in the chapter, when we devote more explicit attention to two specific themes: de-familiarising phenomena and abductive reasoning about them.

Before we do so, however, we return to the set of ideas surrounding the archive and the collection as metaphors for the ethnographer's materials, physical (notes, transcripts) and imaginary (ideas, impressions, memories). We frame our discussion initially by returning once more to the themes of the *collection* and the *archive*. As we have already suggested, the ethnographic frame of mind is often informed by processes and outcomes of collecting. We begin with a consideration of the archive as one way of thinking about ethnographic materials and their care. The idea of the archive certainly gives us one angle on the accumulation of fieldnotes, interviews, images and other materials (drawings, material artefacts and the like). The collector and the collection are key phenomena in the work of Walter Benjamin (Abbas 1988; Holdengräber 1992). Benjamin's mammoth accumulation of extracts and observations make up the materials of his *Passagen-Werk*, or Arcades Project (Hanssen 2006). It is the work of an avid collector, and Benjamin acknowledged his own propensities as a collector, quite apart from his pursuit of modernity in Paris, through the topology of its arcades. No monograph emerged from the collection, meticulously sorted into numerous files, each topic accorded its own *Konvolut* (folder). While it would be wrong to suggest that the accumulation of those notes and fragments was actually an end in itself, it is noticeable that the collection has become treated as a major work of cultural history and a major contribution to the study of modernity by one of the twentieth century's most significant theorists.

Benjamin's own reflections on collecting and collections come from his autobiographical essay on unpacking his personal library (Benjamin 1968). He observes the quality of the collection that resides in its relationship to the owner: 'The phenomenon of collecting loses its meaning as it loses its personal owner. Even though public collections may be less objectionable socially and more useful academically than private collections, the objects only get their due in the latter' (p. 67). Like the ethnographer's hoard, the private collection finds significance through the collector and from the series of personal attachments that permeate it. Benjamin's book collection gives rise to memories:

> Now I am on the last half-emptied case and it is way past midnight. Other thoughts fill me than the ones I am talking about – not thoughts but images, memories. Memories of the cities in which I found so many things: Riga, Naples, Munich, Danzig, Moscow, Florence, Basel, Paris, memories of Rosenthal's sumptuous rooms in Munich, of the Danzig Stockturm where the late Hans Rhaue was domiciled, of Sussengut's musty book cellar in North Berlin; memories of these rooms where these books had been housed, of my student's den in Munich, of my room in Bern, of the solitude of Iseltwaldn on the Lake of Brienz and finally of my boyhood room....
>
> *(p. 76)*

The collection finds its meaning(s) in the collector's memories, which are in turn occasioned by items in the collection. Like the ethnographer's notebooks, items 'come alive' through their author's engagement with them and through them the recorded persons and events. Benjamin himself says: 'Not that they come alive in him; it is he who lives in them'. We would wish to emphasise the dialogues that make things 'come alive'.

We take it that this is one of the key issues illustrated by Wallman (2020) in her layered monograph, revisiting fieldwork in Bellino, an Alpine community in North Italy, conducted over three field trips in the early 1970s. She interleaves passages from her original fieldnotes with reflections nearly fifty years later. Her memories, her hosts' memories and her fieldnotes play against each other. She summarises that ethnographic exercise:

> Essentially this story is built on layers of memory. All of them relate to Bellino, but only a few to direct experience. The things written about happened at different times and to different people; even the shared occasions are not remembered the same way by everyone who was there. Records of the place were kept in the past, first by functionaries or clerics without by-lines, later converted into 'historical documents' by named scholars. Each of them has added a layer to the other's memory of people and events. I even add layers of my own. I catch myself using 'now' memories of that time to fill out notes of what I recalled of the day's happenings 'then'. Some

> entries in my field diaries come back sharp, re-remembered as soon as they are read. Others, just as clearly made by me then, are unrecognisable to me now: I read them like accounts of someone else's experience.
>
> *(p. 156)*

The reactions of memory, notes and other memorabilia constitute the ethnographer's unique collection, which is animated by her or his memory-work and by the occasions of its making and re-making.

We might also want to think of the ethnographer's notes, transcripts and other memorabilia in terms of an *archive*. Farge (2013) is a French social historian, who works on judicial records of the eighteenth century. Her research is archival in the purest sense, and her personal reflections bring vividly to life her encounters with and in those archives, including their materiality. Farge writes vividly on the material, tactile pleasures afforded by the physical archive. The ethnographic cache of materials also invites an embodied engagement, especially with original notebooks and other documents (today, however, often mediated by digital versions of texts and images). She also writes of the temporal flow of the work:

> Combing through the archives – a beautifully evocative term – requires a host of tasks, and no matter how complex the planned intellectual investigation will be, they cannot be bypassed. They are both familiar and simple, and they purify one's thoughts, temper the spirit of sophistication, and sharpen one's curiosity. These tasks are performed without haste, and necessarily so.
>
> *(p. 55)*

But if we treat the ethnographer's work in terms of the archive, then we shall need caution. The archive in this context is not a fixed, or inert body of textual or other materials. It is not something created by others, such as medical, judicial or fiscal authorities, and quite independent of any subsequent research-directed interrogation. It is, after all, created by the ethnographer herself. The materials accumulate dynamically, growing organically as the fieldwork develops and in response to a logic of exploration and discovery. Unfortunately, that is not how practitioners and authors on method often represent the nature of 'data' and its 'analysis'.

We resist the 'archivisation' of ethnographic research if by that we understand a kind of fethishisation of that archive and our relation to it. We avoid that 'archive fever' that treats the archive with an undue reverence, as the only source of knowledge, as a guarantee of authority (cf. Derrida 1996). Furthermore, the ethnographic assemblage is not a dormant one, that Sleeping-Beauty-like awaits the re-animation of analytic searching to excavate its truths. Our ethnographies must also retrieve what was barely noticed at the time, what was absent as well as what was visibly or audibly present and what is only glimpsed askance.

The danger of archivisation derives primarily from a restricted perspective on ethnographic 'data' and consequently on 'analysis'. The implication is that we collect as much information as possible, possibly in different forms (field-notes, interview transcripts, images, documents) and then devote our energies to a separate phase of 'analysis'. Frequently this is based on a technology of coding, usually deploying bespoke software (Computer-Aided Qualitative Data Analysis Software). Now there is nothing intrinsically wrong with searching and indexing one's field materials, or even in conducting the complex sorts of interrogations that the software supports. But overall such an approach can – however inadvertently – subvert the dialectic between fieldwork and ideas, and the conversations between disciplinary ideas and fieldwork-derived understanding. The archive of the ethnography is already imbued with multiple speculations, inferences and maters of potential significance. That web of articulation and interpretation is itself in motion, animated by constant comparisons and speculations. It is interpreted in terms of routines and rituals, encounters and situations, action and organisation. The archive is far from being a lifeless collection of data awaiting a desperate search for meaning. Our ethnographic archive therefore is an active one, and our analytic engagements with it are coterminous with the acts that created it.

Problems arise from a concatenation of shortcomings in the current cultures of analysis. Most egregious is the tacit assumption that the data consist primarily, or even exclusively, of the transcripts of a series of interviews. This is one of the banes of qualitative research. The interviews are treated individualistically, as if they derive from people enrolled serially to a survey-like study. Transcribed, they are then addressed *post hoc*. They are inspected and coded as if encountered by the researcher for the first time. It is as if an analysis were a distinct phase in a production cycle, a phase that comes *after* any data collection, and in which some clerical or graphic manipulation of the data is undertaken. Such a trend is detectable in the recurrent search for 'themes', as revealed in methods texts. Thematic Analysis, derived initially from a social-psychology paradigm is a classic case in point (Braun and Clarke 2006, 2022). A critical reading of its key texts and its apparent usage suggests that, while far from crude, it displays some troubling features. The root image is one of treating datasets as resources to be searched for 'meaning'. The technology of analysis rests on the tasks of coding those data, with or without the use of bespoke software, and using those codes to derive 'themes'. Themes display patterned regularities across the dataset. While in principle it is argued that thematic analysis can be applied to a much wider variety of data types, it is also apparent that it implicitly rests on the assumption that the dataset will normally consist of texts that derive from extended interviews with a series of informants. It is relatively sophisticated form of content analysis.

Although Braun and Clarke are at pains to distance themselves from Grounded Theory, it is clear enough to us that their approach has much in common with many current uses of GT, especially as it is represented in texts of practical advice (e.g. Charmaz 2014) where the implication is that there is a phase of 'analysis' that rests on the inspection and coding of a fixed, complete and static dataset. There has been developed a complex array of coding types, and they have accompanied the expansion of coding-based software. But the underlying assumptions remain. Thematic Analysis and Grounded Theory are both manifestations of a contemporary *coding mania* that characterises so much of what is called qualitative research and qualitative data analysis. It is a form of 'archive fever' (see below). It can be corrosive and inimical to an ethnographic imagination. We exempt the reformulation of grounded theory by Clarke and her co-authors, which retains a strongly interactionist orientation to social organisation and action (Clarke, Friese and Washburn (2018)) in promoting 'situational analysis', based on an exploration of social action and organisation.

While an approach like Thematic Analysis may be appropriate in some circumstances, it does scant service to the ethnographer's collected and curated materials. Ethnography goes well beyond the elucidation of 'meaning' in spoken materials, such as the contents of one-to-one extended interviews. Everyday life is not lived through themes. The ethnographer does not seek simply to elucidate what actors 'mean'. Life is not lived through content analysis. It is organised in terms of interactions, routines, practices, ceremonials, negotiations, disputes, resolutions, turning points, careers, epiphanies and so on. Such events and their intrinsic order are certainly meaningful to the participants. Indeed, they are densely coded in terms of their semiotics and functions. But they are matters of shared, collective action, not 'themes'. Likewise, a blanket appeal to 'meanings' is jejune. Social actors have (or do not have) resources, stocks of knowledge, recipes and strategies for action. They are not revealed through the coding of qualitative datasets and they are certainly not documented through experiential interviews (Atkinson and Silverman 1997). They are not necessarily apparent just from the repeated reading of ethnographic fieldnotes either.

It is, for instance, far from clear that many classic formulations in anthropology or sociology would or could be generated through coding and content analysis. For instance, it seems improbable that Geertz (1973b) would have decided that the Balinese cock-fight was emblematic of a distinctive set of cultural traits through the coding of his fieldnotes and diaries. Goffman's identification of the practice of civil inattention would not have been yielded by similar means, nor indeed would the wealth of ideas and metaphors that he developed (Goffman 1972). Could Douglas's exploration of dirt and pollution have been promoted through similar means (Douglas 1966)? Classics of urban sociology in the tradition of Chicago interactionism were hardly hampered by the absence of coding software. In his most recent monograph, Anderson (2022) develops a powerful ethnographic perspective on African Americans' experience of being black in white spaces apparently without recourse to the dense coding of a mass of data. Like Geertz and so many others, he appreciates the value of the concrete and the specific, not just the recurrence of 'themes' and 'meanings'.

Coding mania echoes Derrida's account of archive fever, insofar as both imply a certain reverence for a textual resource, to be inspected and mined for understandings of everyday life in selected domains and periods. Now archives can be valuable resources for social historians, especially when their subject matter coincides with the social institutions that generated them, such as the law or medicine. But the archive is not the whole story. There are absences, silences and things only partially glimpsed that can escape the record. Especially when we return to our observations after a period, or after we have established some kind of critical distance, we can become aware not just of what is there, but also of what is not there. This is not because we are defective observers or note-takers, but because perspectives shift, and phenomena come to mind in ways that they did not, or perhaps could not, at the originating time of the fieldwork. As the immediacy of observation fades, things can come into focus in a new and different way. We take it that this is partly the inspiration of Carolyn Steedman's reflections on the rag rug (Steedman 2001). The rag rug was a cheap floor covering made by pulling rags, scraps of fabric, through a hessian backing. The result was a rather floppy, multi-coloured object. It had the advantage of protecting floors, from coal-fire ash or burns and the like, and being fairly readily disposable. (PA recalls the presence of rag rugs in family homes when he was young.) Steedman's essay begins from an absence, or rather a misremembrance. Of Mary Gaskell's novel *Mary Barton* (set in Manchester around 1840 and published in 1848), she had clearly recalled the presence of a rag rug in a domestic interior, carefully described in detail. On re-reading the novel, she realises that there was no rag rug, only a piece of oil-cloth (also a cheap floor covering). But it sparks a set of reflections on the description of domestic interiors, Bachelard's poetics of space and the childhood pleasures of miniature worlds. Those reflections arise from something that is not there.

In that spirit, we need, as ethnographers, to be attentive to what is not there, what is absent or overlooked or even abject. Just as we cultivate our competence to observe what is present to our senses, so too we need to be alert to the spaces between things, spaces and actors. It is a point made by Atkinson (2022) in his discussion of the discipline of life-drawing. Observing and drawing demand attention to the spaces between parts of the body and between aspects of the body and the surrounding spaces. It is not just a matter of contrasts between presence and absence, we need to plot the lines of force between and across them, whether they be described by physical spaces, cultural boundaries, or interpersonal fields. Scott (2019) writes persuasively on the significance of absences and nothingness, as being every bit as important as what is present. There is, she suggests, a phenomenology of nothingness, whether that reflects invisibility, silence or emptiness. They are socially produced and enacted; they carry cultural significance. In developing her argument, Scott proceeds from two assumptions. The first is that 'nothing is a form of social action'. The second is that 'nothing is a *social process*' (p. 3, emphases in original). Together these axioms generate an array of research topics:

individual identity and self-identity, situations and interactions, the interaction order and institutions (pp. 17–18). In much the same way, Taussig (2011) reflects on anthropological fieldwork and what was observed/not observed and what is half recalled. We suspect that many ethnographers have similar experiences: the events that are vividly recalled, but in ways that are not recorded in the notebooks or cannot be found in the notebooks at all. Did one fail to record what happened? Or is the memory a false one? Does one use memory to elaborate on a poorly recorded event, or must one stick closely to the inadequate record that was made at the time? The point here is not a simple one concerning the accuracy of notes or of the reliability of memory, but a reminder of the fact that our ethnographic work involves an active, iterative engagement with 'data' and memory. The former is not just an archive of fixed records. Recording, recollection and imagination constantly interact. If 'nothing' is a social phenomenon, then so too is ignorance. We spend a great deal of our efforts examining the competence and knowledge displayed by our hosts. We ought also to explore what is not known or acknowledged. We say this in the spirit of contemporary studies of ignorance. Ignorance studies are far removed from any attribution of deficit to any given group or individual. Rather, it recognises that any contours of the distribution of knowledge must imply blind-spots, and tacit, taken-for-granted but unexamined assumptions. We recognise that there is the equivalent of dark matter in the distribution of knowledge and belief. It is thus fundamental to a phenomenology of everyday life and hence to the ethnographic exploration of knowledge-in-action (cf. Gross 2010; Gross and McGoey 2015). We must equally reflect on the shaping of our own knowledge as ethnographers, acknowledging that blind-spots and spheres of ignorance are implicit in the conduct of fieldwork, while cultural omniscience will also elude us all. In a very different vein, we can learn much from texts like Goethe's memoir of travels in Italy. His tour took him to places that contemporary tourists visit, including Monreale on Sicily. Nowadays, we go there to admire the mosaic decorations in the Norman-Byzantine cathedral. He is silent on them and seems not to have visited them, being interested only in Renaissance art or the classical world. The absence speaks volumes about the nature of artistic taste at the time. Value is expressed as much through what is overlooked or despised as much by what is actively prized. As we inspect and recall persons and events, we are not undertaking the smooth, untroubled traverse of an equally smooth terrain of notes and memory. We need to accept and be alert to the fact that the record – the records we have ourselves created and garnered – are incomplete. Our understanding is equally imperfect, however much we strive towards the desired goals of completeness and comprehension. Moreover, we should be examining the rifts and ruptures, the absences and the puzzles (see Strathern 1988). Ignorance becomes as much a part of our ethnography as it is an inevitable feature of our academic work. We need to incorporate our own ignorance and that of the actors we work with in the course of our fieldwork.

We might think of the ethnographer's cache of materials in terms of an *assemblage*. That term has a particular usage in critical theory – to which we shall return – but to begin with we draw an analogy with the archaeological or ethnological museum assemblage. That is, a collection of artefacts deriving from the same site or the same stratum (archaeology) or from the same culture (ethnology). PA recalls as a student of anthropology at Cambridge having to acquaint himself with the assemblages in the Haddon Museum. The glass cases contained artefacts from a wide variety of 'peoples', from the Northwest Coast of North America, identified as Tlingit or Haida, from the Arctic, identified in those days as Eskimo, from the Plains Indians of North America and so on. In many cases, they had been collected and shipped back to Cambridge many years before. The ethnological assemblages gained their significance by virtue of being collected, arrayed, labelled and displayed. They showed the distinctiveness of the relevant culture, being technically and aesthetically related within the assemblage, and manifestly different from those in other assemblages. Collectively, the vitrines created a topology of otherness, granted importance by their co-location in Cambridge: it could have been reproduced in many national and university museums elsewhere. Now here we are not commenting on the morality of appropriating material artefacts in that way, or on the history of anthropology that generated such displays. Rather, we identify it by way of an analogy to the ethnographic desire for collecting that we have identified in an earlier chapter and in this. No such assemblage could lay claim to being a comprehensive inventory of a given material culture, much less a key to unlock social arrangements. But it evokes a technology, an aesthetic, a mode of subsistence and a belief system. The 'Eskimo' harpoon or spear-thrower, or the 'Plains Indian' bead-worked moccasins potentially provoke much more than their plain material presence. They suggest to the attentive observer a historical and ideological relationship between 'the people' and the collector and between the observer and the collection. In a similar way, we might suggest that the contemporary ethnographer's assemblage evokes and signifies more than it denotes in so many words or images. It calls to mind a web of relationships between the ethnographer, her or his hosts and the potential readers of 'the ethnography'.

We are conscious of the fact that the 'assemblage' has acquired a particular meaning in recent theory, deriving from the work of Deleuze and Guattari (1983, 1987). While that has inspired assemblage theory, the use of the concept is highly variable, to the point of being productively vague, and even seems to be a poor translation of the original French *agencement* (Delanda 2016, p. 1). In any event, as Delanda demonstrates, it has multiple meanings in the work of its originators. It does, on the other hand, have the merit of being susceptible to a range of concrete applications, of different scales and in very different social contexts. As Delanda makes clear in his survey of its applications, in general terms an assemblage brings together a heterogeneous collection of items, and as Deleuze suggests, 'It is a multiplicity which is made up of many heterogeneous terms and which establishes liaisons, relations between them, across ages, sexes and reigns – different natures. Thus, the assemblage's only unity is that of co-functioning …'. So, like the ethnographer's archive, the assemblage is brought together; it is not necessarily a 'natural' family. It is a coming together of recondite elements. A classic Deleuzian example is the soldier, his or her weapons and equipment such as a radio. The nomad warrior (Scythian for example) embodies the triadic assemblage of warrior-horse-bow. These collocations of things are actively brought into conjunction, establishing functional and/or semiotic relations between them. Now we do not need a fully elaborated assemblage theory to recognise that the museum assemblage, a Deleuzian assemblage/agencement, and the ethnographer's archive have family resemblances: collections of sometimes disparate objects, traces and phenomena, actively and purposefully brought into conjunction. They set off resonances and connotations, echoes and cross-references, beyond their purely functional relations.

The motif of collecting, the collector and the collection is another way of thinking about the ethnographer and her materials. Collecting, sorting, classifying and re-ordering are all activities associated with the collection. EMW writes of collecting:

> I rescue other people's photos. I collect other people's memories. I store and play and categorise and embellish the episodes the photos contain. I ponder on their origins and their relationships and their histories. I wonder what they thought of political ineptitude, dance music, daffodils. Like many seemingly new found compulsions it was born from a tangled web of desires and needs, and began in the first UK lockdown of 2020. In that atypical time, when people started daily walking to mete out a rhythm missing in the absence of the commute or school run, I discovered 'found photography'. I didn't know it was called that then. I didn't know about cabinet cards or daguerreotypes, or how Box Brownies democratised how we represented and then saw ourselves. I just saw a job-lot on EBay of black-and-white photos and felt sad about it. Exposed and spread out on the seller's table were men, women, children, dogs, chickens. There were family shots in gardens, holidays by the seaside. The seller guessed they were taken between the 1920s and 1940s. Rather than a single family or personal chain thy were a mishmash, but all centred around the south coast of England. I decided I wouldn't like it if they were all of the same person or family: that would feel too much like theft or voyeuristic intrusion. There were thirty in total and I know I paid over the odds – a standard rookie error when it comes to collecting anything. But I didn't know I was collecting anything then, or that within two years I would become an amateur collector, scouring antique and flea markets and charity shops with increasing confidence, training my 'eye' with each handful sifted and sorted into categories I could work and rework.

The origins of a such collection may be adventitious, but the act of collecting is not random. As the collection itself develops, it can become increasingly focused and purposeful. Collecting can thus be a form of resistance against entropy, creating the appearance of order. The collection itself is never fixed, however. In principle, it can always be extended and expanded in different ways. It can be refreshed, with less valued pieces discarded and/or newer things added. It is rarely, if ever, complete.

The collection finds its significance precisely because it is a collection. The pieces are brought together with intention. The significance of any individual piece is established precisely because of its place within the whole. It may complete a set or a series; it may be a rare piece; it may be typical of a given period or style. Removed from that context, the individual piece is just that – one isolated artefact, or image. Here, therefore, is the parallel between the collection and the ethnographer's materials. The ethnographic cache is incomplete and can always be added to. The significance of any given episode is to be found in relation to its context within the ethnography as a whole. The materials describe a trajectory of their own – an arc of retrieved objects, of lucky finds, of gaps in the record and so on. The collector can also find engagement in the minor details of objects of interest, such as the significance of the boxes that hold Japanese ceramics and that are heedlessly discarded by the uninitiated. The ethnographer too can find significance in such apparently incidental details.

We can all share an interest in ephemera, the discarded, the marginal, detritus. EMW again:

> I started to notice abandoned shoes. I had been spotting them for years and dutifully reporting them to the dedicated Twitter account. I was collecting abandoned shoes as episodes, if not taking the artefacts themselves. I would wonder how they got there, what had befallen the wearer, the context of it all. I discovered that I was not alone. It turned out that a friend and fellow ethnographer was equally fascinated by abandoned shoes. We developed our ideas together. We suggested that the abandoned shoe acts as a cipher: for suddenness, loss, transformation, shock, the unexpected. Something must have happened; shoes are not lost without awareness that they are gone. Abandoned shoes are puzzles and symbolic thresholds. They mark encounters that in some way – mundane or life-changing – have been transformed. As ethnographers, the abandoned shoe seduced us, calling us to imagine the lives prior to and after abandonment; we become attuned to a ground-level parade. In becoming alive to the shoes' presence we see them everywhere. The affective persuasiveness of their ubiquity prompts us to speculate, to imagine, to try to understand. Unfettered and unshackled the work hums between the factions of 'making stuff' and 'making stuff up'. We ask ourselves 'What worlds do these shoes belong to and open up?'

In other words, those abandoned shoes can be what Sherry Turkle (2011) calls *evocative objects* that provoke as many questions as answers. As we shall stress in the remainder of this chapter, the ethnographer's imagination is, or should be, constantly nourished by such speculations. The apparently trivial, the mundane, the overlooked and marginal should all be stimuli to an analytic imagination. They can be just as illuminating and suggestive as the 'bigger picture' topics or more obviously core phenomena. If we let them, stimuli can trigger a wide range of intellectual and imaginative associations. Turkle explores how the simplest of objects, an apple, a diary, a laptop, provoke a world of memories, associations and feelings. We do not, of course, rely solely on physical objects, nor indeed on *objets trouvés*, for ideas. But those lost shoes and Turkle's evocative objects remind us that the ethnographer sweeps up, amasses and reconstructs a great many instances – persons, events, situations, meanings, that form the materials of a collection, and are suggestive of an array of productive ideas.

As we have suggested already, the ethnographic collection is born of a desire to gather and store, but also to return repeatedly, to pick over the contents, and to chart alternative ways of classifying it and to trace multiple ways through it. EMW's anonymous photographs and those abandoned shoes are illustrative of the ethnographer's mode of acquisitive and inquisitive motivations. It is not just a matter of accumulation – of fieldnotes, transcripts, images and the like. It is also a matter of how we conceive and relate to that stuff. We need to *think with* the collections, play with them and move the constituent bits around. We need to do far more than accumulate and also to do more than simply index, catalogue or create inventories of our accumulated materials. We are tasked with having and developing ideas and with inviting others into that understanding.

It is important to consider how we relate to our collections and how we can breathe life into ideas. Thinking about how we relate to our gathered and generated material matters because good ideas do not come from holding a séance with your corpus; you cannot get it to speak. Staring at a collection of artefacts, notes, interviews or maps will not cause 'themes' to levitate from it, contrary to popular assumptions. To commune with your data disconnects the researcher and the project from its roots and bonds. It undermines the work that is needed to tend and yield ideas. It obfuscates rather than reveals. Moreover, we are not engaged in the equivalent of an autopsy or dissection: cutting and dicing may well mask and cut away more than it reveals. Ideas cannot be legislated for and they are not guaranteed by diligently following procedures such as Thematic Analysis. They come from cross-pollination, serendipity, shadows of past projects and fleeting conversations. Our predilections, our reading, our past and present work are all brought to bear on our conversations with fieldwork, notes and the rest of our trove.

Something akin to 'analysis' is clearly close to the catch, in Wolff's sense. But we need to acknowledge the significance of work that goes well beyond just inspecting and trawling through a body of data. We clearly do not commit the considerable amount of time and effort involved in fieldwork, amassing such materials as we can, without the equivalent commitment to making something of them. And that is the point: we *make* something and we can make more than one something. Ethnographic making is what Atkinson (2022) has explored in terms of craft work, distinguishing ethnographic sensibility from stereotypes of both art and science. It is firmly rooted in the everyday world and in its mundane realities. As we have acknowledged, 'the ethnography' has 'literary' antecedents and modalities (cf. Atkinson 2020). But it is far from being pure fiction. Undoubtedly, the ethnographic monograph has to be shaped and sustained through textual and rhetorical devices (Atkinson 1990) but it is not a work of fiction in itself. Equally, the monograph is the outcome of *research* and is a contribution to scholarly knowledge, but its production is not captured by the conventional representation of science (if by that the natural sciences are taken as the model).

Atkinson's treatment is based on his own engagements with craft activities – including ceramics, glassblowing and silversmithing – that form the pretexts for his ethnographic reflections. But he makes clear that his ultimate purpose is to do the ethnography *of* craft in order to explore ethnography *as* craft. Like the skilled craft artist, the ethnographer works with 'base' materials. For the craft worker, they may be wood, sand (glass) or clay (ceramics), while for the ethnographer they are the stuff of ordinary everyday life. The craft artist and the ethnographer alike take their materials and shape them into something transformative. The craft artist makes vessels and objects, the ethnographer shapes her or his gathered materials and from them constructs accounts that make sense of a given social world. The latter is a work of interpretation, but not of pure fiction, any more than the material work of the potter is divorced from material reality. In both cases, there can be a radical act of transformation. The ethnographer and the potter are transcending their base materials, and from them shaping something that is simultaneously faithful to them but also creates something with a new form and texture.

In the case of ethnographic interpretation, analysis involves going beyond the 'data', thinking with them and through them, but not just reproducing them. It involves the exercise of *abductive imagination* (cf. Tavory and Timmermans 2014). Derived from the philosophy of C.S. Peirce, and brought into social-science methods through the original inspiration of Grounded Theory (Glaser and Strauss 1967), it requires an elementary thought-style. As Reichertz (2010) observes, one must recognise that Strauss's understanding of Grounded Theory, informed by Peirce's abductive reasoning, is not an affirmation of purely inductive logic, and that abductive reasoning is especially fruitful in the generation of new theory, or where no existing theory exists that is relevant to the phenomena under scrutiny. It amounts to what good social scientists have done for generations. It implies thinking with the data, but not confining one's perspective simply to their contents. It means asking far more than 'What do they do?' or 'What did they do?' Its results can be far more penetrating than the kind of content-analysis we have already criticised. It relies on something different from inspecting the data –

although there is obviously need for thorough knowledge of one's corpus of materials. So it includes a degree of *inductive* reasoning: identifying regularities and multiple occasions is an important part of the work. A purely top-down theory-driven *deductive* approach is too limited in itself, but a thorough engagement with theory is also a prerequisite. Indeed, an abductive approach to the catch means, above all else, a dialogue between 'data' and 'ideas'. From that interaction – which is iterative throughout the ethnographic project – sociological or anthropological ideas can be developed, elaborated and tested. As Timmermans and Tavory (2012) put it, abduction promotes a dialogue of data and ideas:

> Abductive analysis is a qualitative data analysis approach aimed at generating creative and novel theoretical insights through a dialectic of cultivated theoretical sensitivity and methodological heuristics, Abductive analysis emphasizes that rather than setting all preconceived theoretical ideas aside during the research project, researchers should enter the field with the deepest and broadest theoretical base possible and develop their theoretical repertoires throughout the research process.
>
> *(p. 180)*

In thinking abductively, therefore, we are repeatedly asking of ourselves and of any given instance, situation or event: 'What might this be a case of?' (cf. Atkinson 2017). Let us give a very small example, that derives from a personal occasion for PA. He has written, of a day in 2022, on the basis of notes he made then:

> I had occasion to go shopping for a new electric guitar for my adult godson, who is an experienced musician. We met one Saturday morning in a coffee shop near London's Denmark Street. Known as Tinpan Alley, that small 17th Century street had once held a concentration of music engravers, and had then become the centre for sellers of sheet music. It then evolved into a street of musical instrument shops and recording studios. There are several specialist guitar shops. The shops themselves are quite small, as the original buildings had narrow frontages.
>
> We start with some window-shopping (and see some alarmingly expensive guitars on display) and then we spend some time in one of the shops, where electric guitars line the walls. The shop easily became crowded, when one family group entered: I had the feeling that they were primarily sightseeing rather than shopping. One young man was sitting on a stool playing a solid-body guitar. He was playing well, as far as I could judge. He rather dominated that cramped space physically and acoustically. My godson and I had already talked about playing in the shops. He said he was not so proficient as to want to play. I joked, 'So you won't be playing *Stairway to Heaven*, then?' I don't know where that came from, however, as I realise I have no idea who played it or what it sounds like. I think I only know it

has a famous guitar riff. Because the shop is busy I go and wait outside for a bit. When I go back in, my godson is playing a Gretsch [hollow body], handsomely finished in deep red. But it is apparent that he is not really comfortable with the neck, which he says feel short to him. The seller points out that the neck is not really short, but is set deep into the body of the guitar. But I can see perfectly well that this guitar is not 'the one'.

We move on to another of the shops. This one has a different atmosphere and feels more invitingly relaxed. It even has a sofa that I can sit on. It specialises in vintage guitars, some of which I observe are jolly expensive. My godson tries a couple of the guitars. He finds one he seems very comfortable with. It is an Epiphone Les Paul and has a more mellow sound than the Gretsch he had tried earlier. I say I like the sound, but add that I know nothing about guitars. The shop assistant says you don't need to know anything about guitars to hear differences or to prefer the sound of one over another. The shop's owner says that some people never play the guitars they buy; they just hang them on the wall. I say that they are certainly beautiful objects.

Godson points out that one of the guitar's controls is crackly. We are told that there is a workshop downstairs that can service it. Godson goes on playing the guitar, strumming quietly rather than playing flashy riffs. The guitar is a Les Paul Epiphone, finished in black and over twenty years old. As the shop is relatively quiet, I talk to the owner, and on impulse I say I would like to come back and do a study of the shop, and I very briefly describe my recent work. He seems agreeable to the idea, and I add that it would not be an in-out kind of visit, but involve my 'hanging out' for a while. He adds that of course there is the workshop downstairs. I say (truthfully) that I have long wanted to do a study of luthiers. He says they are a special breed. He adds that he is fortunate in his. I take one of his cards. He and godson discuss his other guitar, a Fender Jaguar. They discuss the stringing of the guitar, and godson is asked what strings he uses. He seems a bit nonplussed by the question and needs some prompting to answer and to say whether he uses 'twelves' or 'elevens'. It has now been agreed that the workshop will sort out that crackly control, and it will be done within the hour. So we agree we will go out and find some lunch and then come back. An hour later we return to pick up the guitar, which comes in its rather engagingly battered case. The luthier says he has 'gone in' and cleaned it all up thoroughly. We leave with the Epiphone.

After writing up these notes, I reflect on a number of issues that might inform my interest if I am able to do something more there. They include:

- Are such shops sites of display and 'showing off'?
- I have noticed no women in the shops. Are these strongly gendered environments? How do they deal with women?

- Customers seem to be enthusiasts. How do the shops deal with guitar novices?
- Can such specialist settings be intimidating? Can they be welcoming?
- Are these places where people congregate to share their enthusiasm(s)?
- How do guitar collectors appreciate and select their precious guitars?

So then I think a little about how one might develop such speculations more broadly:

- Might I find comparable phenomena in other specialist places, such as camera shops or commercial art galleries? I know something of both.
- Where else can I find people showing off their virtuoso skills? Skateboarders? Jugglers? Street musicians?
- Where else might one find displays of connoisseurship? Artists' open studios? Collectors of art, craft, rare books etc.? I am a collector (cameras, ceramics, works on paper).

These and similar questions include speculations as to what might prove productive and illuminating. They start to lead me towards ideas about performance and display, about aesthetic judgements and collectors, about the enactment of expertise by participants – shoppers and sellers – and about the role of specialist settings as a focus for enthusiasts.

Although PA did not include this in his notes that day, one can also glimpse how such a setting would respond to a fully sensory engagement, from the aesthetic values of the guitars themselves, to the soundscape of customers and others trying out the instruments. Self-evidently, on the basis of a couple of hours observation, these notes and speculations are rough-and-ready. But they may help to show something of what we mean by abductive reasoning in practice. It means going beyond the 'data' and thinking through them *from the very outset of any involvement in a given field.* We do not wait to amass a large corpus of undigested observations (or conversations) and then plough through them in the search for ideas. Moreover, our iterative engagements between ideas and field(s) can lead towards a developmental fieldwork trajectory. It is a trajectory, rather than a fixed 'research design' and implies many possible routes. In this hypothetical example, it would not be necessary to undertake more fieldwork in all the potentially relevant settings: there are plenty of accounts of collecting, shopping, enthusiasts and so on that can be drawn on. One can perhaps glimpse how these simple speculations about the specialist guitar shop might couple with recurrent sociological interests in the interaction order, with explorations of display, expert knowledge, communities of enthusiasm, commercial and aesthetic values. So far one may not be generating anything particularly novel, but at least things are moving in the right directions. There is an interplay between local enactments and generic ideas. It is a microcosm of the surrender and the catch. We surrender to the local, allowing our observations to provoke speculations. Our catch resides in the sociological or anthropological ideas that can be brought to bear and that are developed further through that process. We create links within and between our observations, between our speculations and ideas and between those two levels of analysis. Here we can see ourselves re-working ideas derived from Erving Goffman, from Gary Alan Fine, or from Susie Scott, among many scholars in the broadly interactionist tradition (Atkinson and Housley 2003). None of this is a matter simply of chance or inspiration. It demands work, just as much as the original fieldwork. Here we have tried to display how one might start a lot from a little, whereas too many 'qualitative' projects seem to derive a little from a lot of 'data' (cf. Atkinson 2022). In this case, PA also notes how the guitar-culture ideas might mesh with some of his personal interests and hence his own stock of knowledge. Of course, reference to collectors and their values also reflexively bears on what we have had to say about the ethnographic corpus and the act of collecting. Note that the comparisons implied in some of those speculations do not necessarily imply whole new fields of fieldwork: 'desk research' can often help to fill in and extend suggestive ideas, while very short field visits can be illuminating.

Timmermans and Tavory (2022) provide a valuable summary of the goals of abductive analysis in the interests of the ethnographic catch:

> The goal of qualitative data analysis is coming up with an answer to the question *what is this data a theoretical case of?* Abductive analysis is a scientific logic of inference aimed at theory construction that involves a recursive process of moving between data and theories. An abductive inference makes a preliminary guess of what kind of case you have when surprising or unexpected findings occur.
>
> *(p. 156, emphasis in original)*

We would emphasise that 'surprises' (a recurrent theme for Timmermans and Tavory) are not just odd or deviant happenings in the field that are self-evidently striking. We need to work, phenomenologically, at making the most mundane, ordinary and routine of actions 'surprising'. Analytic surprise is not a given or a knee-jerk response, but the outcome of our ethnographic commitment to making everyday life anthropologically strange.

It follows that abductive reasoning must be accompanied by an ethnographic commitment to de-familiarisation. If we repeatedly ask ourselves 'What might this be a case of?' then we shall discover nothing if our sociological imagination does not free itself from the taken-for-granted, even obvious. If we study a classroom, or a lesson, then we may not 'discover' much if all we can think of is 'This is a case of pedagogy'. We might start to explore things more productively if we allow ourselves to think that the class might be a site of frustration, or of linguistic violence, or of empty procedural display, or frittering time away while time passes unenduringly slowly. And so on. Those kinds of thoughts could open up further avenues of development: a study of frustration could take us in many directions, from queues to flat-packed furniture, to workplace complaints, to inquiry desks. The classroom might turn out to have parallels with the airport as a site of frustration, tedium, impotent rage and so on.

The imaginative direction of abductive reasoning resonates with psychological work on 'convergent' and 'divergent' styles of thought (Hudson 1966). Those categories were based on projective psychological tests, such as the 'uses of an object'. Respondents (in Hudson's case boys in selective secondary schools) were asked to think of as many uses as they could, such as a brick or a golf ball. Convergent thinkers come up with few ideas, and they were close to the original object (a brick might be used to build a wall, or to make a raised flowerbed), while divergent thinkers suggest idiosyncratic and creative uses (a brick might be thrown at an unpopular politician, or used to smash one's sister's annoying mobile phone). Now we do not think that these styles, or something like them, are in any sense fixed. No more did Hudson. Indeed, so-called convergents, when shown examples of the sort of thing that might be possible, can perform in more 'creative' ways. And we are certainly not going to suggest that qualitative researchers are inherently more 'creative' than their quantitative counterparts. But we are suggesting that something like a 'divergent' mode of thought can be cultivated, and certainly should be encouraged among all researchers, ethnographers in particular.

The abductive approach to 'analysis' therefore depends on the capacity to resist the familiarity of everyday scenes and actions. Fighting familiarity (Delamont and Atkinson 1995, 2021) is an intellectual discipline enjoined on all ethnographers. It calls for the imaginative capacity to ask oneself some basic – sometimes apparently simple or even naïve – questions. It calls for an imaginative mobility, in examining phenomena from different perspectives and standpoints. It means asking oneself how something could be different or could be experienced differently. One needs to ask how a phenomenon is constituted: by what methods and using what means. We need to pay extraordinarily close attention to the *whatness* of things and equally close attention to what social actors are actually *doing*. This amounts to treating everyday life – wherever it is found – as *anthropologically strange*. It needs to be made sufficiently strange as to promote detailed examination, while being made sufficiently familiar to allow sufficient acquaintance for thorough exploration. The word *extraordinary* here emphasises that this calls for something more sustained and profound than ordinary everyday curiosity. It is noticeable that explicit calls to fight familiarity are to be found in educational research (Delamont 2014), perhaps because educational processes and institutions are part of every researcher's and reader's personal experience. It is sometimes assumed that anthropologists working in other cultures do not need to fight familiarity, because they are natural strangers. But after months or even years of fieldwork their adoptive culture may come to be as much taken for granted as their home culture. They may need to work just as hard as the ethnographer at home to achieve sufficient estrangement.

In essence, this returns us to the phenomenological roots of our arguments and of Wolff's contribution. A phenomenological intervention requires a suspension (bracketing) of our cherished, taken-for-granted presuppositions and categories of perception. It is a mode of deliberate alienation from mundane thought. It turns out that surrender and catch are two sides of the same coin. Surrender and openness to the phenomena must always be tempered with the self-critical attitude of the reflective craft practitioner and depends on the oscillation between familiarity and strangeness. The catch is sustained by our further efforts towards imaginative estrangement that casts phenomena is new light, and thus encourages their assimilation into social-scientific forms of understanding, and hence of a transposed familiarity.

8

EPILOGUE

Are there conclusions? Not in any simple sense. As we have stated, this is not intended to be a prescriptive book that insists on simple precepts for the conduct of research. Indeed, we have been at pains to introduce tensions, ambiguities and complexities. In themselves, they are not easily, perhaps ever, resolved. We see ethnography as being suspended, as it were, in the force-fields that such tensions imply. Ethnographers work somewhere between strangeness and familiarity, the local and the generic, and intimacy and distance: both 'stranger' and 'friend' (Powdermaker 1966). In this book, we seek to encourage ways of thinking about ethnographic fieldwork and its possibilities. We return to Rilke's advice to a would-be-poet: It is better to live in or with the questions rather than seeking out definitive answers. In the same way, there are rarely simple 'conclusions' to any ethnography. Often one wishes to say to readers: Learn to see a social world and its actors in this way. There is no QED, no null hypothesis to be rejected. Ethnography is a matter of exploration, and in the course of this book we ourselves have explored a number of key issues that have informed ethnographic work for many years.

Our own perspectives in the course of this book are driven as much by values as by methods, and it is appropriate that we should make explicit what has perhaps been implicit in the various chapters. We do not think that any approach to social research can claim to be the queen of the sciences, but we do think that ethnography rests on a number of core values that escape simple methodological formulae. One ought to affirm and celebrate the extent to which ethnographic and similar qualitative research is especially 'ethical' by virtue of its methodological, existential and interpersonal commitments. Ethnographers commit themselves to spending extended periods of time with their hosts. They commit themselves to sharing with their hosts key features of their everyday lives, including the longueurs and the boredom, the mundane

DOI: 10.4324/9780429056802-8

as well as the dramatic or the startling, the distressing or unpleasant as well as the pleasant. We grow old together by sharing the flow of time, events and experiences. As field researchers we surrender, however temporarily, to the shared everyday social world. Whatever analytic catch that fieldwork yields up is dependent entirely on those processes of personal commitment and interpersonal conduct.

As ethnographers we pay close and serious attention to other actors' everyday life. Seriousness has a distinctive meaning in this context. It calls for intellectual and personal openness, a willingness to engage with – though not necessarily endorse – the ways of life that are sustained locally in a social world by its members. Phenomenologically, it calls for a sustained empathy that goes beyond the somewhat jejune, bloodless notion of 'rapport' and transcends the pragmatic connotations of 'access'. (Though in earlier decades, one 'negotiated access' to a setting, rather than gaining 'informed consent' from a series of individuals.) It is an empathy that recognises and learns from a shared humanity in all its guises, its strengths and its frailties, it goodness and its evils, and its heroism and its weakness.

We need to conduct ourselves, and hence our relations in the field, with honour. We ought, therefore, to embody the values of courtesy and tact. We ought to be able to draw on our expert understanding of the interaction order and its ceremonial enactments, in order to comport ourselves in locally appropriate ways. Such courtesy implies attentive listening and speaking with our hosts with respect. Being honourable means finding ways for our fellow men and women to express their chosen or preferred identities and respecting those performances. And if the connotations of honour sound a bit patrician, so be it: intellectuals have obligations as well as licence, and a duty of reciprocal respect. To behave honourably might also be expressed in more mundane, if old-fashioned, terms such as decency and tact. Such values encourage us to aspire to an openness of mind and spirit, and a degree of generosity towards our hosts (institutions and person). Such generosity suggests not blind acceptance, but the intellectual and imaginative capacity to comprehend a range, a variety, of cultural and organisational arrangements. Surrender to the field and to its phenomena depends ultimately upon such generosity of spirit and intellect. Decent and honourable conduct are among the obligations of being an intellectual. Now it is becoming harder and harder to maintain the position of an intellectual in contemporary neoliberal academic institutions and on the face of increasing external political interference. Yet these underlying values need to be re-stated.

It will be clear that these commitments and values escape the confines of contemporary guidelines and obligations set by ethics committees and institutional review boards. Like so much that is inappropriate, they deal in checklists, protocols and procedures. Ethnographers are not resistant to such perspectives because they are libertarians or are harking back to simpler times (though both are possible). But we resist such impositions because we are forced to. Fieldwork is founded on trust. The procedures of institutional ethical review are based on an institutional absence of trust and a consequent avoidance of risk and legal liability.

The surrender we have discussed and alluded to throughout the book is not passive, as we do not abandon our sociological or anthropological imagination. The counterpart of Wolff's surrender is the catch. If we find productive ways of getting lost and losing ourselves, then the catch implies rediscovery. We have to work, imaginatively and intellectually, to achieve the right degree of estrangement from what and whom we encounter. Our surrender is therefore always tempered by resistance. That is, the kind of resistance that brings us up short that makes us question what we know and how we have learned it. It is also a resistance that makes us critically self-aware.

We do not endorse some versions of 'reflexivity' that result primarily in autobiographical accounts, or emotionally driven confessions. We do, however, recognise that ethnographic research *can* be a transformative experience. As we have indicated, it can be a period of biographical interruption for ourselves just as much as it is an interruption or imposition for those we encounter. Consequently, the catch and its intellectual resistance can also be a matter of self-scrutiny. Ethnography is an intensely personal activity, involving as it does personal, embodied and sensory work. In crafting the ethnography, therefore, we are also working on ourselves. The self and the other(s) are inextricably linked in mutual appraisal and empathetic understanding.

The making of the ethnography demands that we craft texts, and that in the process we craft ourselves as authors. If the ethnography does not exactly produce conclusions, it certainly generates texts that can be of abiding significance. There are multiple frames of reference, multiple webs of significance, in everyday life. Ethnographers therefore should be able to explore the possibilities of textual conventions and literary genres. This, again, is the *work* of the ethnographer as an intellectual. We do not advocate the wholesale adoption of 'alternative' ways of writing ethnography, and we certainly do not endorse the emergence of auto-fiction in the form of autoethnography as an alternative to making sense of others' lives. But we do want to encourage the creative reading of multiple kinds of text – fiction and factual – in the interest of understanding how everyday life can be reconstructed. Textual exploration is one area in which two meanings of reflexivity can come together: an appreciation that any mode of observation and representation helps constitute the phenomena so described, and a self-conscious awareness of one's own involvement in the ethnographic crafting. The worlds we observe and reflect on can be absurd in key aspects, can be suffused by magical and extraordinary happenings, and can endow small things with great significance. Sometimes we need to find appropriate ways to convey and reconstruct such actions and beliefs.

Our account of ethnography has been characterised by some disjunctures. We write about working and writing with and against the grain of everyday life, and we write about ethnographic fieldwork as a series of interruptions. We interrupt the lives of our hosts. However, accommodating and welcoming they may be – and we must not underestimate just how helpful people can be – we are an extraneous presence, a stranger in the midst. And just as we interrupt others, so fieldwork can be thought of as an interruption in the life of the ethnographer herself. Time out and time away can be fruitful, both in the present of fieldwork itself and in the future when the fruits of fieldwork can be brought forth in the form of theses and monographs. But mutual interruption can bite deeper: fieldwork is rarely, if ever, a smooth process of time with our hosts, a period without its hiatuses, its periods of intense and focused attention, and its times of boredom. To a considerable extent, therefore, ethnographic understanding can be episodic in nature. Claims for holistic understanding of a given culture or social world can be illusory. Partial and fragmented comprehension is often nearer the truth. There is no shame in that realisation. Partial understandings are the best that all disciplines and any methods can aspire to. Partial connections and incomplete accounts are our stock in trade.

Lastly, in celebrating ethnography, whatever its vicissitudes and shortcomings, it remains to assert that we do not equate it with 'qualitative research' or 'qualitative inquiry'. Qualitative research is broad and encompasses many research strategies, which in turn rest on different kinds of presuppositions and goals. In general, we believe that the value of ethnographic fieldwork sometimes needs to be affirmed. Fieldwork can include interviewing, but they are not equivalent. Extended, life-history interviewing is undoubtedly an important research strategy, and the narratives it generates are among the most important of sociological or anthropological texts. But fieldwork it is not. Likewise, critical self-reflection is important throughout social research, and autobiographical writing *per se* is not in itself ethnography. The social worlds of others should always be of greater interest than the experiences or feelings of social scientists themselves. Introspection does not substitute for sustained fieldwork. Consequently, while the virtues of ethnographic fieldwork should be celebrated, it sometimes needs to be rescued from 'qualitative research' or 'qualitative inquiry'.

BIBLIOGRAPHY

Abbas, A. (1988). Walter Benjamin's collector: The fate of modern experience, *New Literary History*, 20, 1: 217–237.

Adams, P.J. (2018). *Navigating Everyday Life: Exploring the Tension Between Finitude and Transcendence*. Lanham, MD: Lexington Books.

Agamben, G. (1986). The eternal return and the paradox of passion, *Stanford Italian Review*, 6, 1–2: 9–17.

Allan, A. and Cole, S. (in press). Finishing fieldwork in less than perfect circumstances: Lessons learned in 'labyrinth' exiting, in R.J. Smith and S. Delamont (eds). *Leaving the Field*. Manchester: Manchester University Press.

Allen-Collinson, J. and Hockey, J. (2010). Feeling the way: Notes towards a haptic phenomenology of scuba diving and distance running, *International Review for the Sociology of Sport*, 46, 3: 330–345.

Altork, K. (1995). Walking the fire line: The erotic dimension of the fieldwork experience, in D. Kulick and M. Willson (eds). *Taboo: Sex, Identity and Erotic Subjectivity in Anthropological Fieldwork*. New York, NY: Routledge, pp. 107–139.

Ames, R.T. (ed) (1994). *Self as Person in Asian Theory and Practice*. New York, NY: SUNY Press.

Anagnostou, Y. (2006). Metaethnography in the age of 'popular folklore', *Journal of American Folklore*, 119, 4: 381–412.

Anderson, E. (2022). *Black in White Space: The Enduring Impact of Color in Everyday Life*. Chicago, IL: University of Chicago Press.

Archetti, E.P. (ed) (1994). *Exploring the Written: Anthropology and the Multiplicity of Writing*. Oslo: Scandinavian University Press.

Ardener, E. (1972). Belief and the problem of women, in J. Lafontaine (ed). *The Interpretation of Ritual*. London: Tavistock, pp. 135–158.

Ardener, E. (1985). Social anthropology and the decline of modernism, in J. Overing (ed). *Reason and Morality*. ASA Monograph 24. London: Tavistock, pp. 47–70.

Ardener, S. (ed) (1975). *Perceiving Women*. London: Dent.

Atkinson, P. (1981). *The Clinical Experience: The Construction and Reconstruction of Medical Reality*. 2nd edition, Farnborough: Ashgate, 1997.

Atkinson, P. (1990). *The Ethnographic Imagination: Textual Constructions of Reality.* London: Routledge.

Atkinson, P. (1992). The ethnography of a medical setting: Reading, writing and rhetoric, *Qualitative Health Research*, 2, 4: 451–474.

Atkinson, P. (1996). *Sociological Readings and Re-Readings.* Aldershot: Avebury.

Atkinson, P. (2006). *Everyday Arias: An Operatic Ethnography.* Lanham, MD: AltaMira Press.

Atkinson, P. (2012). Ethnographic writing: The avant-garde and a failure of nerve, *International Review of Qualitative Research*, 6, 1: 19–36.

Atkinson, P. (2015). *For Ethnography.* London: SAGE Publications.

Atkinson, P. (2017). *Thinking Ethnographically.* London: SAGE Publications.

Atkinson, P. (2020). *Writing Ethnographically.* London: SAGE Publications.

Atkinson, P. (2022). *Crafting Ethnography.* London: SAGE Publications.

Atkinson, P., Coffey, A. and Delamont, S. (1999). Ethnography: Post, past and present, *Journal of Contemporary Ethnography*, 28, 5: 460–471.

Atkinson, P. and Housley, W. (2003). *Interactionism.* London: SAGE Publications.

Atkinson, P. and Silverman, D. (1997). Kundera's *immortality*: The interview society and the invention of the self', *Qualitative Inquiry*, 3: 304–325.

Auden, W.H. and Mayer, E. (1970). Introduction to Johann Wolfgang von Goethe, *Italian Journey.* London: Penguin Classics, pp. 7–19.

Babcock, B. (1982). Ritual undress and the comedy of self and other: Bandelier's *the delight makers*, in J. Ruby (ed). *A Crack in the Mirror: Reflexive Perspectives in Anthropology.* Philadelphia, PA: University of Pennsylvania Press, pp. 187–203.

Bailey, M.M. (2013). *Butch Queens Up in Pumps: Gender, Performance, and Ballroom Culture in Detroit.* Ann Arbor, MI: University of Michigan Press.

Barbaras, R. (2006). *Desire and Distance: Introduction to a Phenomenology of Perception.* Trans. Paul B. Milan. Stanford, CA: Stanford University Press.

Barnes, D. (2007). *Nightwood.* London: Faber and Faber. Originally published by Faber and Faber (1936).

Barthes, R. (2018). *A Lover's Discourse.* Trans. Richard Howard. London: Vintage. French edition, 1977, Paris: Éditions du Seuil. Translation first published by New York, Farrar, Straus and Giroux, 1978.

Bateson, G. (1936). *Naven: A Survey of the Problems Suggested by a Composite Picture of the Culture of a New Guinea Tribe Drawn from Three Points of View.* Cambridge: Cambridge University Press. 2nd edition, 1958, Stanford, CA: Stanford University Press.

Battaglia, D. (2005a). "For those who are not afraid of the future": Raëlian clonehood in the public sphere, in D. Battaglia (ed). *E.T. Culture: Anthropology in Outerspaces.* Durham, NC: Duke University Press, pp. 149–179.

Battaglia, D. (ed) (2005b). *E.T. Culture: Anthropology in Outerspaces.* Durham, NC: Duke University Press.

Beard, M. (2000). *The Invention of Jane Harrison.* Cambridge, MA: Harvard University Press.

Becker, H.S. (1967). Whose side are we on? *Social Problems*, 14, 3: 239–247.

Behar, R. (2007). *An Island Called Home.* New Brunswick, NJ: Rutgers University Press.

Belmonte, T. (1979). *The Broken Fountain.* New York, NY: Columbia University Press.

Belsey, C. (2002). *Critical Practice.* 2nd edition. London: Methuen.

Benjamin, W. (1968). Unpacking my library: A talk about book collecting, in H. Arendt (ed). *Illuminations.* Trans. H. Zohn. New York, NY: Schocken Books.

Benjamin, W. (1986 [1932]). A Berlin chronicle, in P. Demetz (ed). *Reflections: Essays, Aphorisms, Autobiographical Writings.* New York, NY: Schocken Books.

Benjamin, W. (2002). *The Arcades Project*. Trans. Howard Eiland and Kevin McLaughlin, Rolf Tiederman (ed). New York, NY: Belknap Press.

Berlina, A. (ed and trans.) (2017). *Victor Shklovsky: A Reader*. London: Bloomsbury.

Blackwood, E. (1995). Falling in love with an-other lesbian, in D. Kulick and M. Willson (eds). *Taboo: Sex, Identity and Erotic Subjectivity in Anthropological Fieldwork*. New York, NY: Routledge, pp. 51–75.

Bleakley, A. (2000). Writing with invisible ink: Narrative, confessionalism and reflective practice, *Reflective Practice*, 1, 1: 11–24.

Blumer, H. (1954). What is wrong with social theory? *American Sociological Review*, 19: 3–10.

Boyd, V. and Clinton, C. (2003). *Wrapped in Rainbows: The Life of Zora Neale Hurston*. New York, NY: Simon and Schuster.

Braun, V. and Clarke, V. (2006). Using thematic analysis in psychology, *Qualitative Research in Psychology*, 3, 2: 77–101.

Braun, V. and Clarke, V. (2022). *Thematic Analysis: A Practical Guide*. London: SAGE Publications.

Brettell, C.B. (ed) (1993). *When They Read What We Write: The Politics of Ethnography*. Westport, CT: Bergin & Garvey.

Briggs, D. (2013). *Crack Cocaine Users: High Society and Low Life in South London*. London: Routledge.

Buck-Morss, S. (2006). The flâneur, the sandwichman and the whore: The politics of loitering, in B. Hanssen (ed). *Walter Benjamin and the Arcades Project*. London: Continuum, pp. 33–65.

Bullivant, B.M. (1978). *The Way of Tradition*. Melbourne: Australian Council for Educational Research.

Büscher, M. and Urry, J. (2009). Mobile methods and the empirical, *European Journal of Social Theory*, 12, 1: 99–116.

Butler, J. (1987). *Subjects of Desire: Hegelian Reflections in Twentieth-Century France*. New York, NY: Columbia University Press.

Buzard, J. (2005). *Disorienting Fiction: The Autoethnographic Work of Nineteenth-Century British Novels*. Princeton, NJ: Princeton University Press.

Carpentier, M.C. (1994). Jane Ellen Harrison and the ritual theory, *Journal of Ritual Studies*, 8, 1: 11–26.

Carson, A. (2000). *Plainwater: Essays and Poetry*. New York, NY: Vintage Books.

Carpentier, A. (1957). *The Kingdom of This World*. Trans. H. de Onis. New York, NY: Alfred Kopf. Originally published in 1949.

Carter, I. (1990). *Ancient Cultures of Conceit: British University Fiction in the Post War Years*. London: Routledge.

Casteneda, C. (1968). *The Teachings of Don Juan: A Yaqui Way of Knowledge*. Berkeley, CA: University of California Press.

Cavafy, C.P. (2009). *Collected Poems: Bilingual Edition*. Trans. and ed E. Keeley and P. Sherrand. Princeton NJ: Princeton University Press.

Charmaz, K. (2014). *Constructing Grounded Theory*. 2nd edition. Thousand Oaks, CA: SAGE Publications.

Chernoff, J.M. (1979). *African Rhythm and African Sensibility: Aesthetics and Social Action in African Musical Idioms*. Chicago, IL: University of Chicago Press.

Chin, E. (ed) (2014). *Katherine Dunham: Recovering an Anthropological Legacy: Choreographing Ethnographic Futures*. Santa Fe, NM: School for Advanced Research Press.

Chryssides, G. (2003). Scientific creationism: A study of the Raëlian church, in C. Partridge (ed). *UFOReligions*. London: Routledge, pp. 45–61.

Clarke, A.E., Friese, C. and Washburn, R.S. (2018). *Situational Analysis*. Thousand Oaks, CA: SAGE Publications.

Classen, J. (ed) (2005). *The Book of Touch*. Oxford: Berg.

Clifford, J. (1988). *The Predicament of Culture: Twentieth-Century Ethnography, Literature, and Art*. Cambridge, MA: Harvard University Press.

Clift, B.C., Gore, J., Gustafsson, S., Bekker, S., Battle, I.C. and Hatchard, J. (eds) (2021). *Temporality in Qualitative Inquiry: Theories, Methods and Practices*. London: Routledge.

Clough, P.T. (2000). *Autoaffection: Unconscious Thought in the Age of Technology*. Minneapolis, MN: University of Missouri Press.

Coffey, A. (1999). *The Ethnographic Self*. London: SAGE Publications.

Coffey, A. (2018). *Doing Ethnography*. London: SAGE Publications.

Coffey, A. and Atkinson, P. (1996). *Making Sense of Qualitative Data*. Thousand Oaks, CA: SAGE Publications.

Coleridge, S.T. (1840). *The Works of Samuel Taylor Coleridge, Prose and Verse: Complete in One Volume*. Philadelphia, PA: Thomas, Cowperthwait and Co.

Cooley, C.H. (1902). *Human Nature and the Social Order*. New York, NY: Scribners.

Corbin, J. and Strauss, A. (1998). *Basics of Qualitative Research*. 2nd edition. Thousand Oaks, CA: SAGE Publications.

Crang, M. (2003). Qualitative methods: Touchy, feely look-see? *Progress in Human Geography*, 274: 494–504.

Csordas, T.J. (1994). *The Sacred Self: A Cultural Phenomenology of Charismatic Healing*. Berkeley, CA: University of California Press.

Curran, K. (ed) (2019). *Renaissance Personhood: Materiality, Taxonomy, Process*. Edinburgh: Edinburgh University Press.

Czaplicka, M. (1914). *Aboriginal Siberia: A Study in Social Anthropology*. Oxford: Clarendon Press.

Delamont, S.W. (2009a). Neo-pagan narratives, *Sociological Research Online*, 14, 5: 213–222, https://doi.org/10.22582/am.v9i1.62.

Delamont, S. W. (2009b). The only honest thing, *Ethnography and Education*, 4, 1: 51–64.

Delamont, S. (2014). *Key Themes in the Ethnography of Education*. London: SAGE Publications.

Delamont, S. (2018). Fieldnotes and the ethnographic self, in R. Jeffrey and L. Russell (eds). *Ethnographic Writing. Stroud*. Gloucestershire: Ethnography and Education Publishing, pp. 33–44.

Delamont, S. (ed) (2019). *Lo Spirito Esplorativo Libero*. Lecce, Italy: Kurumuny.

Delamont, S. and Atkinson, P. (eds) (1995). *Fighting Familiarity*. New York, NY: Hampton Press.

Delamont, S. and Atkinson, P. (2021). *Ethnographic Encounters*. London: Routledge.

Delamont, S., Atkinson, P. and Parry, O. (2000). *The Doctoral Experience: Success and Failure in Graduate School*. London: Falmer-Routledge.

Delamont, S. and Smith, R.J. (in press). Leaving the field: An editors' introduction, in R.J. Smith and S. Delamont (eds). *Leaving the Field: Methodological Insights from Ethnographic Exits*. Manchester: Manchester University Press.

Delamont, S., Stephens, N. and Campos, C. (2017). *Embodying Brazil*. London: Routledge.

Delanda, M. (2016). *Assemblage Theory*. Edinburgh: Edinburgh University Press.

Deleuze, G. and Guattari, F. (1983). *Anti-Oedipus*. Minneapolis, MN: University of Minnesota Press.

Deleuze, G. and Guattari, F. (1987). *A Thousand Plateaus*. Minneapolis, MN: University of Minnesota Press.

Deloria, E.C. (1988). *Waterlily*. Lincoln: University of Nebraska Press. New edition, 1990.

DeNora, T. (2000). *Music in Everyday Life*. Cambridge: Cambridge University Press.
Derrida, J. (1996). *Archive Fever: A Freudian Impression*. Chicago, IL: University of Chicago Press.
Douglas, M. (1966). *Purity and Danger*. London: Routledge and Kegan Paul.
Douny, L. (2018). A praxeology and phenomenology of Dogon landscape: Fieldwork practice, kinesthetic experience and embodies knowledge, in T. Rakowski and H. Patzer (eds). *Pre-Textual Ethnographies: Challenging the Phenomenological Level of Anhropological Knowledge-Making*. Canon Pyon: Sean Kingston Publishing, pp. 94–115.
Downey, G. (2005). *Learning Capoeira: Lessons in Cunning from an Afro-Brazilian Art*. Oxford: Oxford University Press.
Dubish, J. (1995). Lovers in the field: Sex, dominance, and the female anthropologist, in D. Kulick and M. Willson (eds). *Taboo: Sex, Identity and Erotic Subjectivity in Anthropological Fieldwork*. New York, NY: Routledge, pp. 29–50.
Duneier, M. (1992). *Slim's Table: Race, Respectability, and Masculinity*. Chicago, IL: University of Chicago Press.
Dunham, K. (1969). *Island Possessed*. Garden City, NY: Doubleday.
Dunham, K. (1983). *Dances of Haiti*. Los Angeles, CA: University of California Center for Afro-American Studies.
Dutkiewicz, J. (2015). Pretzel logic: An embodied ethnography of a rock climb, *Space and Culture*, 18, 1: 25–38.
Edensor, T. (2010). Walking in rhythms: Place, regulation, style and the flow of experience, *Visual Studies*, 25, 1: 69–79.
Edmondson, R. (1984). *Rhetoric in Sociology*. London: Macmillan.
Eickelman, D. (1978). The art of memory: Islamic education and its social reproduction, *Comparative Studies in Society and History*, 20, 4: 485–516.
Eliade, M. (1954). *The Myth of the Eternal Return: Cosmos and History*. Princeton, NJ: Princeton University Press.
Elkin, L. (2016). *The Flâneuse*. London: Chatto and Windus.
Evans-Pritchard, E. (1937). *Witchcraft, Oracles and Magic Among the Azande*. Oxford: Clarendon Press.
Fabian, J. (1983). *Time and the Other: How Anthropology Makes Its Object*. New York, NY: Columbia University Press.
Fallon, S. (2019). *Paper Monsters: Persona and Literary Culture in Elizabethan England*. Philadelphia, PA: University of Pennsylvania Press.
Farge, A. (2013). *The Allure of the Archives*. Trans. T. Scott-Railton. New Haven, CT: Princeton University Press.
Favret-Saada, J. (1980). *Deadly Words*. Cambridge: Cambridge University Press.
Ferrell, J. (2018). *Drift: Illicit Mobility and Uncertain Knowledge*. Berkeley, CA: University of California Press.
Fiedler, L.A. (1973). *The Stranger in Shakespeare*. London: Croom Helm.
Field, A. (1985). *Djuna: The Formidable Miss Barnes*. Austin, TX: University of Texas Press.
Fine, G.A., Campion-Vincent, V. and Heath, C. (eds) (2005). *Rumor Mills: The Social Impact of Rumor and Legend*. Piscataway, NJ: Aldine Transaction.
Foucault, M. (1981). *The History of Sexuality*. Harmondsworth: Penguin, Vol. 1.
Freeman, D. (1983). *Margaret Mead and Samoa: The Making and Unmaking of an Anthropological Myth*. Cambridge, MA: Harvard University Press.
Fortune, R. (1932). *Sorcerers of Dobu: The Social Anthropology of the Dobu Islanders of the Western Pacific*. London: George Routledge and Sons.
Fowles, J. (1963). *The Collector*. London: Jonathan Cape.

Fugard, A.J.B. and Pots, H.W.W. (2021). Thematic analysis, in P. Atkinson, S. Delamont, A. Cernat, J.W. Sakshaug and R.A. Williams (eds). *SAGE Research Methods Foundations*. London: SAGE Publications, Vol. 10, pp. 4876–4880

Gascoigne, N. and Thornton, T. (2013). *Tacit Knowledge*. Durham: Acumen.

Geană, G. (2018). The phenomenological programme and anthropological research, in T. Rakowski and H. Patzer (eds). *Pre-Textual Ethnographies: Challenging the Phenomenological Level of Anthropological Knowledge-Making*. Herefordshire: Sean Kingston Publishing, Canon Pyon, pp. 40–57.

Geertz (1973a). *The Interpretation of Cultures*. New York, NY: Basic Books.

Geertz, C. (1973b). Deep play: Notes on the Balinese cockfight, in *The Interpretation of Cultures*. New York, NY: Basic Books.

Gere, C. (2009). *Knossos and the Prophets of Modernism*. Chicago, IL: University of Chicago Press.

Ghent, E. (1990). Masochism, submission, surrender, *Contemporary Psychoaalysis*, 26, 1: 108–136.

Gherardi, S. (2015). Why Kurt Wolff matters for a practice-based perspective of sensible knowledge in ethnography, *Journal of Organisational Ethnography*, 4, 1: 117–131.

Gill, J. (2004). Anne Sexton and confessional poetics, *The Review of English Studies*, 55, 220: 425–445.

Gill, J. (ed) (2006). *Modern Confessional Writing: New Critical Essays*. London: Routledge.

Girard, R. (2004). *Oedpis Unbound: Selected Writings on Rivalry and Desire*. Trans. and ed Mark Anspach. Stanford, CA: Stanford University Press.

Glaser, B. (2001). *The Grounded Theory Perspective: Conceptualization Contrasted With Description*. Mill Valley, CA: The Sociology Press.

Glaser, B. and Strauss, A.L. (1967). *The Discovery of Grounded Theory*. Chicago, IL: Aldine.

Goffman, E.W. (1961a). *Asylums: Essays on the Social Situation of Mental Patients and Other Inmates*. New York, NY: Doubleday Anchor.

Goffman, E. W. (1961b). *Encounters: Two Studies in the Sociology of Interaction*. Indianapolis, IN: Bobbs-Merrill.

Goffman, E. (1967). *Interaction Ritual: Essays on Face-to-Face Behavior*. New York, NY: Doubleday Anchor.

Goffman, E. (1972). *Relations in Public*. New York, NY: Basic Books.

Gorton, K. (2008). Desire, Duras, and melancholia: Theorizing desire after the "affective turn." *Feminist Review*, 89, 1: 16–33. doi: 10.1057/fr.2008.10

Goslinga, G. (2012). Spirited encounters: Notes on the politics and poetics of representing the uncanny in anthropology, *Anthropological Theory*, 12, 4: 386–406.

Goulet, D.E. and Young, J.-G. (eds) (1994). *Being Changed by Cross-Cultural Encounters*. Peterborough, ON: Broadview Press.

Graham, S.B. (1981). Social networks and community administration: A comparative study of two mining towns, in D.A. Messerschmidt (ed). *Anthropologists at Home in North America: Methods and Issues in the Study of One's Own Society*. New York, NY: Cambridge University Press, pp. 106–120.

Grande, P.B. (2020). *Desire*. East Lansing: Michigan State University Press.

Greenfield, S.M. (2008). *Spirits With Scalpels: The Cultural Biology of Religious Healing in Brazil*. Walnut Creek, CA: Left Coast Press.

Gregory, E. (2006). Confessing the body: Plath, Sexton, Berryman, Lowell, Ginsberg and the gendered poetics of the 'real', in J. Gill (ed). *Modern Confessional Writing: New Critical Essays*. London: Routledge, pp. 33–49.

Grimshaw, A. (2001). *The Ethnographer's Eye: Ways of Seeing in Anthropology*. Cambridge: Cambridge University Press.

Grindal, B.T. (1983). Into the heart of Sisala experience: Witnessing death divination, *Journal of Anthropological Research*, 39, 1: 60–80.

Gross, M. (2010). *Ignorance and Surprise*. Cambridge, MA: MIT Press.

Gross, M. and McGoey, L. (eds) (2015). *Routledge International Handbook of Ignorance Studies*. London: Routledge.

Grosz, E. (1994). Refiguring lesbian desire, in L. Doan (ed). *The Lesbian Postmodern*. New York, NY: Columbia University Press, pp. 67–84.

Haddon, A.C. (1901). *Head-Hunters: Black, White, and Brown*. London: Methuen.

Hall, T. (2017). *Footwork: Urban Outreach and Hidden Lives*. London: Pluto.

Hancock, B.H. (2013). *American Allegory: Lindy Hop and the Racial Imagination*. Chicago, IL: University of Chicago Press.

Hancock, B.H. (2018). Embodiment: A dispositional approach to racial and cultural analysis, in C. Jerolmack and S. Khan (eds). *Approaches to Ethnography: Analysis and Representation in Participant Observation*. New York, NY: Oxford University Press.

Hanssen, B. (ed) (2006). *Walter Benjamin and the Arcades Project*. London: Continuum.

Haraway, D. (2018). *Modest_Witness@Second_Millennium. FemaleMan_Meets_OncoMouse: Feminism and Technoscience*. 2nd edition. London: Routledge.

Harper, S. (2019). All acts of love and pleasure are my rituals: Fieldwork and erotic subjectivity in an American neopagan community, in R.J. Martin and D. Haller (eds). *Sex: Ethnographic Encounters*. London: Routledge, pp. 101–114.

Harrod, M.B. (2007). Making confessions: The confessional voice found among literary genres. MA thesis, SUNY College at Brockport.

Hart, S.M. (2003). Magical realism in the Americas: Politicised ghosts in *one hundered years of solitude, the house of the spirits*, and *beloved*, *Journal of Iberian and Latin American Studies*, 9, 2: 115–123.

Hart, S.M. and Ouyang, W.-C. (eds) (2005). *A Companion to Magical Realism*. Woodbridge, Suffolk: Tamesis.

Hartman, T. (2007). Beyond Sontag as a reader of Lévi-Strauss: 'Anthropologist as hero', *Anthropology Matters*, 9, 1.

Heaney, S. (1999). *Beowulf: A New Verse Translation*. London: Faber and Faber.

Herzfeld, M. (2003). *The Body Impolitic: Artisans and Artifice in the Global Hierarchy of Value*. Chicago, IL: University of Chicago Press.

Heuston, S. (2011). *Modern Poetry and Ethnography: Yeats, Frost, Warren, Heaney, and the Poet as Anthropologist*. New York, NY: Palgrave.

Hillyard, S. (2010). What's (still) wrong with ethnography?, in S. Hillyard (ed). *New Frontiers in Ethnography*. Bingley Yorks: Emerald, pp. 1–18.

Hockey, J. (2006). Sensing the run: The senses and distance running, *Senses and Society*, 1, 2: 183–202.

Hoffman, S.K. (1978). Impersonal personalism: The making of a confessional poet, *English Literary History*, 45, 4: 687–709.

Holdengräber, P.B. (1992). Between the profane and the redemptive: The collector as possessor in Walter Benjamin's "Passagen-werk", *History and Memory*, 4, 2: 96–128.

Horsley (2012). 'How dead the dead are': Sensing the science of death, *Qualitative Research*, 12, 5: 540–553.

Hudson, L. (1966). *Contrary Imaginations: A Psychological Study of the English Schoolboy*. London: Methuen.

Hurston, Z.N. (1937). *Their Eyes Were Watching God*. New York, NY: J.B. Lippincott.

Iversen, R.R. (2020). Leaving the field, in P. Atkinson, S. Delamont, A. Cernat. J. Sakshaug and R. Williams (eds). *SAGE Research Methods Foundations*. London: SAGE Publications, Vol. 10, pp. 2749–2755.

Jackson, J. (1990). Déja Enterndu: The liminal qualities of anthropological fieldnotes, *Journal of Contemporary Ethnography*, 19, 1: 8–43.

Jackson, M. (1986). *Barawa and the Ways Birds Fly in the Sky*. Washington DC: Smithsonian Institution Press.

Jackson, M. (2017). After the fact: The question of fidelity in ethnographic writing, in A. Panadian and S. McLean (eds). *Crumpled Paper Boat: Experiments in Ethnographic Writing*. Durham, NC: Duke University Press, pp. 48–67.

Jamie, K. (2012). *Sightlines*. London: Sort of Books.

Janeja, M.K. and Bandak, A. (2019). Introduction, in M.K. Janeja, M.K. and A. Bandak (eds). *Ethnographies of Waiting: Doubt, Hope and Uncertainty*. London: Bloomsbury.

Jennings, G., Brown, D.H.K. and Sparkes, A.C. (2010). It can be a religion if you want', *Ethnography*, 11, 4: 533–557.

Jerolmack, C. and Khan, S. (2018). Introduction: An analytic approach to ethnography, in C. Jerolmack and S. Khan (eds). *Approaches to Ethnography: Analysis and Representation in Participant Observation*. New York, NY: Oxford University Press, pp. xi–xxx.

Josipovici, G. (2010). *Whatever Happened to Modernism*. New Haven, CT: Yale University Press.

Kakavoulia, M. (2008). The ethnographer's 'gaze': Some notes on visuality and its relation to the metalanguage of anthropology, in N. Panourgiá and G.E. Marcus (eds). *Ethnographica Moralia: Experiments in Interpretive Anthropology*. New York, NY: Fordham University, pp. 213–216.

Kenna, M. (2005). Why does incense smell religious? Greek Orthodoxy and the anthropology of smell, *Journal of Mediterranean Studies*, 15, 1: 50–69.

King, N. (1984). *Abel Gance*. London: British Film Institute.

Knorr-Cetina, K. (1999). *Epistemic Cultures: How the Sciences Make Knowledge*. Cambridge, MA: Harvard University Press.

Krautwurst, U. (2014). *Culturing Bioscience: A Case Study in the Anthropology of Science*. Toronto: University of Toronto Press.

Kuklick, H. (1997). After Ishmael: The fieldwork tradition and its future, in A. Gupta and J. Ferguson (eds). *Antropological Locations: Boundaries and Grounds of a Field Science*. Berkeley, CA: University of California Press, pp. 47–65.

Kulick, D. (1995). The sexual life of anthropologists: Erotic subjectivity and ethnographic work, introduction, in D. Kulick and M. Willson (eds). *Taboo: Sex, Identity and Erotic Subjectivity in Anthropological Fieldwork*. New York, NY: Routledge, pp. 1–28.

Kusenbach, M. (2003). Street Phenomenology: The go-along as ethnographic research tool, *Ethnography*, 4, 3: 455–485.

Laing, O. (2016). *The Lonely City: Adventures in the Art of Being Alone*. London: Picador.

Lane, N. (2016). Bringing flesh to theory: Ethnography, black queer theory, and studying black sexualities, *Feminist Studies*, 42, 3: 632–648.

Laplantine, F. (2015). *The Life of the Senses: Introduction to a Modal Anthropology*. Trans. Jamie Furness. London: Bloomsbury. Originally published *Le social et le sensible*. Paris: Téraèdre.

Larson, F. (2021). *Undreamed Shores: The Hidden Heroines of British Anthropology*. London: Granta.

Latour, B. (1993). *We Have Never Been Modern*. Trans. Catherine Porter. Cambridge, MA: Harvard University Press. Originally published *Nous n'avons jamais été modernes*. Paris: La Découverte.

Latour, B. (2004). How to talk about the body? The normative dimension of science studies, *Body & Society*, 10, 2–3: 205–229.

Lawrence, C. and Shapin, S. (eds) (1998). *Science Incarnate: Historical Embodiment of Natural Knowledge*. Chicago, IL: University of Chicago Press.

Lefebvre, H. (2004). *Rhythmanalysis*. London: Continuum.

Leeds-Hurwitz, W. (2021). Thick description, in P. Atkinson, S. Delamont, A. Cernat, J.W. Sakshaug and R.A. Williams (eds). *SAGE Research Methods Foundations*. London: SAGE Publications, Vol. 10, pp. 4894–4902.

Leibing, A. (2007). The hidden side of the moon, or 'lifting out' in ethnographies, in A. McLean and A. Liebing (eds). *The Shadow Side of Fieldwork: Exploring the Blurred Borders Between Ethnography and Life*. Malden, MA: Blackwell, pp. 138–156.

Leiris, M. (2017). *Phantom Africa*. Trans. Brent Hayes Edwards. Calcutta: Seagull.

Lepselter, S. (2005). The license: Poetics, power and the uncanny, in D. Battaglia (ed). *E.T. Culture: Anthropology in Outerspaces*. Durham, NC: Duke University Press, pp. 130–148.

Lewis, J., Featherstone, K. and Atkinson, P. (2012). Representation and practical accomplishment in the laboratory: When is an animal model good-enough? *Sociology*, 47, 4: 776–792.

Liebow, E. (1967). *Tally's Corner*. London: Routledge & Kegan Paul.

Loughran, T. and Mannay, D. (eds) (2018). *Emotion and the Researcher: Sites, Subjectivities and Relationships*. Bingley: Emerald.

Lorde, A. (1984). *Sister Outsider*. Berkeley, CA: The Crossing Press.

Lorde, A. (2006). The uses of the erotic: The erotic as power, reprinted, in K.E. Lovaas and M.M. Jenkins (eds). *Sexualities and Communication in Everyday Life: A Reader*. Thousand Oaks, CA: SAGE Publications, pp. 87–91.

Löwstedt, M. (2015). Taking off my glasses in order to see': Exploring practice on a building site using self-reflexive ethnography, *Construction Management and Economics*, 33, 5–6: 404–414.

Lundberg, A. (2000). Journeying between desire and anthropology: A story in suspense, *The Australian Journal of Anthropology*, 11, 1: 24–41.

Luria, A.R. (1987). *The Mind of a Mnemonist*. Trans. Lynn Solotaroff. Cambridge, MA: Harvard University Press.

MacDougall, D. (2019). *The Looking Machine: Essays on Cinema, Anthropology and Documentary Filmmaking*. Manchester: Manchester University Press.

Malinowski, B. (1922). *Argonauts of the Western Pacific*. London: G. Routledge & Sons.

Malinowski, B. (1935). *Coral Gardens and Their Magic*. London: Routledge.

Malinowski, B. (1967). *A Diary in the Strict Sense of the Term*. London: Routledge and Kegan PauL

Mann, C. (2012). *Mosaic of Fire: The Work of Lola Ridge, Evelyn Scott, Charlotte Wilder and Kay Boyle*. Columbia, SC: University of South Carolina Press.

Manganaro, M. (1990). *Modernist Anthropology: From Fieldwork to Text*. Princeton, NJ: Princeton University Press.

Mannheim, K. (1936). *Ideology and Utopia*. London: Kegan Paul.

Mannheim, K. (1993). The sociology of intellectuals, *Theory, Culture and Society*, 10, 1: 69–80.

Marchand, T. (2008). Muscles, morals and mind: Craft apprenticeship and the formation of person, *British Journal of Educational Studies*, 56, 3: 245–271.

Marcus, G.E. (1985). A timely rereading of Naven: Gregory Bateson as oracular essayist, *Representations*, 12, Autumn: 66–82.

Marcus, G.E. (1990). The modernist sensibility in recent ethnographic writing and the cinematic metaphor of montage, *Society for Visual Anthropology Review*, 6, 1: 2–12.

Marcus, G.E. (2015). The legacies of *writing culture* and the near-future of ethnographic form: A sketch, in O. Starn (ed). *Writing Culture and the Life of Anthropology*. Durham, NC: Duke University Press, pp. 35–51.

Marquez, G. (2000). *One Hundred Years of Solitude*. Trans. Gregory Rabassa. London: Penguin Modern Classics.

Martin, R.J. and Haller, D. (eds) (2019). *Sex: Ethnographic Encounters*. London: Routledge.

Marton, Y. (1994). The experiential approach to anthropology and Castaneda's ambiguous legacy, in D.E. Goulet and J.-G. Young (eds). *Being Changed by Cross-Cultural Encounters*. Peterborough, ON: Broadview Press, pp. 209–236.

Mason, J. (2018). *Living the Weather: Voices from the Calder Valley*. Manchester: University of Manchester Press.

Matthews, C.R. (2021). *Doing Immersive Research: Using Social Science to Understand the Human World*. Beeston: CRM Publishing.

Mauss, M. (2006). *Techniques, Technology and Civilisation*. Trans. D. Lkussier and J. Redding, N. Schlanger (ed). Oxford: Berghahn Books. Originally published in 1935.

McLean, S. (2017). *Fictionalizing Anthropology: Encounters and Fabulations at the Edges of the Human*. Minneapolis, MN: University of Minnesota Press.

Mead, G.H. (1934). *Mind, Self and Society: From the Standpoint of a Social Behaviorist*. Chicago, IL: University of Chicago Press.

Merleau-Ponty, M. (1962). *Phenomenology of Perception*. Trans. D.S. Landes. London: Routledge and Kegan Paul. Originally published in 1945.

Meskus, M. (2018). *Craft in Biomedical Research: The iPS Cell Technology and the Future of Stem Cell Science*. New York, NY: Palgrave Macmillian.

Michailova, S., Piekkari, R., Plakoyiannaki, E., Ritvala, T., Mihailova, I. and Salmi, A. (2014). Breaking their silence about exiting fieldwork: A relational approach and its implications for theorizing, *Academy of Management Review*, 39, 2: 138–151.

Miller, M.J. (1985). *The Poetics of Nikki Bungaku: A Comparison of the Traditions, Conventions, and Structure of Heian Japan's Literary Diaries With Western Autobiographical Writings*. New York, NY: Garland.

Mills, C.W. (1940). Situated actions and vocabularies of motive, *American Sociological Review*, 5: 439–452.

Moeran, B. (2007). Marketing scents and the anthropology of smell, *Social Anthropology/ Anthropologie Sociale*, 15, 2: 153–168.

Moody, J. (2003). *Sentimental Confessions: Spiritual Narratives of Nineteenth-Century African American Women*. Athens: University of Georgia Press.

Dove, M. (1927). *Cogewea, The Half-Blood: A Depiction of the Great Montana Cattle Range*. Boston, MA: Four Seas.

Muniesa, F. and Trébuchet-Breitwiller, A.-S. (2010). Becoming a measuring instrument: An ethnography of perfume consumer testing, *Journal of Cultural Economy*, 3, 3: 321–337.

O'Connor, E. (2005). Embodied knowledge: The experience and the struggle towards proficiency in glassblowing, *Ethnography*, 6, 2: 183–204.

O'Connor, E. (2006). Glassblowing tools: Extending the body towards practical knowledge and informing a social world, *Qualitative Sociology*, 29: 177–93.

O'Connor, E. (in press). Materia erotica: Making love among glassblowers, in R.J. Smith and S. Delamont (eds). *Leaving the Field: Methodological Insights from Ethnographic Exits*. Manchester: Manchester University Press.

Papagaroufaki, E. (2008). Carnal hermeneutics: From "concepts" and "circles" to "dispositions" and "suspense, in N. Panourgiá and G.E. Marcus (eds). *Ethnographica Moralia: Experiments in Interpretive Anthropology*. New York, NY: Fordham University Press, pp. 113–125.

Paterson, M. (2009). Haptic geographies: Ethnography, haptic knowledges and sensuous dispositions, *Progress in Human Geography*, 33, 6: 766–788.

Peppis, P. (2014). *Sciences of Modernism: Ethnography, Sexology, and Psychology*. Cambridge: Cambridge University Press.

Perec, G. (2010). *An Attempt at Exhausting a Place in Paris*. Trans. M. Lowenthal. Cambridge, MA: Wakefield Press. Originally *Tentative d'épuisement d'un lieu parisien*, 1975.

Pink, S., Hubbard, P., O'Neill, M. and Radley, A. (2010). Walking across disciplines: From ethnography to arts practice, *Visual Studies*, 25, 1: 1–7.

Powdermaker, H. (1950). *The Hollywood Dream Factory: An Anthropologist Looks at the Movie-Makers*. Boston, MA: Little, Brown.

Powdermaker, H. (1966). *Stranger and Friend: The Way of an Anthropologist*. New York, NY: W.W. Norton.

Preston, C.J. (2016). *Learning to Kneel: Noh, Modernism, and Journeys in Teaching*. New York, NY: Columbia University Press.

Probyn, E. (1996). *Outside Belongings*. New York, NY, and London: Routledge.

Purser, A. (2018). Getting it into the body': Understanding skill acquisition through Merleau-Ponty and the embodied practice of dance, *Qualitative Researchin Sport, Exercise and Health*, 10, 3: 318–332.

Putnam, R.D. (2000). *Bowling Alone: The Collapse and Revival of American Community*. New York, NY: Simon and Schuster.

Rabinow, P. (1977). *Reflections on Fieldwork in Morocco*. Berkeley, CA: University of California Press.

Rasmussen, S. (1999). Making better "scents" in anthropology: Aroma in Tuareg socio-cultural systems and the shaping of ethnography, *Anthropological Quarterly*, 72, 2: 55–73.

Reichertz, J. (2010). Abduction: The logic of discovery of grounded theory, Forum: Qualitative Social Research, 11, 1, Art. no.13. http://nbn-resolving.de:0114-fqs1001135.

Reyes, V. (2020). Ethnographic toolkit: Strategic positionality and researchers' visible and invisible tools in field research, *Ethnography*, 21, 2: 220–240.

Reynolds, D.F. (2001). *Interpreting the Self: Autobiography in the Arabic Literary Tradition*. Berkeley, CA: University of California Press.

Rilke, R.M. (2016). *Letters to a Young Poet*. Trans. Charlie Louth. London: Penguin Classics.

Roberts, R.A. (2014). Research to performance methodology: Embodying knowledge and power from the field to the concert stage, in E. Chin (ed). *Katherine Dunham: Recovering and Anthropological Legacy, Choreographing Ethnographic Futures*. Santa Fe NM: School for Advanced Research Press, pp. 17–30.

Rocha, C. (2016). *John of God: The Globalization of Brazilian Faith Healing*. New York, NY: Oxford University Press.

Rollins, H.E. (ed) (1958). *The Letters of John Keats*. Cambridge, MA: Harvard University Press.

Roth, C.F., Samuels, D. and Lepselter, S. (eds) (2006). *ET Culture: Anthropology in Outerspaces*. Durham, NC: Duke University Press.

Roth, J. (1963). *Timetables: Structuring the Passage of Time in Hospital Treatment and Other Careers*. Indianapolis, IN: Bobbs-Merill.

Routledge, K. (1919). *The Mystery of Easter Island*. London: Sifton, Praed & Co.

Rutherford, D. (2015). Kinky empiricism, in O. Starn (ed). *Writing Culture and the Life of Anhropology*. Durham, NC: Duke University Press, pp. 105–118.

Saldaña, J. (2021). *The Coding Manual for Qualitative Researchers*. Thousand Oaks, CA: SAGE Publications.

Salerno, (2007). *Sociology Noir: Studies at the University of Chicago in Loneliness, Marginality and Deviance, 1915-1935.* Jefferson, NC: McFarland & Co.
Sarraute, N. (2015). *Tropisms.* Trans. Maria Jolas. New York, NY: New Directions. Originally published *Tropismes*, Paris: Les Editions de Minuit, 1957.
Scheler, M. (1954). *The Nature of Sympathy.* Trans. P. Heath. London: Routledge and Kegan Paul.
Schmerler, G. (2017). *Henrietta Schmerler and the Murder That Put Anthropology on Trial.* Eugene, OR: Scrivana Press.
Schütz, A. (1967). *Phenomenology of the Social World.* Evanston, IL: Northwestern University Press.
Schütz, A. (1971). The stranger: An essay in social psychology, in A. Broderson (ed). *Alfred Schutz: Collected Papers II – Studies in Social Theory.* The Hague: Martinus Nijhoff, pp. 92–105.
Scott, S. (2019). *The Social Life of Nothing: Silence, Invisibility and Emptiness in Tales of Lost Experience.* London: Routledge.
Serres, M. (2016). *The Five Senses.* London: Bloomsbury.
Shepherd, N. (2011). *The Living Mountain.* Edinburgh: Canongate.
Sheringham, M. (2006). *Everyday Life: Theories and Practices from Surrealism to the Present.* Oxford: Oxford University Press.
Sherwin, M. (2011). *Confessional' Writing and the Twentieth-Century Literary Imagination.* London: Palgrave.
Shortt, H. (2015). Liminality, space and the importance of 'transitory dwelling places' at work, *Human Relations*, 68, 4: 633–658.
Silverman, D. (1975). *Reading Castaneda: A Prologue to the Social Sciences.* London: Routledge and Kegan Paul.
Sinclair, I. (2002). *London Orbital.* London: Granta Books.
Sinclair, I. (2021). *The Gold Machine: In the Tracks of the Mule Dancers.* London: Oneworld Publications.
Smith, R.J. and Delamont, S. (eds) (2019). *The Lost Ethnographies: Methodological Insights from Projects That Never Were.* Bingley: Emerald.
Smith, R.J. and Delamont, S. (eds) (in press). *Leaving the Field.* Manchester: Manchester University Press.
Snyder, C.J. (2008). *British Fiction and Cross-Cultural Encounters: Ethnographic Modernism from Wells to Woolf.* London: Palgrave.
Solnit, R. (2006). *A Field Guide to Getting Lost.* Edinburgh: Canongate.
Sontag, S. (1966). *Against Interpretation.* New York, NY: Farrar, Straus and Giroux.
Sontag, S. (2001). *After Confession*, ed. K. Sontag and D. Graham. Minneapolis, MN: Graywolf Press.
Sontag, S. (2012). *As Consciousness Is Harnessed to Flesh: Diaries 1964-1980.* New York, NY: Farrar, Straus and Giroux.
Souhami, D. (2021). *No Modernism Without Lesbians.* London: Head of Zeus.
Sparkes, A.C. (2009). Ethnography and the senses: Challenges and possibilities, *Qualitative Research in Sport and Exercise*, 1, 1: 21–35.
Spinney, J. (2006). A place of sense: A kinaesthetic ethnography of cyclists on Mont Ventoux, *Environment and Planning D: Society and Space*, 24: 709–732.
Spivak, G. (1988). Can the subaltern speak? in C. Nelson and L. Grossberg (eds). *Marxism and the Interpretation of Culture.* Basingstoke: Macmillan, pp. 271–313.
Stanley, L. and Wise, S. (1983). *Breaking Out.* London: Routledge and Kegan Paul.
Stanley, L. and Wise, S. (2002). *Breaking Out Again: Feminist Ontology and Epistemology.* London: Routledge.

Stavrides, S. (2010). *Towards the City of Thresholds.* Professional Dreamers Wick, Nr Bath.

Steedman, C. (2001). *Dust.* Manchester: Manchester University Press.

Stein, E. (1989). *On the Problem of Empathy.* Trans. Waltraut Stein. 3rd edition. Washington DC: ICS Publication. Originally published in 1917.

Stephens, N., Glasner, P. and Atkinson, P. (2011). Documenting the doable and doing the documented, *Social Studies of Science*, 41, 6: 791–813.

Stewart, K. (1996). *Space on the Side of the Road: Cultural Poetics in an 'Other' America.* Princeton, NJ: Princeton University Press.

Stewart, K. (2007). *Ordinary Affects.* Durham, NC: Duke University Press.

Stoller, P. (1989). *The Taste of Ethnographic Things: The Senses in Anthropology.* Philadelphia, PA: University of Pennsylvania Press.

Stoller, P. (1997). *Sensuous Scholarship.* Philadelphia, PA: University of Pennsylvania Press.

Strathern, M. (1988). Commentary: Concrete topographies, *Cultural Anthropology*, 3, 1: 88–96.

Strathern, M. (1999). *Property, Substance and Effect: Anthropological Essays on Persons and Things.* London: Athlone Press.

Sudnow, D. (1978). *Ways of the Hand: The Organization of Improvised Conduct.* London: Routledge and Kegan Paul.

Swartz, L. (1994). Being changed by cross-cultural encounters, in D.E. Goulet and J.-G. Young (eds). *Being Changed by Cross-Cultural Encounters.* Peterborough, Ontario: Broadview Press, pp. 209–236.

Taussig, M. (1987). *Shamanism, Colonialism and the Wild Man: A Study in Terror and Healing.* Chicago, IL: University of Chicago Press.

Taussig, M. (1993). *Mimesis and Alterity: A Particular History of the Senses.* London: Routledge.

Taussig, M. (2011). *I Swear I Saw This: Drawing in Fieldwork Notebooks, Namely My Own.* Chicago, IL: University of Chicago Press.

Tavory, I. and Timmermans, S. (2014). *Theorizing Qualitative Research.* Chicago, IL: University of Chicago Press.

Teil, G. (1998). Devenir expert aromaticien: Y-a-t-il une place pour le goût dans les goûts alimentaires? *Sociologie Du Travail*, 4, 98: 503–522.

Tester, K. (ed) (1994). *The Flâneur.* London: Routledge.

Thomas, G. (in press). Unfinished business: A reflection on leaving the field, in R.J. Smith and S. Delamont (eds). *Leaving the Field: Methodological Insights from Ethnographic Exits.* Manchester: Manchester University Press.

Thoreau, H.D. (2000). *Walden.* London: Arcturus.

Thrift, N. (2004). Intensities of feeling: Towards a spatial politics of affect, *Geografiska Annaler*, 86, 1: 57–78.

Timmermans, S. and Tavory, I. (2012). Theory construction in qualitative research: From grounded theory to abductive analysis, *Sociological Theory*, 30, 3: 167–186.

Timmermans, S. and Tavory, I. (2022). *Data Analysis in Qualitative Research: Theorizing With Abductive Analysis.* Chicago, IL: University of Chicago Press.

Todorov, T. (1970). *Introduction à La Litterature Fantastique.* Paris: Éditions du Seuil.

Torgovnick, M. (1990). *Gone Primitive: Savage Intellects, Modern Lives.* Chicago, IL: University of Chicago Press.

Travers, M. (2009). New methods, old problems: A sceptical view of innovation in qualitative research, *Qualitative Research*, 9, 2: 161–179.

Turkle, S. (2011). *Evocative Objects: Things We Think With.* Cambridge, MA: MIT Press.

Turner, E. (1994). A visible spirit form in Zambia, in D.E. Goulet and J.-G. Young (eds). *Being Changed by Cross-Cultural Encounters.* Peterborough, ON: Broadview Press, pp. 71–95.

Underman, K. (2020). *Feeling Medicine: How the Pelvic Exam Shapes Medical Training*. New York, NY: New York University Press.
Van Maanen, J. (1988). *Tales of the Field*. Chicago, IL: University of Chicago Press.
Van Maanen, J. (2011). *Tales of the Field*. 2nd edition. Chicago, IL: University of Chicago Press.
Vernant, J.-P. and Detienne, M. (1978). *Cunning Intelligence in Greek Culture and Society*. Atlantic Highlands, NJ: Humanities Press.
Videen, H. (2021). *The Wordhord: Daily Life in Old English*. London: Profile Books.
Visweswaran, K. (2015). Dying worlds, in O. Starn (ed). *Writing Culture and the Life of Anthropology*. Durham, NC: Duke University Press, pp. 204–220.
Wacquant, L. (2005). *Body and Soul: Notebooks of an Appretice Boxer*. New York, NY: Oxford University Press.
Wallman, S. (2020). *Sometime Kin: Layers of Memory, Boundaries of Ethnography*. Oxford: Berghahn Books.
Waskul, D. and Waskul, M. (2016). *Ghostly Encounters: The Hauntings of Everyday Life*. Philadelphia, PA: Temple University Press.
Weston, K. (2008). "Real anthropology" and other nostalgias, in M. Panourgiá and G.E. Marcus (eds). *Ethnographica Moralia: Experiments in Interpretive Anthropology*. New York, NY: Fordham University Press.
Whitaker, E.M. and Atkinson, P. (2019). Surrender, catch and the imp of fieldwork, *Qualitative Inquiry*, 25, 9–10: 936–944.
Whitaker, E.M. and Atkinson, P. (2021). *Reflexivity in Social Research*. London: Palgrave.
Whitaker, E.M. and Atkinson, P. (2022). Reflexive ethnography, in A. Poferl and N. Schröer (eds). *Handbook of Sociological Ethnography*. Wiesbaden: Springer.
White, G. (1977). *The Natural History of Selbourne*. London: Penguin Classics.
Whyte, W.F. (1943). *Street Corner Society: The Social Structure of an Italian Slum*. Chicago, IL: University of Chicago Press.
Winn, R. (2018). *The Salt Path*. London: Michael Joseph.
Winterson, J. (2007). *Preface to Djuna Barnes Nightwood*. London: Faber and Faber.
Wohlfarth, I. (2006). Et cetera? The historian as chiffonier, in B. Hanssen (ed). *Walter Benjamin and the Arcades Project*. London: Bloomsbury, pp. 12–32.
Wolff, K.H. (1976). *Surrender and Catch: Experience and Inquiry Today*. Dordrecht: Reidel.
Young, D.E. and Goulet, J.-G. (eds) (1994). *Being Changed by Cross-Cultural Encounters: The Anthropology of Extraordinary Experience*. Peterborough, ON: Broadview Press.

INDEX